A BANTAM TRAVEL GUIDE

LONDON

1990

W9-BEL-818

BANTAM

NEW YORK • TORONTO • LONDON • SYDNEY • AUCKLAND

LONDON 1990
A Bantam Book/April 1990

ISBN 0–553–34842–6

Published simultaneously in the United States and Canada

Bantam Books are published by Bantam Books, a division of Bantam Double-
day Dell Publishing Group, Inc. Its trademark, consisting of the words "Ban-
tam Books" and the portrayal of a rooster, is Registered in U.S. Patent and
Trademark Office and in other countries. Marca Registrada. Bantam Books,
666 Fifth Avenue, New York, New York 10103.

LONDON 1990

THE CONTRIBUTORS

Melanie Menagh, who wrote most of the chapters in this book, is a New-York-based writer who spends much of her time in Great Britain. Ms. Menagh has contributed to books on Italy, Mexico, and New York City, and her articles have appeared in *Omni, Savvy, Travel & Leisure,* and *Vanity Fair.*

The restaurant section was contributed by **Helen Varley,** London restaurant critic and writer on consumer affairs. She has been editor of the annual *Time Out Guide to Eating Out in London* and its offshoots for several years and is a regular contributor to *Time Out* magazine's food columns.

Contributor of the *Business Brief,* **James Louttit,** an author, publisher, and travel writer, was president of Fodor's Travel Guides and David McKay Company, Inc. until he retired to North Carolina in 1986. His experience in "doing business in Great Britain" covers the 15 years that Fodor's/McKay was owned by a British parent company.

Carl Nagin, who contributed the *Cultural Timeline,* is a free-lance journalist who teaches writing at Harvard. Mr. Nagin has written for *New York* magazine, the *Christian Science Monitor, Interview, Geo, Reader's Digest, Art and Auction,* and the *Boston Globe.*

Editors are Audrey Liounis and Deborah Jurkowitz; assistant editor is Charlotte Savidge. Maps are by Swanston Graphics and R.V. Reise and Verkehrsverlag. Project management by Madigan Editorial Services.

CONTENTS

FOREWORD   vii

1. TRAVELING TO LONDON IN 1990   1

2. ORIENTING YOURSELF   8

    Map of London Neighborhoods 10–11

3. HOTELS   14

4. PRIORITIES   31

5. TRANSPORTATION   36

6. TOURING   38

7. LONDON BY NEIGHBORHOOD   46

  The City 46
    Map of the City 48
    Plan of the Tower of London 50
    Plan of St. Paul's Cathedral 61
  Westminster and Whitehall 70
    Map of Westminster and Whitehall 71
    Plan of Westminster Abbey 81
  Soho and Covent Garden 88
    Map of Soho and Covent Garden 89
  Belgravia, South Kensington, and Chelsea 102
    Map of Belgravia, South Kensington, and
    Chelsea 103
  St. James's, Mayfair, and the Parks 115
    Map of St. James's, Mayfair, and the Parks 116
    Plan of Hyde Park 125
  Bloomsbury and Marylebone 127
  Clerkenwell and Holborn 138
  Kensington 147
    Map of Kensington 149
  The South Bank 155

8. SHOPPING   164

9. RESTAURANTS   175

10. ENTERTAINMENT   197

    Map of the Theater District 200

11. SHORT TRIPS FROM LONDON   203

Greenwich   203
Map of Greenwich   204
Hampton Court Palace   205
Hampstead   205
Kew Gardens   206
Windsor and Eton   207
Stratford - upon - Avon   207
Oxford   208
Cambridge   209
Bath   209
Salisbury   210
Stonehenge and Avebury Stone Circles   210
Brighton   211

12. CITY LISTINGS   212

13. TRAVEL ARRANGEMENTS   219

For Information . . .   219
Transportation   220
Formalities   224
The Seasons in London   224
Money Matters   225
1990 Events   227

BUSINESS BRIEF   231

CULTURAL TIME LINE   233

VITAL INFORMATION   238

INDEX   241

ATLAS

London,   1
The Underground,   7
Greater London,   8
Great Britain,   9
Windsor and Eton,   10
Stratford-Upon-Avon,   11
Oxford,   12
Cambridge,   14
Bath,   16

FOREWORD

How can a travel guidebook help you?

At a bare minimum it should 1. Help you plan your trip, and 2. Help you make choices during that trip. Of course, any good guidebook can be useful, but the guide you're holding, one of Bantam's growing new series of travel guides, does it better. During our first year of publication, the critics raved about us. The public is reacting even better than we dared hope when we embarked on this bold new publishing venture in late 1987. That both the critics and public alike have judged us so favorably is gratifying for us and good news for you. Our efforts have been recognized, and that's nice. But there are good reasons for that, and you benefit by having chosen this guide.

Here are just a few of the solid reasons why, as one critic put it, "Bantam has themselves a winner!"

- Bantam guides are affordable. You get more information for your dollar than you do with most other guidebooks.
- The books are up-to-date. Since they're revised annually, they'll always be more current than the vast majority of guidebooks.
- Each Bantam guide includes a full-color travel atlas with maps detailed enough for the most demanding travel needs. These are supplemented with black-and-white maps throughout the text.
- Upon close examination you'll see that your Bantam guidebook is organized geographically rather than alphabetically. What this means is that descriptions of what's available in a contiguous geographical area make it easier to get the most out of a city neighborhood or country region. For those who still need to locate a place alphabetically, we provide a detailed index.
- Restaurants, hotels, and shops are keyed into the maps so that you can locate these places easily.
- You'll find a feature called City Listings where museums, churches, and major sites are listed with their addresses, phone numbers, and map-location code.
- Finally, we think you'll enjoy reading our guidebooks. We've tried hard to find not only informed writers, but good writers. The writing is literate and lively. It's honest. Most of all it's a good read.

Yet no matter how good a guidebook is it cannot cover everything. It can't include every good restaurant, and it can't do justice to everyone's favorite place—though we believe we come closer than anyone else. Bear in mind, too, that prices can change at any time, and today's well-managed restaurant or hotel can change owners or managers tomorrow. Today's great food or service can be tomorrow's disappointment. We've recommended places as they are now and as we expect them to be in the future, but there are no guarantees. We welcome your comments and suggestions. Our address is Bantam Travel Guides, 666 Fifth Avenue, New York, N.Y. 10103.

Richard T. Scott
Publisher
Bantam Travel Books

TIPS ON GETTING THE MOST OUT OF THIS GUIDE

Bantam Travel Guides are designed to be extremely user friendly, but there are a few things you should know in order to get the maximum benefit from them.

1. You'll find a special **Travel Arrangements** section toward the back of the book. This section can be invaluable in planning your trip.
2. The **Priorities** chapter will insure that you see and do the most important things when you visit your destination. Whether you're spending two days or two weeks there, you'll want to make the most of your time and certainly not miss the musts.
3. Note that in addition to our main selection of important restaurants you'll also find described in the text informal places to stop for lunch, a snack, or a drink. To help you instantly identify these places as well as restaurant and hotel write-ups, whether they're in a list or mentioned in the text, we've designed the following two symbols which will appear at the beginning of restaurant and hotel lists and in the margin of the text whenever a restaurant or hotel is described there.

Hotels

Restaurants

1

TRAVELING TO LONDON IN 1990

London is a city at the epicenter of controversy and change. The "big bang" of 1986, which essentially deregulated all money matters, blasted the city into the stratospheric realms of highest finance. The "every man for himself" creed of Margaret Thatcher's government is diligently dismantling the welfare state by privatizing industry, slashing government subsidies to health and education, and severely restricting the heretofore free-for-all system of dole (welfare) in an incessant series of measures even her own education minister has characterized as Draconian. Everyone on the streets of London has a passionate conviction on Thatcherism either pro or con, and since all the PM's essential tenets are being played out in London, the city is being transformed from a gentle, genteel, not-quite-Continental capital to a bustling, hustling metropolis based more on New World models than on Old.

Whether you love or loathe the principles of Mrs. Thatcher's philosophy, you must concede that the 1990s find London more alive, active, and exciting than at any time since the days of the Empire. And London is always a city that relishes her role as fulcrum for great forces. In the heady days of the 1590s, formerly second-rate England was mad with pride and excitement at having defeated the most powerful naval force in the world—the Spanish Armada. The alehouses and coffeehouses were full of talk of politics and poetics. Londoners of all classes convened at the theaters on the south bank of the city to watch a round of bearbaiting or perhaps the latest offering of Mr. Shakespeare or Mr. Marlowe.

For the next two hundred years or so London's spirits dampened as her coffers were emptied by the Civil War and a series of foreign campaigns. But in the early 19th century Admiral Nelson's victory at Trafalgar and General Wellington's at Waterloo brought an end to Continental opportunism and enabled Britain to turn her money and manpower to the business of establishing an empire. For the 63-year reign of Queen Victoria, London was the First City of the Empire upon Which the Sun Never Set.

It's important to remember that previous to the present U.S./U.S.S.R. scenario, the last superpower was Great Britain and Great Britain alone for very close to a century, from the end of the Napoleonic Wars to the beginning of World War I. London is very used to being the center of global attention, practiced at posing in the limelight. London is likewise used to being the center of national attention. London is the indisputable hub of England. Government is here, fashion is here, the Queen is here, the media are here, finance is here, art and music are here. If any young Briton has a notion of making it in the world, he or she must make the inevitable pilgrimage to the capital to seek his or her fortune. It is this convergence of ideas and temperaments that makes London so lively—and so volatile.

As with the opportunists of the nation, so too the opportunists of the (former) Empire have immigrated to the capital in search of employment. Black people from Africa and the West Indies, brown people from India and Pakistan, tawny people from China and Southeast Asia now make up (unfortunately) much of the impoverished classes of London, living in neighborhoods, like the East End and Brixton, once occupied by their predecessors in disenfranchisement, the Jews and the Irish. But the situation is not uniformly depressing; on the contrary, they add to the rich spectrum of cross-cultural cuisine, fashion, music, and philosophy that makes London truly a cosmopolitan city. London is long-practiced in the art of accommodating foreigners, either as visitors or as eventual citizens. London, above all other cities, is supremely complacent about the movements of the populace, be they natives or tourists. The strongest impression many people take away from London is its pleasantness, its amiability, and, oddly enough for the world's largest city by area, its manageability. Much of the center of town is still dominated by four- or five-story buildings built a hundred or more years ago. The vast expanses of the Royal Parks, Regent's Park, Holland Park, and Hampstead Heath provide a verdant sanctuary for birds, bunnies, squirrels, and, of course, the citizenry who flock thither in droves to sun, chatter, row, ride, bike, court, fly kites, play tennis, picnic, and generally disport themselves about the greensward. And the Thames provides a liquid link to the outside world and to the city's past.

Another important factor contributing to the humanness of the city is indeed her human element. Londoners, for the most part, aren't at all the archetypal imperious upper-class twits caricatured in the mind of the rest of the world. The average Londoner is as down-to-earth and sociable (not to be confused with social) as you please. If you pull up next to one in a pub,

he or she will most likely favor you with all kinds of suggestions of where to go, what to do, what to think about the prime
minister; hold forth with a history lesson, a literary survey,
several personal anecdotes; and manage to buy you a pint of
beer before you can get your pounds out of your pocket in
protest. As mentioned, many if not most Londoners were not
born here, and consequently even those with an obviously
extra-Britannic accent are simpatico with strangers.

In fact, it is this very discrepancy of accent that can cause
the most confusion. Not, as you might suspect, because the
accents are different, but because the accents are the same.
One of the greatest causes of confusion for the North American and South Pacific visitor to London arises when the visitor
mistakes London for an extension of his or her homeland, or
vice versa. Unless you are from Britain (and in many cases
even if you are), London is a city in a foreign country. The
common language and the common democratic and literary
history can be very deceiving, lulling you into the erroneous
belief that when you arrive in London, you've really never left
home. Make no mistake about it, London is a foreign city, and
unless you are a true-blood Brit, you are a foreigner in it. This
is, of course, not at all a bad thing. One assumes if you have
flown all the way from another continent, you are looking for
a change. London will provide just that. You won't have to
deal with a completely different language, but you will have
to deal with different currency, different habits, and a different
heritage and point of view.

Probably the most salient difference between Britain and
newer-world countries is her class system. The class system
is alive and well in the Old Country. It of course exists in
every country on the planet, but elsewhere class distinction
is handled considerably more subtly than here where dukes
and marquises roam freely about the land. Probably the most
conspicuous element of the British class system is the royal
family. They're present at opera galas, at the opening of
Ascot, and at center court at Wimbledon. They do a lot of
goodwill work, raising money and consciousness, as the theo-
ry goes. The world thrills to the latest scrapes of Di and Fergie and wonders how such spunky girls put up with those dull
Windsor boys. It is all quite enchanting and fairy-tale—the flying lessons for the Duchess of York, and the shopping sprees
of the Princess of Wales. On the other hand, in this kingdom
of grossly inequitable distribution of resources, Queen Elizabeth and her brood are by far the largest landowners. The
Queen is easily the wealthiest woman in the country and one
of the wealthiest women in the world. And all of it is tax-free.
This rather sticks in the craw of Brits being asked to buckle
down and do some "serious" work rather than live off the fat
of the welfare system.

The point about the British class system that separates it from others is that it is a class system of blood. In the United States and elsewhere, the class system is based on money and power, and, therefore, theoretically anyone can become an aristocrat. In Britain, with very few exceptions, one must be born an aristocrat, one cannot become one by virtue of virtue or hard work. Thus the country has survived and prospered for centuries. The vast changes that Britain is currently undergoing, however, have not bypassed the upper classes. Even the blue-blood, old-family aristocracy is beginning to show signs of weakening against the unremitting onslaught of new wealth generated by the financial community flourishing in the City under the nurturing influence of Thatcherism. The situation is more than a little ironic when you consider that the prime minister's supporters (the Tories) are staunchly conservative. Tories, historically, have always come down on the side of upholding the pomp and circumstance of monarchic England. Yet it is Thatcherism's laissez-faire policy toward the financial frenzy in the City that is abetting a burgeoning upper middle class whose emphasis on hard work and fast money implicitly calls into question all the basic underpinnings of English aristocracy.

Commenting on all these convolutions and fueling London's rocket back to international prominence is the local press. In the case of London, however, the local newspapers constitute the national voice. Since *The Guardian* opted for printing an edition in the capital as well as in its hometown of Manchester, with *very* few exceptions the print medium is exclusively installed and wrapped up in London. As preparation for your voyage, one of the best things you can do is to take up reading the London dailies for a few weeks before your departure and to continue this when you are here.

You'll find a variety of opinion expressed in the popular press. Of course conservatives (and Conservatives) read the *Times*es, regular and *Financial.* People to the left of center swear by *The Guardian.* And just in the past few years, another entity, *The Independent,* has captured the interest and respect of liberals (its natural constituency) and conservatives alike for its tough line and excellent reportage. In Britain you are what you read, and one of the best ways to appreciate the national mind is to acquaint yourself with current national events and with the variety of papers covering them.

In fact, there is a lot of reading you can do in anticipation of your trip. There are excellent histories by A. L. Rowse, Barbara Tuchman, and G.M. Trevelyan that are interesting to read and widely available. There are novels from the picaresque 18th-century antics of Henry Fielding's *Tom Jones* to the cautionary Victorian comedy of Charles Dickens's *David Copperfield* to the chilling humor of the post-Thatcherist future in Pete Davies's *The Last Election.* Of course many guidebooks will counsel you to read the complete works of Chaucer, Shakespeare, and Milton, then work your way up through the Romantic poets. While we would be the first to applaud anyone with the time and perseverance to embark on such a program, we would also like to suggest a few more accessible and up-to-date sources of information and opinion on the London scene. Aside from reading newspapers, try to pick up a few issues of London magazines before your trip. Some we would suggest as particularly useful and enlightening are: *Harpers & Queen,* which is essentially a chat sheet for the upper classes, discusses important matters such as society weddings, country-estate real-estate opportunities, art auctions, gemstones, etc., etc. *The Tatler* covers much the same ground as *H&Q* but does so with tongue wagging in cheek. Undergraduate parties at Oxford are not so much celebrated as sent up. It's always fun to have a laugh at the aristocrats if there's not the slightest chance of your becoming one. *The Face* is London's style sheet par excellence. Its superslick graphics and jaded voice have been often imitated but never equaled—except by its own founders when they created *Arena,* a *Face* for men covering everything from comic-book culture to riots in Soweto. And when you're in London, *Time Out* (one of whose editors kindly contributed the restaurant chapter to this effort) is absolutely essential equipment for anyone attacking the city, with complete listings of all events, all day, every day—"eight days a week."

Another effortless exercise you can do to psych yourself up for the trip is to rent some movies on London specifically, or Britain generally, to give you a visual sense of what you're getting into.

If you get into the habit of reading the daily papers and monthly magazines and if you bring home a couple of movies to watch each week, you will quickly understand that this is, to borrow the phrase of a previous Londoner, the best of times to come to London. And it is the best of times for precisely the same reason Mr. Dickens observed when he discussed the state of the world at the beginning of *A Tale of Two Cities:* It is the best of times to be in London because it is the best of times and it is the worst of times. It is a great time of action and upheaval in the life of London.

The story of London itself in 1990 is a tale of two cities. London is a city trying, quite successfully, to yank itself into the world of international investment and financial services in order to bring badly needed capital back home. London is a city that's decided to crack down on an entire generation that has been raised under the misconception that there's no need to work if the government will pay you more to live on the dole than an employer will pay you to be on the job. London is a city finally giving tax relief to the young professionals so as to stem the tide of English financial whizzes fleeing the country in order to retain some of the wealth they've accumulated. London is also a city in which youth unemployment is often a whopping forty percent. London is a city whose truly needy are having their financial support system stripped as viciously as are those who are living needlessly on the dole. London is a city whose recent rash of BMW thefts is referred to as "yuppie taxation." London is a city whose most beautiful monuments are being obscured by the cheerless, uninspired architecture of buildings designed for upscale office space, not for low-income housing. London is a city on the brink of a brave new world, and as such, London is a city you'll find endlessly intriguing, invigorating, and exciting.

A Glossary of British Terms

Many of the words listed here under the "King's or Queen's" English are not found in the *Oxford English Dictionary* (arbitrator of such things) because many of them are slang—often derived from Cockney expressions. We have included them because visitors will, in all likelihood, hear them. It could save a spot of bother.

"Queen's" English	American English
ta	thanks, so long
cheers	goodbye, a toast
biscuit	cookie
chips	french fries
crisps	potato chips
cuppa	cup of (tea or coffee)
bangers	sausages
tatties	potatoes
loo, w.c.	toilet
hire/let	rent
flat	apartment
knackered	exhausted
kip	sleep
pissed	drunk
knickers	undies (female)
lift	elevator
telly	television
wireless	radio
lorry	truck
coach	bus
bonnet	hood of a car
boot	trunk of a car
bike	motorcycle
push bike	bicycle
roundabout	traffic circle
subway	underground passageway
tube	subway
bobby	police officer
single	one-way ticket
return	round-trip ticket
queue	to wait in line
quid (*never* plural-"2 quid")	pound (or pounds) sterling

2

ORIENTING YOURSELF

London is an ovoid shape running east to west along the Thames River. Most of the city's important sights are on the northern bank, although the south bank is rapidly being developed as an arts, business, and residential area since space is growing more and more scarce on the opposite shore.

Place names in London can be a bit confusing. The East End is in fact in the east and the South Bank is indeed to the south; however, the West End, where you'll find the theaters, is actually in central London. Then to further confuse things, there is the matter of the City, as opposed to the city. The city is a generic term and can be applied to the urban parts of London generally. The City, on the other hand, is a specific (and extremely ancient and important) neighborhood, its square mile recognized as a discrete entity by royal warrant since 1215.

Another important point to be made is the changing direction of the Thames. Although in general terms it runs in an easterly direction through the city, it takes a sharp turn to the left at Waterloo Bridge and runs in a southerly direction past Westminster and Pimlico until it makes another pronounced right-hand turn at Vauxhall Bridge and continues along its east/west axis.

The other outstanding natural feature of London is her parks. The largest area of green is a grouping of what are known as the Royal Parks—St. James's Park, Green Park, Hyde Park, and Kensington Gardens—beginning roughly at the geographical center of London and from there fanning out west and northward. The other great park is Regent's in the north-central part of town; it provides a pleasant pastorale for the inhabitants of Marylebone.

London is a sprawling city; within its confines proper are Wimbledon and Chiswick to the southwest and Hampstead and Highgate to the northeast. What would normally be counted as suburbs in other cities are all part of the urban fold here in London. It can all be quite dizzying in its geographical greatness and its concurrent intimate intricacy; even native Londoners are kidding you if they claim to know the city inside and out. The reason this city above all others in the world is so large is that over the years it has spread from the little Saxon fishing village the Romans called Londinium when they moved there in A.D. 43 to include a host of surrounding populaces. The first significant outpost was established at Westminster when Edward the Confessor built his abbey and palace there in the late 11th century. The city filtered southward across the Thames to Southwark, a major stop on the pilgrimage trail, and westward from the City toward Westminster. These little villages were bounded by the network of rivers and burns that once zigzagged its way through the Thames valley, quite literally islands in many streams. The suffix "ey" in Anglo-Saxon means island, and areas like Hackney, Stepney, and possibly Chelsea and Battersea were named for the islands on which they began.

After the double blow of the Great Plague in 1665 and the Great Fire of 1666, people fled the City in droves and filled up the gaps between what had been separate, self-contained towns, even as their watery parameters were filled in, paved over, and diverted through underground pipes. The estates of kings and nobility were broken up, sold off, and developed. By the days of Dickens, Victoria, and the Empire, what had been a loose conglomeration of unconnected towns had become a teeming, massive city.

Yet the towns still retain a bit of their original identity and integrity to this day. We have tried to respect and celebrate the uniqueness and historical richness of the old English towns in our organization of this volume.

So many visitors to London begin their day at the Changing of the Guard, then walk across to Trafalgar Square, down the Strand and Fleet Street to St. Paul's, and from there past the City to the Tower—cutting through at least five distinct neighborhoods in their path. Obviously there are time constraints on many tourists, and they want to see as many "important" London sights as they can in their limited time. But to merely hit the hot spots as randomly as a pinball bangs into bumpers is to miss the "real" London, the Londoner's London. A Londoner knows that Westminster and St. James's near Buckingham Palace stand for different things as do Soho, Holborn, and the City. If you get nothing else from this book, let it be that we have helped a bit in your vision and understanding of London as a group of little cities within a big city, each with its own character and history to be savored.

We have divided up London into nine areas. These follow roughly the traditional lines of the towns that have been incorporated into the city of London. We have broken down official

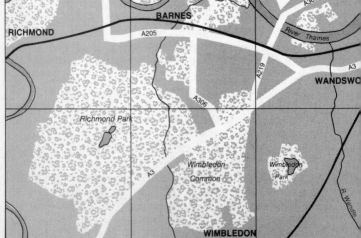

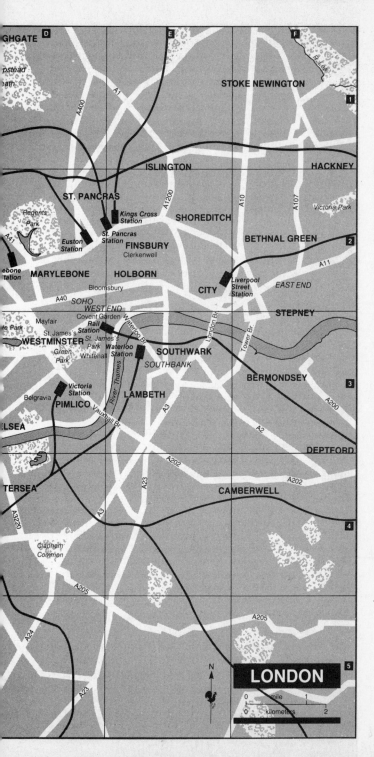

boundaries, such as the City of Westminster and the Royal Borough of Kensington and Chelsea, into smaller units when they were too large to be managed reasonably in a day or two of touring. And we have lumped together neighborhoods actually in two different districts, such as Holborn in Westminster and Camden and Clerkenwell in Islington, when the areas had much in common and made sense together from a historic and atmospheric point of view. Otherwise we have tried as much as possible to present London as the confederation of towns that it is.

Try as much as possible to do your touring neighborhood by neighborhood so you can get the feel of intellectual St. Marylebone and Bloomsbury or official Westminster and Whitehall or residential South Kensington, Belgravia, and Chelsea. You could easily spend your entire visit exploring the City of London alone and never set foot in another district. So much the better. London is not a city known quickly or easily. It takes time and effort but will reward the traveler whose energy and enthusiasm allow for an intelligent, appreciative approach.

The logical place to begin is **the City,** where the city itself began. Here you'll find the Tower, remnants of the London Wall that surrounded what was then the entirety of Londinium, St. Paul's, and a score of Christopher Wren–designed churches erected after the Great Fire. The City is also London's business address, where you'll find the Stock Exchange, the Bank of England, and all the important financial institutions of Britain.

Next is **Westminster and Whitehall.** Although the City of Westminster is a clearly defined area in London, it is too large and unwieldy to consider touring in a day or two, so our definition of Westminster is the area bounded by Buckingham Palace, the Houses of Parliament, and Trafalgar Square, where most of the country's governmental business is attended to.

Soho and Covent Garden are the sensuous and artistic hubs of London where you'll find most of her important commercial theaters, smart shops, and important galleries.

Belgravia, South Kensington, and Chelsea are the lands between park and river chosen by Londoners who like green grass and "blue" waters and who can afford to pay for such luxury. Shops and galleries have followed this sybaritic crew here and cater to their costly, capricious needs.

St. James's, Mayfair, and the Parks are the areas wherein you'll discover the London repositories of upper-class distinction: elegant architecture, consciously conservative shops, and the quiet assuredness only old (i.e. ancient) money can bestow.

Bloomsbury and Marylebone are the provinces of lawyers and professors, writers and students. The presence of

London University, the British Museum, and several small but important art collections perpetuate the intellectual engagement of this north-central sector.

Clerkenwell and Holborn are nuts-and-bolts, no-nonsense neighborhoods full of outspoken tradition, from the monks of the Charterhouse and the knights of the Order of St. John to the lawyers of Gray's Inn to the orations of Marx. Through the years this area has produced a succession of people with a lot to say—and a lot to answer for.

Kensington makes up the western reaches of central London and has usually served as a relatively rural outpost, with pretty Holland Park, antiques shops along Church Street and Portobello Road, several period houses and one palace open to the public.

The **South Bank** cuts across the lower margins of the River Thames and is a good place to see high-minded art at the South Bank Centre or low-brow living at Thames-side pubs and along working-class streets.

3

HOTELS

Finding a good hotel is an especially tricky business in a city: There are thousands, and yet, despite the competition, prices are twice what they are in the country. And ultimately the plethora of choices becomes more of a nuisance than anything else—after all, do you really have time to sift through five thousand brochures or do several hundred on-site inspections? So we have worn out countless pairs of shoes pounding endless miles of pavement, examining each property with a keen and critical eye. We sifted through the masses, adding, subtracting, refining the list down to a couple dozen choices to make the decision just a little bit easier for you.

Despite the number of hotels in London, things get crowded, especially during the busy summer season and around holidays like Christmas and Easter. Do plan to make reservations as far in advance as possible (the hotels we've selected are very popular and fill up fast) so you won't be disappointed.

If you would like information and listings of hotels other than those we've selected, write (at least six weeks in advance) to the **London Tourist Board, Accommodation Services Dept., 26 Grosvenor Gardens, London SW1W 0DU.** There are same-day booking services at both **Heathrow** and **Gatwick airports;** and in London at the **British Travel Centre, 12 Regent St., SW1; tel.** (for information only, no bookings) **730-3400.**

The primary concern most people have about a hotel (other than it be clean and safe) is price or, more correctly, value. Whether you pay £30 per night for a room with a bath down the hall or £250 per night for a room with the Thames out the window, are you getting your money's worth? Or is there another hotel right around the corner that, for an extra £5, will provide a tidy bath en suite to clean yourself up at night and a hearty breakfast to send you off with in the morning?

The best value for the money tends to be found at either end of the price scale. If you're on a tight budget, there are adequate B&Bs (bed-and-breakfast guesthouses) in the northwestern part of town around Paddington and Notting Hill. The streets are literally lined with choices, much like peas lined in the proverbial pod. Even if you have a reservation, insist on seeing the room and the bathroom (and it will be down the hall at these prices) *first.* If anything is not to your liking, ask to be shown another room, and if that doesn't suit, ask to be shown the door. While you can't expect palatial accommodations for thirty quid, you most certainly can insist on a clean, pleasant room in a neat house and a good cup of coffee in the morning.

Several services provide listings of superior B&Bs in the London area (and around the world). A cut well above the usual, these rooms are in homes which often include antiques, luxurious bathrooms and proprietors who treat their guests more like visiting family members than fly-by-night clients. Prices tend to hover in the £20 to £30 per person, per night range, and often minimum (two-night) reservations are required. Write or phone **World Wide Bed and Breakfast Association,** PO Box 134, SW10 E11, 370-7099; **At Home in London,** 70 Black Lion Lane W6 9BE, tel. 748-1943; **London Home to Home,** 19 Mount Park Crescent, Ealing W5 2RN, tel. 567-2998; **The Best Bed and Breakfast in the World,** tel. 351-5846.

We hesitate to recommend any hotels in the middle (£40–£60) range. Most likely they will provide a private bath, although not necessarily. And the private bath may prove to be just that—a tub; if you prefer a shower you may have to use the one down the hall anyway. Service won't be noticeably better— at least not twice as good to justify the doubling in price.

We did manage to find a selection of exceptions to these rules: £60–£80 hotels where service and appointments are clearly superior to a £30 B&B. It wasn't easy, and if you can't get a reservation at one of our selected hostelries in this price category, better to forgo the private bath and find a cosy, economical room at "Mrs. Brown's B&B" and spend the £30 per day you've saved on a terrific meal or in a terrific shop or at a terrific show.

Finally, if your expense account or your trust fund allows you to stay where you please, of course London has a fleet of top-flight hotels for £100 a day on up. Yet in this price category, perhaps more than any other, one must insist on value for money. If you are paying to stay at a deluxe hotel, the service should be stellar, the room should be elegant and comfortable, and the hotel should be equipped to attend to your every wish. There is no room for, and you should have no patience with, a grand hotel grown complacent and careless. A good reputation is not something to be rested on but, rather, something to strive constantly to uphold and even surpass. In all price categories we have tried to find hotels that not only maintain but also seek to surpass the reputation each has already established.

After price, the second consideration is probably the style or atmosphere of a hotel—its feel. The hotels on our list are ones that feel good: the kind of places where you can feel at once the ease and familiarity of being at home as well as the specialness and excitement you came to London to experience.

There is a new breed of inn flourishing in London that is spreading from here around the world: Part town house, part country house, these are small hotels, many with fewer than twenty rooms, that succeed not by accommodating everyone all at once, but rather by concentrating their efforts and attentions on a few visitors at a time. Most of them, in converted residences on quiet streets with access to private gardens, embody a supremely civilized approach to providing a safe haven for the tempest-tossed traveler. These hotels have full concierge services. They may not have a restaurant and most certainly do not have a ballroom—unless it's been converted into a bedroom. For those of you who love a big, bustling hotel in a big, bustling city (and why not?), we've sorted those out for you as well.

Do keep in mind that standards for standard hotel equipment vary greatly from country to country. Most of the hotels we recommend have en-suite bathrooms and air-conditioning, but not necessarily in every room. If these things are important to you, be sure you ask specifically for a room that includes them *when you make your reservation.*

The last consideration is location. And it should be the least important, because public transportation in London is cheap and efficient before midnight, and taxis are, well, efficient anyway, after midnight. The areas with the greatest concentration of hotels are St. James's and Mayfair to the east of the Royal Parks, and Belgravia, South Kensington, and Chelsea to the south of the parks.

St. James's and Mayfair boast the poshest addresses in town—with commensurately elevated price tags and such hotels as Dukes and The Ritz. Here you'll find shopping at the galleries around St. James's and the shops along Regent St. and Piccadilly. Also close by are the West End theaters and the cafés of Soho.

Belgravia, South Kensington, and Chelsea are more residential areas (and the hotels here, like the Beaufort and Fenja, tend to be converted town houses). This neighborhood is where the young upper classes (the pre-Princess Di, for example) have their first flats. The stores are fashionable to funky; the restaurant scene, trendy and turbulent.

In addition to hotels in these clusters of activity you will find Hazlitt's, just down from Soho Square and the Savoy on the Thames, just down from Covent Garden. Both are very convenient to the City's businesses and pleasures. In Marylebone, the north-central part of town near Regent's Park, London University, and some terrific small art galleries, you'll find Dorset Square and Durrant's hotels. In Notting Hill, northwest of the parks, are the Abbey Court, Halcyon, Pembridge Court, and the Portobello hotels in a quiet residential corner of London near beautiful Holland Park and the antique market and shops around Portobello Rd. In the Paddington area north of Hyde Park is the Delmere.

Finally we list a half dozen out-of-town hotels, all approximately an hour's journey from the city. On our list of priorities we propose—even if you're here only a week—that you spend at least one night savoring the charm and ease of an English country house hotel. It is an experience without peer the world over. Most visitors tend to take day-long bus trips or drives out of London anyway; all we're suggesting is that instead of hauling back into town the same night, come back the next morning instead. Or, to save the fuss of checking out of your London hotel only to check back in a day later, we suggest you plan your day or days in the country at the very beginning or the very end of your trip, so you needn't worry about returning to London at all. The only problem with this plan is that these hotels are dangerously seductive. If you spend your first night in the country, you may never make it to London. If you spend your last night in the country, you may never make it to the airport. However you plan to do it, get out of town at least one night; you won't regret it.

🧳 THE SELECTIONS

To the right of each hotel name, you'll find location information: First is the name of the London neighborhood the hotel is in, followed by a reference to the atlas which will give you a more specific idea of location. For example, the key given for The Basil Street Hotel, below, is p. 4, 4B, so you would turn to page 4 in the atlas section and find the square where the coordinates 4 and B meet. A few of London's best hotels are not within the parameters of our street map so only a neighborhood name is given.

All phone numbers for London hotels should be dialed with an 01 prefix. All prices quoted are inclusive of VAT unless otherwise noted. Many hotels accept credit cards. Our abbreviations are as follows: AE—American Express, DC—Diners Club, MC—MasterCard, and V—Visa.

Here then is our list of the best of London's hotels:

The Abbey Court, KENSINGTON
20 Pembridge Gardens, W2 4DU; tel. 221-7518; telex 262 167 ABBYCT; fax 01-792 0858
Singles from £70, doubles from £95, not including breakfast.
Although the location of this delightful newcomer is a bit out of the way, the owners have taken great care to entice prospective guests. The rooms of this Victorian townhouse are beautifully appointed, beginning with the downstairs lobby where an array of papers and magazines awaits the weary tourist. The guestrooms have been returned to their original 19th century luxuriousness and are chockablock with surprises like British mineral water, fine oils, often four-poster beds, and always marble baths *with* Jacuzzi, and stocked with an array of Crabtree and Evelyn toiletries. Breakfast, light snacks, wines and spirits are available and will be delivered to your room in a most attractive presentation. The Abbey manages to combine the Old-World ambience of antiques and faultless service with modern touches like TV, phones, telex and fax service. All major credit cards.

The Basil Street Hotel KNIGHTSBRIDGE; P. 4, 4B
Basil St., Knightsbridge, SW3 1AH; tel. 581-3311; telex 28379
Double room with private bath £110 (without breakfast)
Around the block from Harrods, the Basil Street is one of those English hotels you thought disappeared with hansom cabs and the Empire. Quiet and discreet, they still slice roast beef from a silver trolley in the dining room. You get the strange sensation that Graham Greene is staying in the room next to yours. It's British as the British like it, not gussied up and modernized for

North Americans. This also means that the rooms can be small, and not all of them have private bath, but when it comes to service, everything is just so, from a morning paper with breakfast to a shoe-shining service overnight. The 103 rooms are cheerily furnished with antiques, some with original 1910 marble baths. The public rooms are decorated with a good collection of Oriental porcelain and paintings. The hotel has a restaurant, coffeeshop, wine bar, and lots of repeat customers (who eventually qualify for a discounted rate). All rooms have TV, telephone, and 24-hour room and valet service. All major credit cards.

The Beaufort   KNIGHTSBRIDGE; P. 4, 5A
33 Beaufort Gardens, SW3 1PP; tel. 584-5252; telex 929200; fax (01) 589-2834
Doubles from £120 (including a generous Continental breakfast)
You might easily miss this hotel on one side of a little oval of plane trees tucked just off Brompton Rd. There is only a small brass nameplate to let you know you've arrived. Once inside you may still wonder if you haven't wandered into somebody's house by accident. There's no reception desk, you're simply given a front door key and can come and go as you please. There's no coffeeshop, just help yourself at the honor bar in the drawing room. This is not to say you'll be neglected; the staff will be there at an instant's notice with restaurant reservations, extra towels, or telex assistance. The point is that the Beaufort wants you to feel completely at home, so it's arranged like a home. Waiting in your room will be a decanter of brandy, chocolate eggs (from Lindt, a family connection with the owners), soft bathrobes, and lots of flowers everywhere. The 29 rooms are country-house chintz given a cosmopolitan context: thick carpets, bleached-wood furniture, strong-print floral drapes, TV, phone, and private bath. All major credit cards.

Brown's Hotel   MAYFAIR; P. 5, 3C
Albermarle St. and Dover St., W1A 4SW; tel. 493-6020; telex 28686
Double room from £155 (not including breakfast)
James Brown retired from service as a gentleman's gentleman and, with a tidy sum he had saved, opened a hotel in 1837 so he could continue doing what he knew best: providing a civilized, comfortable town address for the gentry. Over the past dozen years Brown's has become a favorite with an international clientele seeking Victorian elegance and serenity. The hotel expanded from the original row houses (painted coffee brown, of course) on Dover St. to include the St. George Hotel, back-to-back on Albermarle St. The clientele has ranged from Rudyard Kipling to Eleanor and FDR. The guest rooms are off a series of up-and-down halls and stairs. They are decorated for ease rather than elegance and there are occasional mismarriages of old and new, but they are mostly comfortable and restful. All rooms have telephone, TV, and private bath. L'Aperitif restaurant is capably run by chef Michael Davies. Afternoon tea in the lounge is duly celebrated. All major credit cards.

The Capital
Basil St., Knightsbridge, SW3 1AT; tel. 589-5171; telex 919042
HOTCAP; fax (01) 225-0011
Single rooms £125, doubles from £150, suites £210 (exclusive of breakfast)
The Capital is a small, full-service hotel strategically situated for
shopping, museums, and Hyde Park. Much work has been done
recently to attract the international business traveler. Rooms
have been refurbished in a style as comfortable as it is luxurious,
with Ralph Lauren fabrics flown in from 72nd St. in New York
and furniture custom-designed and made in Scotland to a very
high standard of craftsmanship. The colors are deep and
warm—tartans, paisleys, and tweed—and there are original oils
and prints on the walls. Suites have escritoires with desk and
hideaway TV; baths with Italian marble, terry robes, and Capital
cosmetics. Each room is air-conditioned. TV, radio, and light
controls are tucked conveniently next to the bed. The hotel provides 24-hour concierge, room, valet, and laundry services. It
is also one of the few small hotels with a restaurant worth bothering about; Michelin-starred chef John Elliot serves French-ish
food in a formal French setting that is popular with business
lunchers. The wine list is exclusively French and very expensive.
Reservations are necessary. All major credit cards.

The Delmere Hotel
130 Sussex Gardens, Hyde Park, W2 1UB; tel. 706-3344; telex
893857; fax 01-262 1863
**Single room £56, double £68.50 (including a buffet break-
fast)**
On a street lined with standard (shabby) B&Bs, this neat, compact hotel is a real find, outshining its neighbors by a long shot.
Completely redecorated and updated in 1989, the Delmere welcomes with rooms decorated in delicate shades of mauve, jade
and rose softly illuminated by overhead lights and formalized
with heavy swag draperies. Although the rooms are petite,
space has been found for all the necessities: TV, direct-dial
phones, and a kettle if you're keen for an en-suite cuppa. Downstairs is the Sous Sol restaurant, scene of a generous breakfast
buffet, and a lounge with gas fire, chess set, magazines and
books. Crown rooms include Jacuzzi, and rooms at the top of
the house are especially picturesque (tucked under the eaves
with dormer windows). Full laundry and concierge service is
available. Steps away from Hyde Park to the south and Paddington Station to the north, this is a most welcome addition to the
area. All major credit cards.

Dorset Square Hotel
39/40 Dorset Sq., NW1 6QN; tel. 723-7874; telex 263 964 DOR-
SET G; fax (01) 729-3328
**Small doubles £80, luxury suites from £150 (without break-
fast)**
Looking at the map, Dorset Square seems a bit out of the way,
but it is actually within steps of the Underground. The square
in question, aside from being planted with graceful chestnuts
and very quiet, is famous for being the site of Henry Lord's first

cricket ground, which has since developed into Lord's—"the official home of cricket"—just northwest of here. So from the outset, this hotel is set in a place sacred to British tradition. This is a small hotel in two parts occupying several listed Regency buildings, the double rooms at 39/40 and the suites at 25 Dorset Sq. Rooms have hand-painted trim and details in soft shades, and they are often furnished with antique wardrobes that have heaps of hanger space. Marble and mahogany bathrooms are roomy, with Gilchrist and Soames toiletries littered about. The rooms have lots of extras: mineral water, two separate phone lines (in the suites), and bowls of potpourri. Some of the suites have gas-fired marble fireplaces. Cricket memorabilia is deployed throughout. Credit cards: AE, MC, V.

Dukes
ST. JAMES'S; P. 5, 4C

St. James's Place, SW1A 1NY; tel. 491-4840; telex 28283; fax (01) 493 1264

Doubles £170, suites from £310 (not including breakfast)

Secreted down a little passage off St. James's Place is a courtyard brightened by gas lamps and a cascade of potted flowers. Here you'll find Dukes Hotel. Dukes manages, as it has since its beginnings in 1908, to be located in the middle of everything but at the same time to feel private and restful. The clientele tends to be British and European with a smattering of in-the-know Yanks. It is a smallish, personal hotel and vigorously kept that way. Its 58 bedrooms and suites, including a penthouse with patio, all still have the feel of a classic gentleman's club. There are humorous sporting prints on the walls, crisp-cased pillows, antique mahogany reproductions, and fresh freesia adding a touch of softness. The baths are mahogany with old-style chrome fixtures. Suites have brass knockers on the door and a kitchen or kitchenette. Seamless, seemingly effortless service is standard at Dukes. The forty-seat modern-British restaurant with its trompe l'oeil murals and Roland Batchelor watercolors is recommended. Over the years Dukes has had a very loyal following, including Lord Byron, Oscar Wilde, Frédéric Chopin, and Edward Elgar. All major credit cards.

Durrant's Hotel
MARYLEBONE; P. 1, 2B

George St., W1H 6BJ; tel. 935-8131; telex DURHOT 894919; fax (01) 487-3510

Singles with shower from £60, twin with bath from £80— request a room with shower if necessary—(prices do not include breakfast)

Durrant's is steps away from the marvelous Wallace Collection and blocks away from Regent St. shopping in Marylebone. The ceiling of the pine-paneled lobby has a charming sag to it just below the double stairs that join for a single sweep into the room. All the public rooms here are dark, cozy havens in which to enjoy the paper, a G&T, and a moment of quiet before setting out for the evening. This former coaching hotel celebrates its centenary this year. Fortunately, Durrant's is still privately owned and has had a century to work out the perfect equation of upscale service and modest prices. Rooms are decorated in shades of buff and brown with a smattering of Edwardian furniture, TV, radio, phone, and mirrored armoires. Doubles tend to be smaller than twins, so book the latter if you need room to roam. Singles are small but not skimpy, and they are reasonably priced, hence very popular. Amenities include concierge, room, and business services. Credit cards: AE, MC, V.

Ebury Court Hotel
BELGRAVIA; P. 4, 5B

26 Ebury St., SW1W O6U; tel. 730-8147

Doubles with bath (but not necessarily shower) £77

There are several four-poster-bed rooms available for the same price as a standard double, so try to reserve one of these. All prices include full English breakfast served in a sweet little downstairs café. Belgravia is one of London's most exclusive addresses, but surprisingly Ebury Court is neither snooty nor expensive. It appears to be quite a standard, low-cost hotel on a middle-class street within spitting distance of Buckingham Palace, Harrods, and Victoria Station. What is well above standard are the 38 bedrooms, with pastel color schemes, cotton twill bedspreads, radios, phones, and built-in closets. The atmosphere is old-fashioned, like visiting a favorite auntie whose linens were always fresh and soft and who always made a big fuss over you. This hotel offers a very good value for the money, which people know, so book well in advance. Credit cards: MC, V.

Elizabeth Hotel
BELGRAVIA; P. 5, 5C

37 Eccleston Sq., Victoria, SW1V 1PB; tel. 828-6812/3

Double rooms with shower only £48, large double with full bath £61 (including full English breakfast)

Situated in an otherwise busy, bustling precinct is this cosy, simple hotel set at the far end of a garden square, away from all the traffic. The canary yellow townhouse has a prime view of the garden and keys are available to guests who wish to stroll through its flowered paths. This is a perfect place for families on a budget: rooms are not grand, but rather bright with flowery wallpapers, and comfortable with a few nice older pieces scattered among the newer furnishings. The rooms with shower may *not* include in en-suite WC, so be sure to request one if you so desire. The public spaces are decorated with prints and inviting chairs. The location near to Victoria Station and Westminster makes this a perfect touring base for the traveler looking for comfort at a reasonable price. Of special note—garden-view rooms are available at the same rate, so be sure to request one overlooking the square. Credit Cards: MC, V.

The Fenja
CHELSEA; P. 4, 5A

69 Cadogan Gardens, SW3 2RB; tel. 589-7333; telex 934272 FENJA G; fax (01) 581-4958

Single £85, standard double £99, superior twin and suites £160 (additional charge for breakfast)

The Fenja's drawing room welcomes you with the scent of fresh flowers and mellowed leather. Fix yourself a drink at the honor-tab bar and settle in with *The Times.* The Fenja is the closest you can come to finding a private town house in this cosmo capital city. The 14 grandly sized bedroom suites are named for famous writers and painters who previously chose this part of

London for its garden squares, shaded sidewalks, and tranquillity. The Rossetti Room has a triptych of dormer windows overlooking Cadogan Gardens and appropriately Pre-Raphaelite antiques. As in all rooms, there is a tray of liquors in cut-glass decanters. The J. M. W. Turner room has a working fireplace and great folds of curtains tumbling to the floor, and it is decorated in the soft liquid tints favored by the artist. All rooms have a portrait of their namesake and a card explaining his or her importance to the neighborhood and the world of arts and letters. Your every need is anticipated by a small but superior staff: wonderful J. Floris toiletries, fresh flowers, TV, phone, business services, access to private Cadogan Gardens, and a light-meal room service. Breakfasts are worth the extra money. Among the best in its class. All major credit cards.

Forty-Seven Park Street   MAYFAIR; P. 4, 3B
47 Park St., Mayfair, W1Y 4EB; tel. 491-7282; telex 22116 LUXURY; fax (01) 491-7281
One-bedroom suites from £205, exclusive of VAT
This hotel is very convenient to West End theaters, shopping, and galleries. It is an all-suite establishment in a building converted from apartments, so each unit has a large bedroom, sitting and dining room, kitchen, and bath. But if you ask the manager what sets this establishment apart from all the others in London, he'll reply without hesitation, "Room service." You wonder, how special could room service be? Extremely special when it's provided by Le Gavroche, arguably London's finest French restaurant. Le Gavroche shares owner/chef Albert Roux, who is Forty-Seven Park Street's managing director. M. et Mme. Roux have developed a hotel along Parisian lines: chic, dramatic, and extremely luxurious. King-size beds are topped with fluffy duvets, there are Floris cosmetics, robes and towels embroidered with the hotel's signature orchid, Limoges drinking glasses, and a safe for your valuables. The hotel is very expensive, but for some people guaranteed reservations at Le Gavroche—next door through the hotel's private entrance—are worth their weight in gold. All major credit cards.

The Gore   SOUTH KENSINGTON; P. 4, 4A
189 Queen's Gate, SW7; tel. 584-6601; telex 296244
Singles from £69, doubles from £85, deluxe rooms £135 (breakfast not included)
Just down the block from Hyde Park and Kensington Gardens, and around the corner from the Kensington museums, the Gore is a hotel with a penchant for the fun and flamboyant. You're greeted by a profusion of flowers in boxes and planters as you ascend the steps of this 1851 town house built by the marquess of Queensberry and converted to a hotel in 1908. There are standard singles and doubles with above-standard decor. But the real fun happens in the special suites: like No. 211, decorated in Baroque style with a coquettish Venus peering down from the wall, Judy Garland's gilt bed, and a hand-painted Zeus driving his chariot over the tub in the marble bath. The Tiger Room has a rug of the same with amber eyes and a sumptuous bed in a curtained alcove. The Tudor Room has wood floors, stained

glass, beams overhead, and a curtained four-poster bed. All rooms have private bath, phone, and TV. There is a bar and a brasserie-style restaurant. All major credit cards.

The Goring Hotel
BELGRAVIA; P. 4, 5C

Beeston Place, Grosvenor Gardens, SW1W 0JW; tel. 834-8211; telex 919166

Singles from £95, doubles from £138 (breakfast is extra)

Built in 1910, the Goring is one of the best and (sadly) one of the last family-run hotels in this city. Builder O. R. Goring's grandson, George Goring, is still very much in charge of operations, and, a third-generation hotelier, he is much fussier than you could possibly be. That's why the Goring is especially popular with the British—it was Hotel of the Year in 1988. The rooms have deep, rich color schemes, brass beds, and thick royal blue carpets, a shade taken up in the bedspread, canopy, and curtains. Baths are all wood, marble, brass, and Gilchrist and Soames English herb cosmetics. Out back there is a private garden full of flowers and a lawn most spacious for these parts. Rooms overlooking the garden cost no more than others, so request one. Beeston Place is around the corner from Buckingham Palace and Victoria Station. There is a sense of tradition and continuity at the Goring; some of the staff are 15-year veterans. The 24-hour concierge will arrange golf and tennis nearby, swimming down the street, and provide you with a jogging map of the Royal Parks. All rooms have private bath, TV, phones, and most have air-conditioning. All major credit cards.

Halcyon
KENSINGTON

81 Holland Park, W11 3RZ; tel. 727-7288; telex 226721 HALCYON G; fax (01) 229-8516

Singles from £125, doubles from £175, suites from £225

Halcyon occupies a pair of almost-pink town houses with a lacy wrought-iron canopy. Holland Park is London's prettiest, set on the side of a hill in the northwest corner of the city—a supremely secluded location. The signature kingfishers refer to the Greek myth of the beautiful Halcyon, who threw herself into the Aegean Sea when her husband was swept overboard. The gods spared the pair, turning them into kingfishers equally content in water or air. Halcyon is furnished in a style they call Belle Epoch. What used to be one hundred mediocre rooms have been converted into 44 spacious doubles and suites. The walls are covered in fabric hung with Impressionist oils. Bathrooms are elegantly stocked with Czech and Speake toiletries, a scale, bidet, phone, towels, and robes embroidered with the kingfisher; some have Jacuzzis. The Halcyon Suite has its own conservatory. Amenities include satellite TV, air-conditioning, 24-hour concierge, laundry and room services, as well as a wine bar and garden restaurant. All major credit cards.

Hazlitt's
SOHO; P. 2, 3D

6 Frith St., Soho Square W1V 5TZ; tel. 434-1771

Single rooms £65; doubles £75 (excluding VAT and breakfast)

Poet and essayist William Hazlitt entertained many illustrious guests here including Jonathan Swift and Charles Lamb—

names which have been given to the guestrooms in this "hotel of character." An air of civility and gentility still remains here: built in 1718, the rooms maintain many of their 18th century details, (non-working) fireplaces, moldings, woodwork. The current owners have also incorporated over 5,000 prints from their private collection, so every nook and cranny is of special interest. Other (somewhat) more recent arrivals include original Victorian bathtubs, mahogany loos, dried flowers, telephones and full concierge service. The rooms, all different in character and shape, are spread across three connecting townhouses just south of Soho Square. Guests also have access to breakfast, bar and tea service. It's hard to imagine a more perfect retreat in the heart of central London. All major credit cards.

Hyatt Carlton Tower   BELGRAVIA; P. 4, 5B
Cadogan Place SW1X 9PY; tel. 235-5411; telex 21944; fax 01-235 9129

Double rooms from £170; suites from £295 (exclusive of VAT and breakfast)

The Hyatt incorporates all the needs of the modern traveler and all the niceties of an old-fashioned grand hotel. Tradition is celebrated at teatime in the Chinoiserie Lounge where tea comes accompanied not only by scones but also by the strains of a harpist. Service is impeccable from nightly turn-down to full fax, telex and secretarial facilities. The hotel overlooks Cadogan Gardens which contain tennis courts available to guests, but the attention to your health doesn't stop there—a full fitness club (the only one available in-house at any London hotel) with classes, weight machines, bikes and solarium overlooks the gardens from its rooftop perch. The guestrooms, 224 in all, are decorated with reproduction antiques, plush carpeting, and extras like greenery, chocolates, monitor TV, safe, phones in the bedroom as well as in the marble-tiled bath, and of course *The Times* delivered to your door in the A.M. Rooms facing south overlook Cadogan Gardens, ones facing west, Sloane St. and Harrods. The Rib Room and Chelsea Room Conservatory are favorite haunts of the local business community as well as of guests. Non-smoking floors are available. All major credit cards.

Hyde Park Hotel   KNIGHTSBRIDGE; P. 4, 4B
Knightsbridge, SW1Y 7LA; tel. 235-2000; telex 262057; fax (01) 235-2000

Singles from £165, doubles from £190, suites from £475 (not including breakfast); special weekend packages are available

The Hyde Park is one of the few larger hotels listed; it is special in many ways, principally among which is the staff's ease and confidence in delivering country-inn service at a truly grand hotel. Unlike its colleagues along Park Lane, which are separated from the park by multilanes of fast and heavy traffic, the Hyde Park Hotel is right on Hyde Park—right in Hyde Park, actually: A small, unassuming gate leading into the dining room is Royal Park property, and permission must be had from Buckingham Palace each time it is used. The location is superb. On the opposite front of the hotel is Knightsbridge; Harvey Nichols is across the street, Harrods is down the block. London is a city that can bear grand statements, and if you've ever had a yen to stay in an Old World grand hotel, this is a good place to do so. Nothing could be more breathtaking than the view up the entrance's marble stairs to explosions of flowers and a ceiling of luxurious detail. Standard rooms are large enough to accommodate delicate plaster moldings, watered-silk wall coverings, curvilinear closets, satellite TV, antiques, minibar and fridge, and bath with telephone. Nothing could be nicer than watching the horse guards pass by precisely at 10:50 A.M. right outside on their way to Buckingham Palace as you're taking your tea in the Park Room. All major credit cards.

L'Hotel
KNIGHTSBRIDGE; P. 4, 4B
28 Basil St., Knightsbridge, SW3 1AT; tel. 589-6286
Doubles are £100, there is one suite for £135 (breakfast is included)
L'Hotel is a successful hybrid: too luxurious to be called a B&B, too casual to be called a hotel. There are 12 rooms—all with bath, TV, phone, and minibar. The decor is country antique, but the country could be Tennessee or Provence or Wales. There are primitives of farm animals, baskets of dried flowers, stenciling on walls and furniture, straw matting on the floor, and a rocking chair in the tiny reception area. L'Hotel is a new idea in lodging presented by the owners of the Capital up the street, with which there is a reciprocal arrangement for business facilities, laundry, and the like. There is a wine bistro, Le Metro, in the basement for breakfast. Credit Cards: AE, V.

Number Sixteen
CHELSEA; P. 4, 5A
16 Sumner Place, SW7 3EG; tel. 589-5232; telex 266638
Singles from £60, doubles from £125 (including breakfast)
Ask six Londoners where they would send a friend looking for a nice hotel in a good location for a reasonable price, and Number Sixteen will be mentioned a half dozen times. What began at No. 16 now stretches across three Victorian town houses built in 1848, set between the main shopping meccas of Old Brompton and Fulham roads. The rooms are named for colors, among other things. The Olive Room is just that: soft green complemented by antiques, bargello-pattern fabrics, etchings, and Woods of Windsor soaps in the smallish bathrooms. There are TV, phone, fridge with complimentary mixers, and pots of fresh flowers. But speaking of flowers, try to get a room in back, not too high up, in order to get the best view of Number Sixteen's gem of a garden, a fury of color most of the year. Your breakfast will be delightful served here. All major credit cards.

Pembridge Court Hotel
KENSINGTON
34 Pembridge Gardens, W2 4DX; tel. 229-9977; telex 298363
Singles from £55, doubles from £70 (including full English breakfast)
Pembridge Court is just off Pembridge Sq., a garden bordered by the white 19th-century town houses characteristic of the neighborhood, Notting Hill. Pembridge Court is convenient to the Underground, the market at Portobello Rd., and the parks over the hill. Pembridge, the cat, will slip down from his nook

under the stairs to supervise your arrival. The hotel has 25 rooms with phone, TV, hair dryer, trouser press, and private bath or shower. To see how it outshines the competition, you have only to peek in at the other hotels on the street. Pembridge Court is ingeniously decorated with framed theatrical costumes, Victorian slippers, fans, and lace dresses. Baths are comfortably sized with pine appointments, striped towels, and L'Avenie soap. Standard twins are on the small side but serviceable. Singles have double-size beds. Breakfast can be taken at Caps, the downstairs bistro named for jockeys' striped headgear. Pembridge Court offers many amenities for which you'd pay twice as much elsewhere. All major credit cards.

Portobello Hotel   KENSINGTON
22 Stanley Gardens, W11 2NG; tel. 727-2777; telex PORT G
Single £54.05, double £86.25, special rooms from £126.35 (including en-suite Continental breakfast)
Like Pembroke Court, the Portobello Hotel is in Notting Hill and convenient to the same things. The lounge, full of potted ferns and a selection of reverse glass equestrian paintings, opens out to a glorious private backyard garden for the surrounding houses, and it is most popular with the hotel's guests. The feel is one of colonial ease. Bedrooms have been fitted out with custommade mahogany and brass built-in drawers and closets, shirred scalloped curtains, and cream and ecru wall coverings to a most handsome effect. There are several special rooms worth requesting, if you don't mind spending a bit more. The Round Room has a round bed and fixtures. The Bath Room has a Victorian tub in the middle of the room. Some rooms have a Jacuzzi; request one overlooking the garden. All have phone, TV, and bath (some WCs are quite tiny). All major credit cards.

The Ritz   ST. JAMES'S; P. 5, 4C
Piccadilly, W1V 9DG; tel. 493-8181; telex 267200
Singles £155, doubles from £185, suites from £410
Cesar Ritz was a willful man. When Cesar decided he wanted to build a hotel to rival the palaces of imperial France, there was just no stopping him. If Versailles or Chambord appeals to you, the Ritz might be just the thing. The public rooms are beneficently Baroque, with gilt chandeliers and statuary, gold-leaf trim, and frivolous murals in the style of Fragonard. Of course afternoon tea at the Palm Court is an institution: young ladies are treated for their 18th birthday, and older ladies look on conspiratorially, remembering when. Luckily a lot of the original turn-of-the-century details have been retained—most especially the Ritz's signature gold leaf gleaming from moldings, cornices, and ceilings. Some rooms have 1906 brass beds, marble fireplaces, and French vanities. The best rooms face west over Green Park. Bathrooms might be a tad smaller than expected but have Ritz royal blue towels and toiletries, bidets, and phones. All hotel services you'd expect at these prices are provided. A special treat is big-band dancing on Fri. and Sat. from 10 P.M. to 1 A.M. in the Palm Court. All major credit cards.

The Savoy
COVENT GARDEN; P. 5, 3D

The Strand, WC2R 0EU; tel. 836-4343; telex 24234; fax (01) 240-6040

Singles from £140, doubles £165, suites from £250

In the American Bar are hung portraits of famous Savoyards of yore—Fred and Ginger, Bogey and Baby, Hope and Crosby. Looking around the hotel, you can just picture them here, fitting right into the all-out glamour of the place. Garbo stayed here, and the Savoy is very much in the *Grand Hotel* manner. There is still a system of call lights for every chamber whereby you can summon the waiter (red), the maid (yellow), or the valet (green). Every floor has one of each at the ready at all times. The rooms are decorated in sinuous thirties Deco: rounded closets with space enough for grand tour trunks, vast tubs, and cerulean tiles in the blue bathrooms (many guests request blue bathrooms specifically). Of course the Thames suites offer the most spectacular view of any hotel in London, bar none. Impresario Richard D'Oyly Carte built the hotel with money made from his protégés Gilbert and Sullivan. Its prime location is in the center of London theaters, and it is the best hotel close to business in the City. Indeed, many a gray suit can be spotted power-breakfasting at a river-view table. All major credit cards.

OUT-OF-TOWN HOTELS

It is foolish to say that London isn't the "Real England." Of course it is. But London is not the Only England, not hardly. Another equally important England is the England that is, well, Not London. There's a lot of this Not-London England out there, and an afternoon's junket to Windsor Castle just can't quite convey what exurban Britain is all about.

The crash course we recommend—we'd like to make it obligatory with the purchase of this book, but that would be a tad doctrinaire—is to spend a night or two in a country house hotel. We suggest positioning such a visit either at the beginning or the end of your stay to save the extra packing chores.

We have selected a half dozen truly spectacular properties, all of which are less than an hour's journey out of the capital. Since all of them are in the country—some quite completely so—of course it would be best to hire a car and drive; however, if you're unsure about left-hand roads or wish to save the expense, they all can be reached by inexpensive public transportation with perhaps a 10- or 15-minute taxi ride from a bus or rail station. Every one of these hotels is handpicked, deluxe in every way. While they're not inexpensive, if you're staying at a first-class hotel in London, they will probably prove less costly; if you're staying at a moderately priced hotel in town, they will be worth pinching your pence for the splurge.

The Bell Inn

Aston Clinton, Buckinghamshire, HP22 5HP; tel. (0296) 630252; telex 83252 BELINN G

Doubles from £90, four-poster-bed rooms from £110, suites from £110 (including Continental breakfast)

The Bell is easily reached on the A41 from London, or you can take a train from Marylebone Station to Aylesbury and a taxi to the hotel, about 8 miles. Behind the large brass bell on the street is a 16th-century coaching inn on what used to be the main route to London from the northwest. Although the Bell Inn is not way out in the country like some of the other properties mentioned here, it bears including because it, too, is a unique, precious resource. Decorated with fine antiques, and candlelit whenever possible, it is the closest you'll ever come to the feeling of finding a haven of ease along the long ride to London, as did its 16th-century patrons. Rooms are in the main inn or across the street in the cobbled courtyard which now features a sparkling fountain instead of hustling ostlers. Courtyard rooms overlook or open out onto lovely garden patios that lead into the inn's extensive formal and informal gardens.

The rooms are warm and welcoming with antiques—some with four-poster beds—thick carpets, flowers, a lemoned finger bowl, and stationery in water-print boxes. Bathrooms are tiled, with towels, robes, bidet, and Crabtree and Evelyn soaps. The dining room is extraordinary with its wraparound murals of the four seasons and its outstanding menu accompanied by a most reasonable wine list. The Harrises have run the Bell for years with pride and with great concern that every detail should be perfect. They have succeeded brilliantly. Credit Cards: MC, V.

Great Foster's

Egham, Surrey, TW20 9UR; tel. (0784) 433822
Double room from £78, special rooms £110

Great Foster's, in Surrey, southwest of London, is 35 minutes by train and taxi from Waterloo Station, London. Or you can take the Underground to Heathrow and pick up a taxi there—only 7 miles away. If you have a car, it's perfectly situated for visiting Windsor and Eton or Oxford. However, once you arrive you may not want to budge from the 17 acres of gardens. Great Foster's was built as a hunting lodge in 1550. As you enter, you'll be transported to the 16th century. The hall is strewn with Persian carpets, 17th-century antiques, and a plaster ceiling whose color hints at a history of many satisfying pipes. Out the diamond-paned leaded windows is a view to the topiary gardens and the park. There are a total of 45 rooms, twenty in the main building, half of which are period rooms. The Tapestry Room was Charlie Chaplin's favorite for its wide floorboards, plaster ceiling, original fireplace, and, of course, tapestries. The Italian Room is decorated in the Baroque style with patterned silk on the walls and gold velvet on the bed. The Queen Anne Suite has a four-poster overlooking the rooftop and lawns, a brass chandelier, and 17th-century armour.

The restaurant is in the former tithe barn used by the parson for storing grain; a huge sagging fireplace sits below a double-tiered iron chandelier hung from the beamed ceiling. Sat. nights from 8 to midnight there is dancing to an orchestra. All rooms have private bath, TV, radio, and phone. There is a heated pool and a tennis court. All major credit cards except CB.

Inn on the Lake

Godalming, Surrey, GU7 1RH; tel. (04868) 5575/6

Single or double £60, with Jacuzzi £70
By car, A3 to A3100 to Godalming in the southwest in Surrey.
By rail from Victoria Station to Godalming. About forty minutes.
The Cummings, Joy and Martin, have been running the inn to
great acclaim for several years now. Joy attends to decorating
chores and Martin to administration, and everything runs
smooth as silk. The house is a conglomeration of periods: warm
Tudor, formal Georgian, and of course 20th-century TVs,
phones, Jacuzzis, and an inventive menu to keep your palate
tickled. All rooms have lovely views, but request one overlooking
the lake. There are antiques on the one hand, big picture windows on the other for a most fortuitous commingling of the old
and the new. The dining room is alive with the gurgle of an Italian
fountain right in the middle. Dinner will run about £18. The pub
is cosy with fireplace, deer trophies, and even a few family portraits. The Inn on the Lake is south and a little west of London
and is good for exploring the coast from Portsmouth to Brighton.
All major credit cards.

Le Manoir aux Quat' Saisons

Great Milton, Oxfordshire, OX9 7PD; tel. (0844) 278881; telex
837552 BLANC RG
**Doubles from £150, suites from £300 (including an elegant
Continental breakfast). Midweek rate breaks including dinner for two are an excellent value**
Ahhhh, Le Manoir . . . lounging in the Hyacinth Suite swathed
in a fluffy robe, a glass of fine Madeira in hand, nibbling on a
passion fruit, waiting for the Jacuzzi to fill up, peering out the
15th-century casement onto the drive and gardens, anticipating
a glorious meal at Raymond Blanc's stellar restaurant downstairs. Le Manoir might very well be the finest country house
hotel in England. It's an easy 45-minute drive out of London to
the northwest on the M40; or you can take public transportation
to Oxford, 15 minutes away, and a cab from there; or alight in
real style at Le Manoir's private helipad. Set in a stunning 15th-
to-17th-century house surrounded by lawns, park, and water
gardens, it has a swimming pool, a tennis court, and sublime
peace and quiet. The garden is brought indoors by Patricia Col-
beck, Mrs. Blanc's mother, who has "made a spectacle" of the
flowers with fresh, fragrant arrangements all over. Rooms are
named for various flowers and are decorated accordingly. The
older portions of the manor have exposed beams and high ceilings. All rooms overflow with elegance, antiques, rich fabrics,
flowers, mineral water, fruit; bathrooms, with brass fittings and
bidets, some with Jacuzzi. And if this weren't enough, as mentioned, the restaurant is on everyone's list of "musts." M. Blanc
is a self-taught chef from Besançon, and his six-course
menu is worth every farthing of £40. Wine is also pricey, but the
point is, to eat at Le Manoir and to stay at Le Manoir is one of
those once-in-a-lifetime splurges you really do deserve—don't
you? All major credit cards.

Tylney Hall

Rotherwick near Hook, Hampshire, RG27 9AJ; tel. (0256)
764881

Singles from £78, doubles from £92 (including breakfast)
Southwest of London, by car, the M3 to the B3349, located on Basingstoke Road, signposted from Rotherwick. By rail from Waterloo Station to Hook, about 16 miles away; 45 minutes from London. The approach to Tylney Hall is past a vast carpet of perfect croquet-lawn green up to this Tudor-Jacobean-style mansion, shaded by great trees that dwarf even the great house's rows of chimneys. Those chimneys very likely service one of the original fireplaces you'll find in your room. Each room, with high ceilings and rich moldings around the wall and fireplaces, allows enough space to stretch out in. Fabrics are chintz and chinoiserie for floor-to-ceiling drapes and perhaps a four-poster canopy. The dining room is bright, with sun streaming through the windows and the skylight overhead. An à la carte meal will be £25–£35; table d'hôte, £19. The comprehensive wine list ranges all the way from £9–£105. Tylney Hall is open year-round and has indoor and outdoor pools, tennis courts, golf nearby, and of course croquet on the lawn. South and west of London, it is a base for Windsor and Eton, Stonehenge, Winchester, and Salisbury. All major credit cards.

West Lodge Park

Cockfosters Rd., Hadley Wood, Barnet, Hertfordshire, EN4 0PY; tel. (01) 440-8311; telex 24734
Singles from £75, doubles from £90 (including breakfast)
By car, A111 to Hadley Wood. By rail to Hadley Wood Station, about half an hour's journey at most. As you might have guessed from the phone number, West Lodge Park is merely 12 miles northeast of the center of London, but it feels way out in the country. Because it is. Set in 35 quiet, private acres of park, West Lodge sits beside a lake, and its arboretum contains ancient and unusual specimens. The hotel itself was a manor house built in the 16th century but has been modernized to include all the creature comforts you need, including spacious baths, TVs, phones, all overlooking the park and gardens. Rooms combine antiques with some reproduction pieces and display the house's collection of 19th-century country and sporting prints. Being as close to London as it is, West Lodge is a terrific retreat for business travelers who want to be near town but away from the bustle. The dining room offers country-house-haut selections for about £20 per meal. The wine list is large and relatively reasonable. All major credit cards.

4

PRIORITIES

As with every vast and ancient city, London has its list of not-to-be-missed activities—a very long list indeed. If you're new to the city, or if you have only a short time to spend here and don't want to waste it making wrong turns or tracking down dull monuments, have a look at the following suggestions. Most of them are obvious selections, several are not; but certainly there will be a half dozen or so that you will want to explore. Some are evening activities to keep your nights as exciting as your days in London. Along with each item we have included a brief list of other things to do in the neighborhood (when applicable) and given directions on how and when to get there. You will also be gratified to note that many items are free of charge.

To the right of each entry you will find, when applicable, a reference first to the neighborhood tour in the *London By Neighborhood* chapter, where you'll find a more detailed description, then a key to the atlas section so you can locate the sight.

BRITISH MUSEUM
BLOOMSBURY AND MARYLEBONE; P. 2, 2D

This houses collections of objects from ancient civilizations to Beatles' manuscripts, incorporating collections from the British Library. At least a half to a full day to visit. Great Russell St.; tel. 636-1555. Open Mon.–Sat., 10 A.M.–5 P.M., Sun. 2:30–6 P.M.; admission is free. Underground: Russell Square, Holborn, Tottenham Court Rd.
In the area: Percival David Foundation of Chinese Art, Regent's Park.

CHANGING OF THE GUARD
WESTMINSTER AND WHITEHALL; P. 5, 4C

The bearskin hats and scarlet uniforms and horses and bands fete the assembled masses(!) daily at 11:30 A.M., 10:30 on Sun.; during winter, every other day. May be canceled due to inclement weather or special state occasions. Buckingham Palace, the Mall. Underground: Victoria, St. James's Park, Green Park.
In the area: The Queen's Gallery, the Royal Mews, the Mall, Parliament Square, Westminster Abbey, the Royal Parks.

A TOUR OF THE CITY

London's oldest neighborhood established by the Romans. A tour should include St. Paul's and the Tower (see below), the City churches, the Smithfield Meat Market, the financial district. A good tour should take at least a day. Underground: Temple, Blackfriars, Mansion House, Cannon Street, Monument, Tower Hill, St. Paul's, Bank, Liverpool St.

HOLLAND PARK   KENSINGTON

London's loveliest—full of flowers and woodlands, an open-air theater, a cafeteria, and a restaurant. Spend an afternoon here, preferably Sun. when Londoners are out in force. Underground: Notting Hill Gate, High St. Kensington.

In the area: Linley Sambourne House, Leighton House, Kensington Palace, Portobello Rd. Market (Sat.).

MARKETS

To get the flavor of what shopping was like before indoor malls, try an outdoor market. Go early in the morning for the best buys. Some are on the fringes: Brick and Petticoat lanes and Spitalfields are just to the north and east of the City; Camden Lock is north of Bloomsbury; Smithfield Market is in the City; Portobello Rd. is on the northwest edge of Hyde Park in Notting Hill.

Brick Lane and Petticoat Lane. Clothes, records, junk— you name it on Sun. mornings. Underground: Liverpool St.

Camden Lock. Beside a canal; crafts and antiques, Sat. and Sun. Underground: Camden Town, Chalk Farm.

Portobello Road. Famous for antiques, "antiques," junk; on Sat. 8 A.M.–6 P.M. Underground: Notting Hill Gate.

Smithfield. The world's largest meat market is open midnight to 9 A.M., Mon.–Thurs. Underground: Farringdon, St. Paul's.

Spitalfields. London's vegetable market, due to be torn down, so get there before it's gone. 5–9 A.M. weekdays. Underground: Liverpool St.

MUSEUM OF LONDON   THE CITY; P. 3, 2F

A tour through the history of the city from geologic to modern times; a great intro, two hours to tour. London Wall; tel. 600-3699. Open Tues.–Sat. 10 A.M.–6 P.M., Sun. 2–6 P.M.; admission is free. Underground: St. Paul's, Barbican, Moorgate.

In the area: Barbican Centre, St. Paul's, Smithfield Market (mornings only), St. Bartholomew-the-Great.

NATIONAL GALLERY   SOHO AND COVENT GARDEN;
                                                    P. 5, 3D

European and British masterpieces; a stunning collection. Reserve at least an entire morning or afternoon. Trafalgar Square tel. 839-3321. Open Mon.–Sat. 10 A.M.–6 P.M., Sun. 2–6 P.M.; admission is free. Underground: Charing Cross.

In the area: National Portrait Gallery, Piccadilly Circus, Covent Garden, Trafalgar Square.

A NIGHT IN THE COUNTRY

To understand the English, you must spend at least one night out of London. In our *Short Trips from London* chapter, we list day trips out of town; and in our *Hotels* chapter, we list a half dozen hotels within an hour's commute. Pick a destination, pick a country house hotel, and have the time of your life.

ORIGINAL LONDON TRANSPORT SIGHTSEEING TOUR

Departs from various points at various hours; phone 227-3456. The original double-decker bus tours to give you a quick run around the city, so you can plan your more intensive touring from here. Fare: £6.

ROCK AND ROLL LIVE

If you consult your record collection, you'll be reminded how many of the bands represented are British. From the 1960s invasion of the Beatles and the Who and the Stones, to the punk days of the Sex Pistols and the Clash to modern pop from New Order and the Eurythmics, some of the world's best music has been made in Britain. Every week there are dozens of great gigs to choose from, usually at 700–2, 500-person venues where you can see your favorite major acts in an intimate, music-hall setting. Consult our *Entertainment* chapter and *Time Out* for weekly listings. Cost ranges from £3–£15 per ticket.

CHELSEA ROYAL HOSPITAL
AND RANELAGH GARDENS   BELGRAVIA, SOUTH
KENSINGTON, AND CHELSEA; P. 4, 5A

A Wren building inhabited by war veterans, the Chelsea Pensioners, set in a Thames-side garden. Lovely. Royal Hospital Rd., SW3. Open Mon.–Sat. 10 A.M.–noon and 2–4 P.M., Sun. 2–4 P.M.; admission is free. Underground: Sloane Square.

In the area: Shopping on King's and Fulham roads, Chelsea Physic Garden. Open Wed. and Sun. 2–5 P.M. only.

A NIGHT AT THE   SOHO
ROYAL OPERA HOUSE   AND COVENT GARDEN; P. 2, 3D

The Royal Opera, the Royal Ballet, and Sadler's Wells Ballet all call this home; an exquisite European opera house. A night here is a night to remember. Royal Opera House, Covent Garden; tel. 240-1066. Underground: Covent Garden.

In the area: For pre-performance visits, Covent Garden Market, the London Transport Museum, the Theatre Museum.

ST. PAUL'S CATHEDRAL   THE CITY; P. 3, 3F

Wren's masterpiece with interiors by 17th-century masters, whispering gallery, and crypt. Two or more hours depending upon how high you climb in the dome. Come for a service if you can. Admission charges for crypt, ambulatory, and galleries, and for a conducted supertour. Ludgate Hill. Underground: St. Paul's, Mansion House.

In the area: The financial district, the Old Bailey, other City churches.

SHOPPING IN SOUTH KENSINGTON AND CHELSEA

Along King's Rd., Fulham Rd., and Old Brompton Rd. you will find most of London's top shops and designers. Much more fun than a single department store or, worse yet, a shopping mall. Could take you an afternoon or all week depending on the state

of your shoes and your credit cards. Underground: Sloane
Square, South Kensington, Knightsbridge, Gloucester Rd.
In the area: Hyde Park and Kensington Gardens, Chelsea
Royal Hospital, Kensington museums.

TATE GALLERY   WESTMINSTER AND WHITEHALL; P. 5, 5D

Britain's collection of British art and modern European art. Most
famous for its collection of Turners in the newly opened Clore
Gallery. Wonderful restaurant. Half to a whole day. Millbank; tel.
821-1313. Mon.–Sat. 10:30 A.M.–5:30 P.M., Sun. 2–5:30 P.M.; ad-
mission is free with the occasional exception of special exhibits.
Underground: Pimlico, or Vauxhall and walk across the bridge.
In the area: Westminster Abbey and Parliament Sq., the Royal
Mews, and the Queen's Gallery.

TAXI TOUR BY NIGHT

Any cabbie should oblige your request to take a spin around the
capital's monuments and fountains all lit up. A suggested itinerary would be to start on the south side of the Thames (the South
Bank Centre is a good place to find taxis), cross over Waterloo
Bridge, work west along the Embankment, turn right past Parliament Sq. down Birdcage Walk to Buckingham Palace, up Constitution Hill to Hyde Park Corner, around to Park Lane, up to
Marble Arch, right onto Oxford St., right again on Regent St.,
down to Piccadilly Circus, and finish up either at Trafalgar Sq.
or continue down the Mall back to the palace and thence home.
The fare should run you £8–£10, depending on how loquacious
your driver is.

THAMES CRUISES

Departing for various destinations from various locations. Call
the River Boat Information Service, 730-4812, or stop in at any
London Tourist Board Information Centre. The Thames is the
aorta of London, and there is nothing more eye-opening in many
ways than to spend a morning, afternoon, or romantic evening
gliding with the tide watching the skyline change and the city's
most important monuments slip in and out of view. You haven't
seen London till you've seen it from the water. A basic twenty-
minute cruise departs from Westminster Pier, by Westminster
Bridge, to the Tower during spring and summer.

A NIGHT AT THE THEATER

No, we're not going to send you to the West End, although we
won't discourage it. If you really want to get your money's worth
and see a production the quality of which is unequaled elsewhere on the planet, spend a glorious evening with the National
Theatre (tel. 982-2252) at the South Bank Centre, or the Royal
Shakespeare Company (tel. 628-8795) at the Barbican Centre.
Shakespeare and his contemporaries are, of course, featured,
but the NT and the RSC also mount wonderful productions of
modern plays and are responsible for debuting many important
works, so if you don't think you could sit through *King Lear,* not
to worry; there is bound to be something to your taste running
in repertory. Prices, of course, will vary, but these nationally
funded companies' tickets are always well below West End
prices. Underground: for the NT, Waterloo, or Embankment and

walk across the river—most pleasant. For the RSC, Barbican, Moorgate.

THE TOWER OF LONDON
THE CITY; P. 3, 3G

London's most famous sight, complete with beefeaters, halls of armor, the crown jewels, and a grisly history. Very crowded; come early in the day during the week. Should take about three hours to see (almost) everything. Tower Hill; tel. 709-0765. Open Mon.–Sat. 9:30 A.M.–5 P.M., Sun. 2–5 P.M.; winter hours till 4, closed Sun. Admission is £4. Underground: Tower Hill.

In the area: St. Katharine's Dock, Tower Bridge, London Wall, the financial district.

VICTORIA AND ALBERT MUSEUM
BELGRAVIA, SOUTH KENSINGTON, AND CHELSEA; P. 4, 5A

Museum for art and design that was an outgrowth of the 1851 exhibition. *Very* wide variety of paintings, furniture, fashion, etc. At least a half to a full day. Tel. 589-6371. Open Mon.–Sat. 10 A.M.–5:50 P.M., Sun. 2:30–5:50 P.M.; admission by suggested donation. Underground: South Kensington.

In the area: Other Kensington museums, Royal Albert Hall, Hyde Park and Kensington Gardens, shopping in Knightsbridge, South Kensington, and Chelsea.

WESTMINSTER ABBEY AND PARLIAMENT SQUARE
WESTMINSTER AND WHITEHALL; P. 5, 4D

Here are the Houses of Parliament, Westminster Bridge, and Westminster Abbey. Westminster Abbey is the burial place of many of Britain's kings, queens, and august subjects. Scene of coronations and royal weddings (Andy and Fergie's, for example). Tel. 222-7110 for abbey tour information. The abbey is open Mon.–Fri. 8 A.M.–6 P.M., Sat. 9 A.M.–2:45 P.M., and for services on Sun. Try to come for choral evensong weekdays at 5. Admission charge for parts of the abbey or take a supertour. Underground: St. James's Park, Westminster.

In the area: Buckingham Palace, the Tate Gallery, the Cabinet War Rooms, Victoria Embankment.

5

TRANSPORTATION

London is one of the world's largest cities. It has engulfed many surrounding towns to create one vast megalopolis. This means that there is a great variety of landscape and atmosphere within the city limits, but it also means that it can take (quite literally) hours to get from one end of London to the other.

Chances are, however, this is not a problem you will be confronting during your stay. As we have arranged the neighborhoods, you should be able to negotiate each area on foot. And this, of course, is far and away the best way to see London. Unlike many New World cities dependent on their motor arteries, London is a pedestrian city. Its web of back streets with tiny pubs and local shops tucked along each is an enchanting change from the grid form and freeways of more modern burgs.

By all means **walk** whenever and wherever you can; this is the best way to feel at home in the city. It is very easy, however, to become lost. VERY EASY! Streets are not numbered or named in alphabetical or any other kind of order.

Public transportation in London is cheap and reliable. The **Underground** (or **tube**) is London's subterranean rail system (in Britain "subway" means a pedestrian crossing below the street); it is fast and usually quite efficient. The fare within central London is 60 pence for all destinations. Beyond the inner ring, fares increase up to about £2. Be sure you retain your ticket; it will be collected by a machine or an agent as you exit. The Underground is open Mon.–Sat. 5:30 A.M.–12 midnight, Sun. 1:30–11:30 P.M. Each station will have a sign posted shortly before closing listing the departure times for the last trains of the night. **For a map of the Underground, see atlas section.**

Buses are slower, but they service more areas and, of course, are a kick to ride if you've got only the single-decker kind at home. Buses run 24 hours, so they are the only cheap mode of transportation after the tube shuts down at midnight. However, the bus routes change completely at night—usually from about midnight–5 A.M. Night bus routes are denoted by an N before the number (i.e., N2, N93, and so on). The best way to catch a bus at night is to go to Trafalgar Square, around the north and east edges of which are bus stops for nearly all the night routes in central London. Many bus stops are "request stops" and will be so indicated on the sign. If you want the bus to pick you up at one of these, you are obliged to step out into the street and wave it down. Your fare will be collected as you get on and will vary according to the number of zones you will be crossing during your journey, beginning at 40 pence. Most drivers will make change; however, handing them large bills makes them testy. Upstairs is reserved for smokers and tends to attract the kids, so it can be the most fun place to sit (especially at night, but it can get rowdy), and, of course, the view is much better.

It is possible to buy a Travelcard for bus and/or Underground that is good for one day (£2) or for periods up to a month. Single-day passes are economical only if you plan to do a lot of traveling in one day. The weekly Travelcard is much more worthwhile and thrifty (about £6.50). You'll need to bring a passport-size photo (many tube stations have photo booths expressly for this purpose). Passes can be bought at selected travel agents, newsagents (shops), or at bus garages and Underground stations.

For London Transport Information (bus and tube) call 222-1234 toplan your route. Or phone 222-1200 to find out if there are any delays or changes in service. Information on special routes for disabled travelers is available on the 222-1234 line.

Taxis are a good idea if there are two or more of you traveling, if you need to travel a long distance in a hurry, or if you are traveling at night. Do keep in mind, however, that London daytime traffic can be horrific, so if you're just going a short distance, it will probably be much faster to walk or take the tube. There will be extra charges at night and on weekends at a fixed rate. A 10 to 15 percent tip is customary.

Next to walking, our favorite way to get around London is **by bicycle.** As with every city, London traffic has its own "rhythm," and even if you do a lot of biking at home, London biking will be different—for starters, you have to ride on the left side of the road. Motorcycle messengers and taxicabs can be merciless about cutting you off, and if you try to fight them or beat them, you're bound to lose. So just strike up a slow, steady, college-professorish pace and enjoy one of London's rarest treats. Check the London phone book for listings of a bike store near you that provides rentals or call the London Cycling Campaign, 928-7220, for suggestions or try Dial-a-Bike (828-4040). Be sure your bike has a *strong* lock, to be used at all times.

The absolute last option is to **rent a car** in London. As mentioned, London traffic can be dreadful: its streets twist, turn, become one-way in the opposite way you want to go, and are booby-trapped with cutthroat cabbies, maniacal messengers, and oblivious pedestrians. Additionally, parking is scarce and can be expensive, and the "Lovely Ritas" policing no-parking zones are generous in their distribution of parking tickets. The only possible reason for renting a car in London is if you are planning to do any extensive traveling outside the city. In this case, it is better to take the train to your destination and rent a car there, or take the tube to Heathrow and drive from there, thus avoiding the chaos of city driving and the higher prices of hiring a car in town.

6

TOURING

We do not recommend taking organized tours—those tours that cram you onto a bus with four dozen other camera-toting, sensible-shoe-wearing tourists and subject you to the tired jokes of some wag of a tour guide. Such tours invariably rush you through sights at which you'd like to spend more time or leave you yawning over some dreary clinker of a monument. The bus tours, even those arranged by different operators, all tend to hit the same places at the same time (i.e., Westminster Abbey in the morning, the Tower in the afternoon). And, of course, these tours tend to force you to do exactly what we implore you not to do: namely, randomly bounce from one red-letter sight to the next, with complete disregard for the unity and individuality of London's neighborhoods.

London is a big city, but it's not so scary that you can't easily manage it on your own. If you get lost, the townspeople speak your language (at least we assume they do, if you're reading this book). The townspeople and tapsters and shopkeepers and museum guides and tube riders collectively also know a lot more about the city than any one tour guide possibly could, and if you're traveling about on your own reconnaissance, you can tap their collective brain for information, history, local color, anecdotes, and personal recommendations far superior to and more colorful and original than those of someone who recites the same spiel day in and day out.

Now that the whole package tour business and its practitioners have been roundly lambasted, we will note a few exceptions to the rule: tours that are either 1) short and sweet, or 2) focused and specialized; either of these criteria makes them worth your time and money.

ORGANIZED TOURS OF LONDON

Original London Transport Sightseeing Tour is a quick overview of the city, whisking you around on a red double-decker bus. The tours depart daily from various locations at various hours but all follow the same route, take the same amount of time—a painless hour and a half—and charge the same practically painless rate—£6. This tour provides you with a working knowledge of how the city is laid out, what is near what, and what might be worth coming back to for a closer look. For information on times and places of departure convenient for you, call 227-3456.

The other overall sightseeing tours we recommend are those by water. You can chug along the Thames from Hampton Court to Greenwich, during the day's bustle for sightseeing or the night's romance for dinner and music. Although some riverboats run year-round, trips are drastically reduced in number from Oct. to April. For information on all **Thames River cruises,** call the River Boat Information Service at 730-4812.

The other watery part of London not so well known to visitors, but no less intriguing, is her **system of canals.** The Grand, Union and Regent's canals converge in a pretty, aqueous triangle in the northwest part of the city known as Little Venice. It is possible to glide through the back streets of town on any of several different canal barges that service several different destinations. Some boats even offer leisurely dinner cruises. The *Jason* and *Serpens* run along Regent's Canal from Little Venice to Camden Town via Camden Lock daily from Easter to Oct. Call 286-3428 for details and reservations.

The *Jenny Wren* also plies Regent's Canal on a round-trip excursion from Camden High St. past the London Zoo and Regent's Park to Little Venice and back again daily from Easter through Oct. Call 485-4433 or 485-6210 for information.

The *Regent's Canal Waterbus* is a fun way to get from here (Camden Lock) to there (the Zoo or Little Venice) daily April to Oct., weekdays only in winter. Trips eastward to the East End and Docklands are also available. Call 482-2550.

Several crackerjack companies operate **walking tours** that concentrate on one small, specific area at a time. The guides are exceptionally well informed and well read on their territory and can provide you with a rich impression of the intricacies of a particular neighborhood.

Probably the best of the bunch is **Citisights of London,** 145 Goldsmith's Row, E2 8QR (tel. 739-4853). This company employs archaeologists and historians as guides who for £3 will take you on an hour-and-a-half to two-hour stroll through various neighborhoods covering various ages and themes in London's history. Walks depart from either museums or tube stations, rain or shine. They list several dozen different walks: among them are "Lundenwic—in Search of Dark Age London," "London After the Great Fire—the City of Wren & Dr. Johnson," "London and the Big Bang—Brave New World or Rape of London?" "Bawdy House to Opera House: A Covent Garden Pub Walk."

There are also special one-time-only walks geared to holidays such as "William Shakespeare Birthday Walk Special" (April 23), "May Day Radical London Walk Special" (May 1), "Pagan Eostra to Christian Easter in London" (Easter Sun.). The list is very long and intriguing; it's best to write or call for a leaflet.

A similar operation, **Cockney Walks,** 32 Anworth Close, Woodford Green, Essex (tel. 504-9159), also employs teachers and historians and also has a provocative roster of tours, among them "The Jewish East End," "Dickens's and Fagin's Haunts,"

"St. Thomas Becket's Strange Story." Walks meet outside tube stations usually at 11 A.M. and cost £3.

The tours offered by **London Theatrical Walks,** 16 Ridgedale St., Bow, E3 2TW (tel. 980-5565), are conducted by theatrical types who do as much performing as informing along their one-and-a-half to two-hour routes, which cost £2.50. Choices include "London's Magical Theatreland," "Literary and Theatrical Fleet Street," "Shakespeare's London."

There are also several good neighborhood tours sponsored by various local organizations interested in promoting their area. A trio of good ones are: **Clerkenwell,** Clerkenwell Heritage Centre, Clerkenwell Rd. and St. John's Gate, daily walking tours spring and summer at 2:30 P.M., tel. 250-1039; **St. Bart's and Smithfield,** Main Gate of St. Bartholomew's Hospital, West Smithfield, London EC1, Sun. at 2 P.M., April–Oct., £2 (no phone), just meet at Main Gate; **Shakespeare's Bankside and Globe Theatre,** Wed. at 2 P.M. outside London Bridge Underground station, Sun. at 10:30 A.M., same meeting point, two-hour tour, £2. Operated by Learning with Pleasure, tel. 868-5055.

For those who like to live in fear, **Tragical History Tours** (tel. 857-1545 or 467-3318) runs a "Bus Trip to Murder," showing the sinister side of London. These tours depart from the Temple Underground station at 7 P.M. Mon.–Fri. in summer, Mon., Wed., and Fri. in winter. The tour lasts three-and-a-half hours and costs £8.50.

OUR OWN THEMATIC TOURS

We have also come up with some suggestions for special-interest tours based on a particular theme ("Kids' London") or period ("Victorian London") or person ("Hogarth's London"). For those of you with particular literary or artistic interests, there are entire books written on where to find the homes of artists, authors, and their characters or subjects. A good place to find such specialty touring books is Edward Stanford, 12–14 Longacre (Underground: Covent Garden). Or try Dillons The Bookstore, 82 Gower Street (Underground: Goodge Street).

Bird's-Eye London

The following are good places to go for the view:

St. Paul's Cathedral, Ludgate Hill (Underground: St. Paul's).

St. Edward's Tower, Westminster Cathedral, Francis St. (Underground: Victoria, Pimlico).

Tower Bridge (Underground: Tower Hill).

Parliament Hill, Hampstead Heath, Hampstead (Underground: Hampstead).

Golders Hill Park, Golders Green (Underground: Golders Green).

Hogarth's London

The artist William Hogarth was a lifelong resident of London and depicted its teeming bawdiness in his 18th-century engravings.

His legacy can be appreciated at:

Hogarth's House, Hogarth Lane, Great West Rd. (Underground: Chiswick Park, Turnham Green). Artist's home with relics and engravings.

Sir John Soane's Museum, 13 Lincoln's Inn Fields (Underground: Holborn). Hogarth works in the collection.

Thomas Coram Foundation for Children (Foundling Hospital Art Treasures), 40 Brunswick Sq. (Underground: Russell Square, King's Cross). Paintings by Hogarth.

National Gallery, Trafalgar Sq. (Underground: Charing Cross).

St. Bartholomew's Hospital, West Smithfield (Underground: Farringdon). Hogarth murals.

Leicester Square. (Underground: Leicester Sq.). Hogarth lived at No. 30.

Inigo Jones's London

Jones began his career as a scenic designer and grew to be a major architect and eventually surveyor-general. Jones developed the idea of the London square, beginning with his designs for Covent Garden, and was the city's first urban planner. Highlights of Jones's London include:

St. Paul's Church, Covent Garden (Underground: Covent Garden).

Banqueting House, Whitehall (Underground: Westminster, Embankment).

Lincoln's Inn Chapel, Lincoln's Inn, Lincoln's Inn Fields (Underground: Holborn).

Chiswick House, Burlington Lane (Underground: Turnham Green). Jones designed the gates.

Holland Park, off Kensington High St. (Underground: High St. Kensington, Holland Park). Jones designed Holland House gates.

Queen's House, National Maritime Museum, Romney Rd., Greenwich (Underground: Docklands Light Railway to Island Gardens, then walk through the tunnel).

Royal Institute of British Architects, 66 Portland Place, and **Heinz Gallery,** 21 Portman Sq. (Underground for both: Marble Arch). Collection of original drawings and blueprints. To view call 580-5533.

Theatre Museum, Covent Garden (Underground: Covent Garden). Scenic designs on display.

Kids' London

There's lots to do for the little tykes. Get them in the mood by reading them *Mary Poppins,* by P. L. Travers; *When We Were Very Young,* by A. A. Milne; *A Bear Called Paddington,* by Michael Bond, or *Peter Pan in Kensington Gardens,* by J. M. Barrie. You'll enjoy the books and the sights, too.

Changing of the Guard, Buckingham Palace (Underground: St. James's Park, Green Park) daily at 11:30 A.M., Sun. 10:30 A.M. with some exceptions (see *Priorities,* Chapter 4). And at Horse Guards, Whitehall (Underground: Westminster, Charing Cross) daily at 11 A.M., Sun. at 10 A.M.

Thames Cruises, Westminster Pier (Underground: Westminster) or Tower Pier (Underground: Tower Hill). Call River Boat Information Service, 730-4812.

Kite Flying, Parliament Hill, Hampstead Heath (Underground: Hampstead). Buy a kite at the Kite Store, 69 Neal Street (Underground: Covent Garden).

The Crown Jewels, Tower of London (Underground: Tower Hill).

London Zoo, Regent's Park (Underground: Baker St. or Camden Town, then take bus 74 from either). Better yet, take Regent's Canal Waterbus from Little Venice or Camden Lock (482-2250).

Bethnal Green Museum of Childhood, Cambridge Heath Rd. (Underground: Bethnal Green).

Pollock's Toy Museum, 1 Scala St. (Underground: Goodge St.).

Little Angel Marionette Theatre, 14 Dagmar Passage (Underground: Angel, Highbury & Islington). For program call 226-1787.

Hamley's, 188–96 Regent St. (Underground: Tottenham Court Rd.). World's largest toy store, purveyors of toys and games to the Royals.

Natural History Museum, Cromwell Rd. (Underground: South Kensington).

Children's Playground and Peter Pan Statue, Kensington Gardens (Underground: Lancaster Gate, Queensway).

The Book Boat, Greenwich (Underground: Docklands Light Railway, then cross at tunnel). Bookshop on a barge next to the *Gypsy Moth IV.*

Madame Tussaud's and the **London Planetarium,** Marylebone Rd. (Underground: Baker St.).

Mansion Galleries

There are several beautiful houses with fine collections of pictures and/or furniture set in parks and gardens around the outskirts of London:

Dulwich Picture Gallery, College Rd. (BritRail: Victoria Station to West Dulwich, London Bridge Station to North Dulwich).

Syon House and Park, Brentford, Middlesex (Underground: Gunnersbury).

Ranger's House, Chesterfield Walk, Blackheath (BritRail to Greenwich, then 15-minute walk).

Kenwood, Hampstead Lane (Underground: Archway or Golders Green, then bus 210 from either).

Osterley Park House, Thornbury Rd., Osterley, Middlesex (Underground: Osterley).

Rockers' London

Ever since the British Invasion of the sixties, London has been an important hub of the music scene. There are loads of songs referring to it ("London Calling," the Clash; "I Don't Want to Go to Chelsea," Elvis Costello; "Victoria," the Kinks; "Up the Junction," Squeeze; "Street Fighting Man," the Rolling Stones; etc.; etc.). Here are places any true-blue rock-and-roller should check out (see also the *Entertainment* chapter for club listings).

Abbey Rd., Kilburn (Underground: Kilburn). The album was made at No. 3.

Wardour St., Soho (Underground: Tottenham Court Rd.). Home of most big-time record companies.

Camden Lock/Dingwalls, Camden Town (Underground: Camden Town, Chalk Farm). Dingwalls club was an important hangout of early new-wavers like Elvis Costello, Nick Lowe, Blondie, et al. Camden Lock market (Sat. and Sun.) is good for picking up secondhand albums and bootleg tapes.

Cheyne Walk, Chelsea (Underground: Sloane Sq., South Kensington). Home of glimmer twins Jagger and Richards.

Bluebird Records, 376–78 Edgware Rd. (Underground: Edgware Rd.). Best shop in town for R&B and soul.

Rough Trade, 130 Talbot Rd. (Underground: Notting Hill Gate). Good store to find independent labels.

Andy's Guitar Centre & Workshop, 27 Denmark St. (Underground: Tottenham Court Rd.). Big names buy here.

Hard Rock Café, 150 Old Park Lane (Underground: St. James's Park). Dreadfully touristy, but they do have good memorabilia up on the walls and play the music real loud.

King's Road, Chelsea (Underground: Sloane Sq.). Former headquarters for punks, and you can still spot a few posing for photos around Royal Ave.

Science and Technology

Lots of innovations have come out of London, and lots of innovators have lived in London. If the history of high tech is your thing, try:

Science Museum, Exhibition Rd. (Underground: South Kensington).

Faraday's Laboratory, 21 Albermarle St. (Underground: Piccadilly Circus).

Freud Museum, 20 Maresfield Gardens, Hampstead (Underground: Finchley Rd.).

Chelsea Physic Garden, 66 Royal Hospital Rd. (Underground: Sloane Sq.). Open only Sun. and Wed. 2–5 P.M. April–Oct.

Thames Barrier Visitors' Centre, Unity Way, Woolwich (BritRail: Charlton, or by boat from Westminster Pier, call 740-8263). Mammoth Thames flood-control gates.

Old Royal Observatory, Greenwich Park (Underground: Docklands Light Railway, then walk through tunnel, or by boat from Westminster Pier, tel. 730-4812).

London Planetarium, Marylebone Rd. (Underground: Baker St.).

Theatrical London

If you aren't satisfied with seeing your theater from a seat in the auditorium, slake your thespian appetites at:

The Theatre Museum, Covent Garden (Underground: Covent Garden).

Backstage Tours at the Royal Shakespeare Company, Barbican Centre (Underground: Barbican, Moorgate) and at the **Royal National Theatre,** South Bank Centre (Underground: Waterloo).

St. Paul's Church, Covent Garden (Underground: Covent Garden). The actors' church; many give readings at Sun. services.

Westminster Abbey, Parliament Sq. (Underground: Westminster). Tombs of and memorials to great playwrights.

Southwark Cathedral, 1 Montague Pl. (Underground: London Bridge). Shakespeare window and graves of relatives.

Shakespeare Globe Museum, 1 Bear Gardens (Underground: London Bridge).

Victorian London

During the 19th century this was the First City of the Empire, and hence of the world, a time of the greatest flowering of national pride and energy. Some of the Victorians' enthusiasm can be caught at:

The Kensington Museums, Exhibition Rd., South Kensington (Underground: South Kensington). Outgrowth of the 1851 Exhibition; best is the Victoria and Albert Museum.

Leighton House, 12 Holland Park Rd. (Underground: High St. Kensington). Victorian artist's home.

Linley Sambourne House, 18 Stafford Terr. (Underground: High St. Kensington). Artist's home, open only Wed. 10 A.M.–4 P.M., Sun. 2–5 P.M.

Geffrye Museum, Kingsland Rd. (Underground: Old St., Liverpool St.). Period rooms furnished with Victoriana (and other periods).

Albert Memorial, Kensington Gardens (Underground: South Kensington). Monument to Victoria's beloved Prince Consort.

William Morris Gallery, Water House, Lloyd Park, Forest Rd., Walthamstow (Underground: Walthamstow Central). Pre-Raphaelite mecca.

The Operating Theatre of Old St. Thomas's Hospital, St. Thomas St. (Underground: Waterloo). 19th century surgery and accompanying museum. Open Mon., Wed., Fri. 12:30–4 P.M.

Christopher Wren's London

Wren is all over the map here, but we've selected some highlights:

St. Paul's Cathedral, Ludgate Hill (Underground: St. Paul's).

Chelsea Royal Hospital, Royal Hospital Rd. (Underground: Sloane Sq.).

Kensington Palace, Kensington Gardens (Underground: High St. Kensington, Queensway).

Hampton Court Palace, East Molesey Surrey, Hampton Court (BritRail: Waterloo Station to Hampton Court).

St. Mary Abchurch, Abchurch Lane, Cannon St. (Underground: Cannon St.)

Monument, Monument St. (Underground: Monument).

Ye Olde Watling, 29 Watling St. (Underground: Bank, St. Paul's). Used by Wren as an office during St. Paul's construction, now a pub.

Royal Institute of British Architects (see entry under "Inigo Jones's London," above). Drawings and blueprints available to view by appointment; tel. 580-5533.

7

LONDON BY NEIGHBORHOOD

The City

The City of London is the most important part of London; it is the heart of London. Within the City—a constitutionally defined entity granted privileged status in 1215 by King John—the Lord Mayor's position precedes that of Princes of the Blood and is second only to the reigning sovereign. Most tourists come dashing through this distinct precinct, cutting an abysmal swath across the core of the City on their headlong tear from Trafalgar Square to St. Paul's to the Tower.

DON'T DO IT! Of all the neighborhoods of London—most of whose parameters have shifted, amoeba-like, from one century to another—only the City has remained unchanged from the almost perfect square mile colonized by the Romans. They named the fishing village they found here Londinium, around which they, as was their wont, erected a wall in the second century A.D.—a wall that remained intact, in one form or another, for the next sixteen hundred years. The medieval incarnation of the wall was punctuated by a series of gates, echoes of which have filtered down in street names and Tube stations: Aldgate, Bishopsgate, Cripplegate, Aldersgate, Moorgate, Newgate, Ludgate. The wall girdled the Roman citadel, ran along the river, and was in turn ringed on the landward side by a particularly pernicious ditch into which the locals dispatched rubbish and corpses of diseased livestock.

It is via the original route of the Wall that you should mark the boundaries of the City, to get a tangible and spiritual sense of where and how this town has stood down through the millennia. There is a marked walking tour, appropriately named the London Wall Walk, which enables you to do just that, see the City from its perimeter, running from the Tower around to the Temple, and you should proceed in this westerly direction. A series of plaques, with text, drawings, and diagrams germane to each point of interest, has been set up at regular intervals en route. These also direct you by marked street map to the next stop. Nonetheless, the tour can be a bit tricky. You are sent down back streets, examining modern office blocks where you expected ancient ruins, and you may lose the thread of the trail due to a quick turn or a plaque obstructed by construction. Stick with it, and you'll be given an on-the-ground sense of the encyclopedic collection of elements essential to London that the City encompasses. Among the sites, ancient and modern, are the Tower of London, the Bank of England, the Old Bailey, the Guildhall, St. Paul's Cathedral, St. Bartholomew-the-Great, the Temple, the Barbican Centre, the Museum of London, the Stock Exchange, and the Smithfield Market.

Smithfield Market

Your day could dawn (literally) at this last, **Smithfield Market.** Smithfield is the largest and one of the last of its kind in the world, and you can only hope it'll be around for your kids (or grandkids) to see. Smithfield is a meat market, pure and simple. It's not some fustian, fossilized museum with glass cases and a gift shop. Smithfield is a working market, a place of business. And you'll have to get up pretty early in the morning to find men who work harder at their business than do the butchers who ply a convivial, cacophonous trade here; in fact, you'll have to get up last night. Servicing these ten acres, trucks come rattling in at midnight, and Smithfield's "day" begins officially at 5 A.M. You don't have to arrive quite that soon, 7:30 to 8 A.M. (Monday through Thursday) will do.

Built on the former site of grisly executions and an equally gruesome livestock market, the vaulted Victorian eastern wings were erected in 1868. Of a dark northern morning the place is lit by bowls of lamps, as the sun rises to the slap of marbled carcasses, the squeal of barrow wheels, and the Tower-of-Babel bickering of the lads. If you're stalking the Wild Cockney, he is alive and well here as at no other place—whistling, singing, hollering at his mates in an accent as thick as the rashers he's porting.

While the banter is local, the barter is international: lamb from Aberdeen and New Zealand, chickens from Oxford and Grampian, York hams, Norfolk ducklings, Gascony foie gras. I [heart] SMITHFIELD stickers and girly posters adorn the stalls' walls. It's a kingdom sui generis, quite literally.

Smithfield has its own law—a private police force employed by the market owner, the City of London Corporation—and its own time clock, as you'll find at the **Fox and Anchor,** and the **Smithfield Tavern,** where special license has been granted to serve spirits to those "following their lawful trade at Smithfield" from 6–9 A.M. For a few bob you too can have the Best

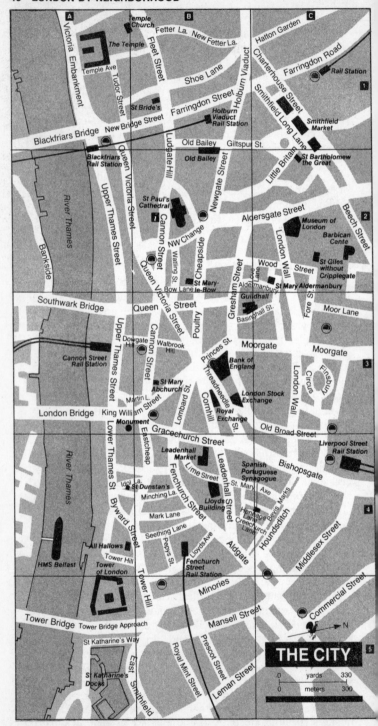

Breakfast in London of eggs, tomato, mushrooms, and fresh-from-the-market bacon, ham, and sausage—accompanied, as the barrow boys do, by a wasser, or whisky with tea. Not only does the odd tourist turn up to bend the tradesmen-only drinking rules, but lately lots of the City's three-piece suiters have discovered the real business of breakfast and can be found rubbing their gray-flannel elbows with the boys in the blue jumpsuits.

Fortified by your rasher and wasser, skirt the market and scoot down Smithfield Street, where, just on your left, you'll see a half-timbered structure above a gateway. This building's true Elizabethan character was revealed by an exploding zeppelin bomb during the First World War. Through the gateway is London's second oldest house of worship, the **Priory Church of St. Bartholomew-the-Great.** Like the neighborhood's pubs, the neighborhood's church opens early, about 7:45 A.M. on weekdays. You enter through a courtyard garden, where the original nave stood. The structure standing today contains portions of the 1123 Norman choir along with a host of subsequent ramifications that are explained, dated by part, in a diagram on your left as you enter, hung on the southside of the second bay.

A great friend and court jester of Henry I, Thomas Rahere lay feverish and dying in Rome when he envisioned St. Bartholomew rescuing him from evil. Rahere vowed to erect a monument to the saint if allowed to live. He returned home fully recovered, obtained a land grant from the king, and founded St. Bartholomew's Hospital (across the street) and an Augustinian priory, of which he became canon.

The present church, capped by a ceiling upheld by tremendous wood beams, is considerably smaller than Rahere's, much of it destroyed during Henry VIII's Dissolution of the Monasteries. The bells in the tower date from 1510 and are rung Sundays from 5:50 to 6:30 P.M. The church is noted for its music: 11 A.M. choral matins, 6:30 P.M. choral evensong. Special programs are staged around holidays. Free lunchtime recitals are held most Thursdays at 1:10 P.M. Schedules of events are available at the shop desk.

Not to rush you through the market or matins, but it is essential to be heading down the hill in time to get to the Tower around opening time.

The Tower

Her Majesty's Tower of London (the official title) is open 9:30 A.M. to 5 P.M. Monday through Saturday, 2 to 5 P.M. Sunday; (closed Sundays in winter); £3.50 admission. Even if you've been here before, there is something you're bound to have missed, and if you've never been . . . well, you simply must go. Your jaded London friends will probably point out the crush of crowds, the lines, the goading of the guards as

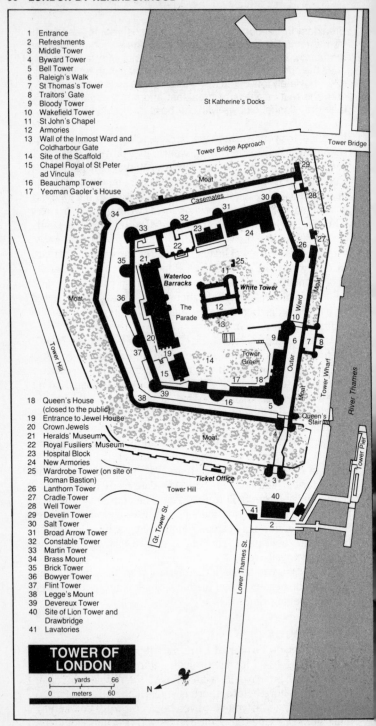

1 Entrance
2 Refreshments
3 Middle Tower
4 Byward Tower
5 Bell Tower
6 Raleigh's Walk
7 St Thomas's Tower
8 Traitors' Gate
9 Bloody Tower
10 Wakefield Tower
11 St John's Chapel
12 Armories
13 Wall of the Inmost Ward and
   Coldharbour Gate
14 Site of the Scaffold
15 Chapel Royal of St Peter
   ad Vincula
16 Beauchamp Tower
17 Yeoman Gaoler's House

18 Queen's House
   (closed to the public)
19 Entrance to Jewel House
20 Crown Jewels
21 Heralds' Museum
22 Royal Fusiliers' Museum
23 Hospital Block
24 New Armories
25 Wardrobe Tower (on site of
   Roman Bastion)
26 Lanthorn Tower
27 Cradle Tower
28 Well Tower
29 Develin Tower
30 Salt Tower
31 Broad Arrow Tower
32 Constable Tower
33 Martin Tower
34 Brass Mount
35 Brick Tower
36 Bowyer Tower
37 Flint Tower
38 Legge's Mount
39 Devereux Tower
40 Site of Lion Tower and
   Drawbridge
41 Lavatories

St Katherine's Docks

Tower Bridge

Tower Bridge Approach

Moat

Casemates

Waterloo
Barracks

White Tower

The
Parade

Tower
Green

Outer Ward

Moat

Moat

Tower Wharf

River Thames

Queen's
Stair

Tower Hill

Moat

Ticket Office

Tower Hill

Gt. Tower St.

Lower Thames St.

Tower Pier

**TOWER OF
LONDON**

0   yards   66
0   meters   60

N

The East End

We can't really tell you how to get to the East End, precisely. It is an area roughly delineated by Bishopsgate and Kingsland Road on the western border; east of the City and Clerkenwell, the East End is somewhat misrepresented by the telly soap named for its supposed inhabitants ("Eastenders"). It's not one single neighborhood, but a raucous, raunchy conglomeration of same. The East End sprawls over Hackney, Stepney, Shoreditch, spreading riverward toward Docklands. And this is only a partial listing, for the East End proper is as much a state of mind as a place, and there can be arguments made for East-Ender mentality flourishing in the City and elsewhere. The East End has become the repository for cockney culture. Although tradition was that you weren't a true Londoner if you weren't born within the sound of the Bow church's bells, the latest judgment has come to include those born within earshot of Shoreditch Church's carillon as well.

The East End's down-and-dirty rep has been somewhat diluted by the recent arrival of the press, business offices, and yuppie loft living in Docklands. In fact much of traditional East End roguishness is being supplanted by the influx of high-power, high-finance businesses which are inimical to all that the East End has traditionally represented. The mom-and-pop stores, the working-class rough and tumble, the chipper seediness are all giving way under pressure from the real-estate speculators who would turn this (undeniably underutilized) domain into an extension of the new-money fast-track City scene.

Additionally, the East End (as has been the case time out o' mind) is the home of as many immigrants as "natives." The air is filled less and less with the whimsical strains of cockney and more and more with the clack of Pakistani and the lilt of West Indian accents and tongues. The developers still have a long way to go to convert the council housing (including London's most notoriously bad "project," Tower Hamlets) and postwar tenements into postmodern offices and flats.

If you'd like to visit the neighborhood, try coming on a Sunday morning to the markets at Brick and Petticoat lanes. Stop in at the Beigel Shop on the former for the London version of the NYC favorite. Wander up to the Bethnal Green Museum of Childhood or Victoria Park to check up on how the locals are amusing themselves. During the week, in the earlier A.M., Spitalfields Market (produce) is a must-see. Must-see because it is shortly scheduled to be transformed into office space. Nearby are the Whitechapel Art Gallery and the Geffrye Museum exhibiting off-center modern art works and a series of period rooms, respectively. Have a pint o' at the Prospect of Whitby Pub in Wapping, or sample the traditional fare at Cook's Eel and Pie house on Kingsland Road in Dalston. These are places to stop at ASAP, because much of the East End is in a frenetic state of flux, and it's entirely possible that before long the only place you'll be able to find Eastenders will be on the telly.

you try to linger over the Crown Jewels, and suggest politely that you'd do best to skip this miasma of the masses altogether. *Rubbish.* Not only does the Tower have crimson-chested beefeaters and tales of blood and gore galore, it is the most architecturally, historically, geographically important structure in all of Britain. The crowds can be tiresome, the guards do rush you past the Crown Jewels too fast to allow for a good gawk, but this should not dissuade you from coming.

It should, however, persuade you to come armed with a plan of attack. The plan includes arriving around 9:45 A.M., allowing a little time for the preopening line to lessen, and arriving only during the week—don't even think about coming here on a weekend. Begin your tour with the most popular exhibitions and work your way around the more crowded indoor installations, saving the outdoor activities—beefeater photo opportunities, parapet perambulations—for later.

During the summer Yeomen Warders (in the black uniforms) give quickie tours that begin at the Bell Tower, or you can gather some background info at the history gallery, down the stairs by the Tower Bridge corner. Nearby are the Tower's famous ravens. They are maintained for more than ornithological curiosity: From the time of Charles II, it has been said that if the Tower's ravens become extinct, the White Tower will fall and the empire will dissolve.

The Ceremony of the Keys

If you really want to escape the crowds at the Tower, you can come by at 9:35 P.M., present your pass, and witness the Ceremony of the Keys. This is a seven-hundred-year-old tradition involving the locking of the gates and the setting of the watch, and the half-hour ritual is most impressive and relatively private. To obtain a pass, make application *in writing* to The Resident Governor, Queen's House, HM Tower of London, EC3N 4AB. Include a stamped, self-addressed envelope, and they will send you an application form.

The site was originally commandeered by the Romans, but it wasn't until after the Conquest that William I, Duke of Normandy, decided in 1078 to hang his helmet here. He arrived in London wooing the populace with promises, but just in case this didn't win them over, he built himself a fortress designed by a Norman monk called Gundolf to remind the Londoners which side had won at Hastings.

Henry III made significant improvements including the addition of a moat, which was in use until the 19th century but is now given over to grass and tennis courts; and a menagerie with leopards, an elephant, and a polar bear that was provided with a chain long enough to allow it to fish in the Thames.

The Tower's menagerie was later removed to Regent's Park and formed the nucleus of the London Zoo.

Although the Tower had always done double duty as a residence and jail, it was the Tudors—a bloody bunch, to be sure—who made the place notorious as a prison for all manner of nefarious characters—murderers, traitors, nephews, spouses. The Tower tended to be reserved for prisoners of good blood, royal and otherwise. Really important personages were privileged to be executed in the relative privacy of Tower Green, rather than in front of the roiling mobs on Tower Hill as was the usual practice.

Make a beeline for the **Crown Jewels** and join the line twisting through the waiting maze along which they've thoughtfully installed swords of state, candlesticks, punch bowls to beguile the time. Downstairs in the mammoth Chubb vaults you'll have to plow your way through school kids ogling and Parisians ooh-la-la-ing to get a glimpse of Her Majesty's eye-popping baubles. The queue on the lower level next to the display cases must be kept in perpetual motion; the upper level is raised for stopping and staring. No doubt about it, you too will be mesmerized, bewitched by the glitter.

In contrast to this extravagance is what ought to be your next stop, the **Chapel Royal of Saint John the Evangelist,** upstairs through the armories in the **White Tower** (the oldest surviving Norman structure in London). Henry IV invited 46 gentlemen to attend him here on the eve of his coronation and knighted them. Whereupon they bathed, prayed, and spent the night in 46 beds, thus beginning the Ceremony of the Bath.

One of the Tower's most famous components is the **Bloody Tower.** Originally known as the Garden Tower, the more titillating title dates from the time of the Little Princes, the boy-king Edward V and the Duke of York. The brothers were incarcerated here and then murdered, most likely by order of their uncle, Richard III. It was published that they were buried in the Wakefield Tower and thence removed to consecrated ground. In 1674, however, a pair of small skeletons were found beneath a staircase of the White Tower. The bodies were brought to Westminster for reentombment. When the bodies were exhumed in 1933 for dating, it appeared likely that these were in fact the bones of the unfortunate Little Princes.

On into The City

Now that you've done the City sights which must be done early in the day, you're at leisure to reconnoiter what you will in this treasure trove of essential London. If you'd like a bird's-eye-view of the Thames, **Tower Bridge's towers** and connecting skywalk are now open to the public. If you're hungry, stroll over to **St. Katharine's Dock,** on the other side of Tower Bridge, and stop at one of the many shops and pubs overlooking an impressive collection of antique and modern sailing ships.

Or if you're keen to press on, you might like to set off on the London Wall Walk (see above), which begins its westerly route at a series of explanatory wall panels in a below-ground passageway across the street by the Tower Hill Tube station. Along the Walk you'll come to the **Barbican Centre,** a concrete fortress of a place—built on blitz-leveled land—which incorporates towers of flats, the Royal Shakespeare Company theaters, the London Symphony Orchestra hall, an arts complex, and the Museum of London.

The **Museum of London** (open Tuesday through Saturday, 10 A.M. to 5:30 P.M., closed Monday; admission free) is a great place to explore on the first days of a visit to London. It begins at the beginning with geologic history and works itself up to the Stone Age, Roman, Saxon, Medieval, Tudor London forward to the present, using artifacts, paintings, dioramas, and multimedia presentations. Especially energizing is a booth with a sound and light re-creation of the Great Fire. Much more palatable than any dry historic tome, this is a marvelous way to set yourself straight on the whens and wherefores of London's past. Check out the Lord Mayor's State Coach and the Victorian storefronts downstairs.

As for the other public sections of the Barbican, you'll certainly want to return in the evening to see the Royal Shakespeare Company or hear the London Symphony, and you can pick up tickets while you're here. There are plenty of daytime amusements as well. **The Arts Centre** is a multifloor building, including several subterranean levels, so you may find yourself walking in from the sidewalk onto Level 5, where you'll find the main lobby with entrances to the main theater, and where there is often free music at lunchtime or after 5 P.M.

The complex has galleries, theaters, restaurants, and shops littered liberally about its precincts. The best way to sort out what's on when and where is to head for the info desk on Level 7, which has a question-answering staff and a board listing the day's events throughout the building.

Take some time to visit the gallery on Level 8; it devotes its two floors to visiting exhibitions, which change every couple of months. (Gallery hours are Monday through Saturday, 10 A.M. to 6:45 P.M., Sunday 12 to 5:45 P.M.; £3.) Also on Level 8 you'll find the Conservatory (admission 50 pence), a two-story hothouse with a crisscrossing network of walkways, planted with flowers of the season, trees, fountains—a great escape. As the signs advise, the paths can be quite wet, so be careful not to spoil your shoes.

If you prefer to take five outdoors, undoubtedly you'll have noticed the plaza with its fountains, cascades, and reflecting pools. Tables are set up in summer so you can bring out your food from the café or bring your own.

At the center of it all, looking a bit beleaguered by the concrete incursions, is **St. Giles Cripplegate Church,** which manages nevertheless to maintain its medieval integrity even as it puts its cheerless, colorless 1980s neighbors to shame. Some vestiges—the base of the tower and parts of the nave—of the original 1390 construction survive. The rest is a jumble of cross-century restorations necessitated by a 1545 fire and heavy bombing during World War II. Parish members included Oliver Cromwell (married here), John Milton (buried here), John Bunyan, and Daniel Defoe.

It is high time to discuss the City's other churches. As you will have learned at the London Museum, after the Great Fire in 1666 only 11 of the City's churches remained standing. Sir Christopher Wren and others built 51 churches on existing property but by the 1930s only 43 were left. During the Axis bombings of London, barely a single one came through unscathed. Today the tally rests at 39 City churches, many heavily restored in the forties and fifties; of this final number, 23 buildings and six standing towers were designed by Wren.

All of these several dozen houses of worship within the City's limits are worth visiting, each is architecturally and historically unique, and as a group they reveal the marvelous, multifaceted artistic and spiritual life of the City. Obviously, though, most visitors won't have time to see them all, and for those people a list of several that are of particular interest follows. As mentioned, all have been partially destroyed at one or more points in their histories, so most have been restored several times from the 17th century onward.

All-Hallows-by-the-Tower, Byward Street. A Saxon church stood here circa 1000. Legend has it that Richard I built a Lady Chapel next to the church and had his heart buried in it. After an accidental explosion of gunpowder nearby, the church was rebuilt in the 1650s. The bombs of 1940 left only the walls and the tower. Donations for reconstruction—accomplished in the fifties—poured in from all over the world.

The seams of endless rebuilding show in the somewhat mismatched interior. Of interest are a font cover by Grinling Gibbons and a font carved from stone taken from the Rock of Gibraltar. Also, there's a collection of ship models commemorating the church's long-standing ties with the Port of London Authority. William Penn was christened here and John Quincy Adams was married here. There are organ recitals on Thursdays at 12:15 and 1:15 P.M.

Spanish and Portuguese Synagogue, Heneage Lane Bevis Marks. Open 7:30 to 8:30 A.M. for services, or call for

The 1660s: Contagion and Conflagration

Late in 1664 London barbers and physicians were reporting cases of patients taken with fever and delirium who developed a red rash and finally black sores around their joints as the sign of impending death. The Great Plague of 1665 was a strain of bubonic plague (named for the "buboes" or black sores, whence also the name "Black Death"). By the spring of 1666 more than one hundred thousand Londoners had succumbed.

The plague was transmitted by infected rats and their fleas, and quickly spread through the crowded, filthy streets of London. There was hardly a street that didn't have its house with the red cross of quarantine painted on the front door. The inmates of the stricken house were locked inside in appalling conditions for forty days after the infected person had died. The aristocracy fled to their country estates, Charles II decamped to Hampton Court, Parliament was suspended. In one week of September 1665, about twelve thousand Londoners died. Thankfully, the winter weather brought the mortality rate down. The court returned to Whitehall in February 1666.

Things were just returning to normal by the end of the summer, when on the morning of September 2nd, a little bakeshop in Pudding Lane caught fire (Robert Hubert, a Frenchman, subsequently confessed to arson and was executed). The Great Fire spread as quickly as had the plague. The lord mayor and the king himself pitched in to help pull down houses in the fire's path, transport water, and attend to victims. But the situation was hopeless; by the time the wind changed on September 7th, four hundred acres, two-thirds of the City, had been laid to ruin. To everyone's amazement only nine people had died.

The double dose of plague and fire in a little over a year had left its mark on the face of London and on the minds of her populace. Eighty-seven churches had been destroyed, and many public buildings were reduced to rubble. Although he wasn't permitted to carry out his master plan for rebuilding London (see box, "Sir Christopher Wren and the City That Almost Was," below), Sir Christopher Wren—and his cronies Nicholas Hawksmoor, and Grinling Gibbons—did manage to rebuild the town in a Neoclassical, "Enlightenment" style.

The aristocrats had been shaken by the swiftness with which both flames and pestilence tore through the city, and the poor whose houses had been the first to go also felt the need to rebuild away from the dirt and danger. The City of London had burst its seams, it seemed, and the plague and fire were merely a predictable outcome of the massive problems caused by overcrowding and concomitant overtaxing of the water supply, sanitation facilities, and medical and city services. Many citizens chose not to return to the City but instead began to settle in the fields and woods between the City and its satellite towns, filling up the unpopulated, in-between land. This was the beginning of the building of London into the city of many cities that it is today.

appointment 289-2573. If the gates are locked, try ringing the bell at door marked Abraham Lopes-Dias Hall around the corner on Heneage Lane. Ironically, perhaps, this 1701 structure was built by a Quaker, Joseph Avis, and the simple rectangular design with its tiers of windows and handsome, low-slung chandeliers closely resembles contemporary Christian churches.

St. Bride's, Fleet Street. St. Brigit was a sixth-century Irish saint to whom this Wren church was dedicated. It is said to support Wren's most exquisite steeple, touted as his "madrigal in stone," completed in 1703.

Most interesting is the museum in the crypt, which exhibits artifacts uncovered when the church was gutted by World War II bombs. Archaeologists found evidence of Roman and Saxon activity, adding to the already available knowledge of the church as a Norman structure wherein King John held Parliament in 1210. St. Bride's is most famous, however, for her contributions to the beginnings of the Fleet Street press here in the late 15th century, when printing presses were set up to accommodate the churchmen—who were practically the only people who could read. The area eventually attracted the likes of Chaucer, Shakespeare, Milton, and Pepys (who was christened here). It is, therefore, not surprising that Wren produced one of his most elaborate designs for this church. The post-war restoration work (the primary share of which was paid for by the newspapers) was carried out according to Wren's existing plans and completed in 1957.

St. Dunstan in the East, Idol Lane, St. Dunstan's Hill, Lower Thames Street. The ruins of this church, all but obliterated by air raids, have become a haven of quiet greenery in the hectic heart of the financial district. An award-winning garden has been planted with a fountain bubbling and birds twittering in the creepers climbing the ruined walls.

Only the tower remains of the 1697 church, a circumstance that would not have surprised Wren in the least; the structure had already confirmed his confidence in its solidity. The story runs that after the hurricane of 1703, a messenger ran to Wren with the news that the winds had wreaked havoc with every one of his beloved steeples. To which the architect replied with great sangfroid, "Not St. Dunstan's, I am sure."

St. Mary Abchurch, Abchurch Lane, Cannon Street. The pedestrian exterior of St. Mary's (1686) in no way gives away the beauty and uniqueness of its interior, one of Wren's finest. A crowning achievement, its glories include a magnificent (unbuttressed) dome decorated by William Snow, original 17th-century woodwork, and a reredos firmly documented as being the work of Grinling Gibbons. Discovered in literally thousands of pieces after a 1940 raid, the reredos was painstakingly pieced back together. If you only have time to visit one church, make it this one. The elegance and effortlessness of design and the quality of workmanship make it the finest (and thankfully least altered) of Wren's City churches.

St. Mary Aldermanbury, Aldermanbury and Love Lane. Much like St. Dunstan's, St. Mary provides a green and pleasant escape from the glass and concrete Barbican. Where the church once stood is a tiny boxwood garden and cherry trees, with a bust of Shakespeare in their midst.

Originally a Saxon church stood here, and before the war a Wren church occupied the spot. After it was damaged by bombs, the remains were numbered, dismantled, and sent to Westminster College in Fulton, Missouri, where the church was reconstructed as a memorial to Sir Winston Churchill, who made his "Iron Curtain" speech at the college.

St. Mary-le-Bow, Bow Lane and Cheapside. Other than the outstanding Wren steeple (1680), this church is architecturally disappointing, owing to its near destruction in the blitz. The restorations were a bit heavy-handed, with the exception of the stained glass by John Hayward. It should be included in any comprehensive tour, however, because of the essential role it has played in many stages of London's history.

Most important of all is the matter of the Bow Bells. From 1334 to 1874 the Great Bell of Bow (and her descendants) rang reveille at 5:45 A.M. and curfew at 9 P.M., regulating the lives of all the City's citizens. Tradition came to be that a true cockney, a full-blooded Londoner, was any man or woman born within the sound of the pealing of the Bow Bells. It was the sound of the Bow Bells that convinced a discouraged Dick Whittington to return to the City to become "thrice mayor of London Town."

The original Great Bell was destroyed in the Great Fire, as were subsequent models in 1941. Luckily, however, the BBC had previously recorded the Bells and had been using them as a time signal. During the war the BBC again broadcast the Bow Bells as a recognition signal in occupied countries to bolster the embattled spirits of the soldiers and the populace, thus earning them the reputation of having "the most famous peal in all Christendom."

The most interesting (visible) aspect of the church is the Norman crypt. Constructed in 1090, it is among London's oldest religious remnants. Its configuration of Norman arches or "bows" is whence derived the church's name. Musical recitals are held here most Thursdays at 1:05 P.M.

These houses of worship are merely a prelude (as they were in Wren's own education and work) to the grandest by far of all London churches, St. Paul's Cathedral.

Sir Christopher Wren and the City That Almost Was

The City of London would be a completely different place if Sir Christopher Wren had been given free rein to rebuild it as he wished after the Great Fire of 1666. Wren was born in Wiltshire in 1632 and during his school years quickly absorbed all the knowledge imparted to him by a series of brilliant mentors in fields ranging from physiology to astronomy. During his student days at Oxford, he joined other like-minded scholars in a loose confederation of scientists and philosophers that eventually became the Royal Society, of which Wren was a founding member and president. A true citizen of the Age of Enlightenment, Wren was both a professor of anatomy at Gresham College in London and of astronomy at Oxford University. In 1665 he journeyed to France and was much impressed by Bernini's work for Louis XIV at the Louvre and Versailles. No English architect was producing any work so grand and imaginative at the time.

The following year the Great Fire broke out on September 2nd, destroying most of the City. Thrilled by the prospect of a clean-slate reconstruction, between September 5th and 11th Wren journeyed to London from Oxford, surveyed the land to be reclaimed, and drew up a program of sumptuous new proportions for doing just that.

Wren's was a visionary design, with ambitions to make London rival the famous capitals of the Continent. Wren's city was to incorporate the spatial relationships demonstrated by astronomy and the Italianate principles he had so admired in Bernini's work. Wren envisioned a grand, ordered city in the Classical style, with wide, tree-lined boulevards radiating from various focal points; an opulent, open-plan city with elegant public spaces, parks, and gardens.

On September 13th, King Charles II proclaimed that a plan would be adopted for rebuilding the city, and several other prominent architects submitted proposals along with Wren. Ultimately, however, none were adopted. The exchequer groused about the cost, there were squabbles over property rights, but perhaps the strongest arguments were heard from the City guilds and merchants, who complained that all these grandiose building schemes would waste time and tie up traffic. They wanted to get business rolling again as quickly as possible.

In 1667 a building act was passed, but its scope was severely limited, only calling for a widening of some streets, requiring all structures henceforth to be made of stone, not wood, and imposing a coal tax for the Port of London—revenues from which eventually financed the reconstruction of St. Paul's. If the warring factions hadn't been so vociferous, if the king hadn't been so indecisive, Christopher Wren might have won out, and London would be a very different city indeed. (See City neighborhood listing of Wren churches and the *Touring* chapter for a tour of Wren-connected sights.)

St. Paul's

The picture most of us carry in our minds is that of the dome, worried by Luftwaffe bombs, wreathed in smoke, floating somehow serene yet determined above the pall of destruction, the appalling wreckage. (You can buy the postcard at the shop.) This nearly nightly tableau was no accident. Hitler's air force had direct orders to destroy the cathedral. Churchill gave equally adamant orders to "save St. Paul's" at all costs. Thus Christopher Wren's masterpiece, became an irreplaceable symbol of the struggle of will between an apparently unstoppable blitzkrieg, bent on breaking the back of British resistance by destroying its morale, and the dogged, besieged Britons fighting (almost single-handedly by this time) for their lives and the way of life embodied in Wren's moving, immovable church.

Hitler almost succeeded. In one night alone, at Christmastime 1940, 28 incendiary bombs fell in the area. In 1941 the east end and north transepts were hit by high-explosive bombs which did acute but limited damage; a third struck the east end but did not detonate, was dug out, and disarmed.

How did St. Paul's remain standing, against all odds, to buttress the tattered, tottering spirits of London and the nation? Luck? Surely. Providence? Probably. The efforts of the RAF intercepting bombers? Certainly. But primarily the cathedral was saved by the St. Paul's Watch, a fire brigade largely consisting of older men, past the age of soldiering, many of whom had daytime jobs and families to attend to. These Londoners volunteered to keep vigil night after night, to disarm the bombs that didn't explode, and to contain the fires of the ones that did.

Not surprisingly, many of the remaining veterans of the St. Paul's Watch are among the most vocal and zealous of the factions fighting the current battle (some would say already lost) with the developers who have now besieged St. Paul's iconic dome with a ring of steely office blocks. Joining the anti-development ranks more recently is a powerful, albeit some say misdirected ally, the Prince of Wales. Prince Charles may well succeed where others have failed in preserving what's left of London's traditional skyscape.

The story of Churchill's iron will, of the fire brigade's valor, and the depressing sequel in which latter-day capitalist greed may well succeed in obliterating the cathedral's visual impact where fascist bombs failed, is essential to understanding the powerful spiritual and visceral hold St. Paul's has on Londoners and on the nation. The site alone is fraught with historic significance. Its position atop Ludgate Hill, best appreciated when approached from Fleet Street, has proved irresistible to builders of would-be landmarks down through the centuries. There is a tradition (disputed by Wren, among others) that a Roman temple to Diana stood here, making it a focal

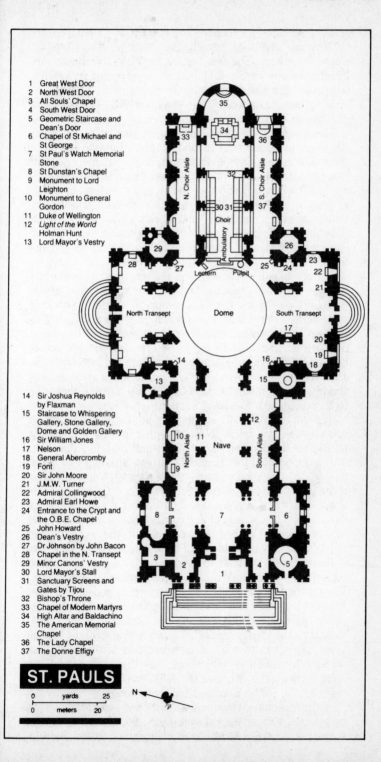

1 Great West Door
2 North West Door
3 All Souls' Chapel
4 South West Door
5 Geometric Staircase and Dean's Door
6 Chapel of St Michael and St George
7 St Paul's Watch Memorial Stone
8 St Dunstan's Chapel
9 Monument to Lord Leighton
10 Monument to General Gordon
11 Duke of Wellington
12 *Light of the World* Holman Hunt
13 Lord Mayor's Vestry

14 Sir Joshua Reynolds by Flaxman
15 Staircase to Whispering Gallery, Stone Gallery, Dome and Golden Gallery
16 Sir William Jones
17 Nelson
18 General Abercromby
19 Font
20 Sir John Moore
21 J.M.W. Turner
22 Admiral Collingwood
23 Admiral Earl Howe
24 Entrance to the Crypt and the O.B.E. Chapel
25 John Howard
26 Dean's Vestry
27 Dr Johnson by John Bacon
28 Chapel in the N. Transept
29 Minor Canons' Vestry
30 Lord Mayor's Stall
31 Sanctuary Screens and Gates by Tijou
32 Bishop's Throne
33 Chapel of Modern Martyrs
34 High Altar and Baldachino
35 The American Memorial Chapel
36 The Lady Chapel
37 The Donne Effigy

ST. PAULS

0 yards 25
0 meters 20

N

point in the life of Londinium. The present St. Paul's (properly, New St. Paul's) is actually the fourth or fifth Christian church built here. The first, quoth the Venerable Bede, was founded in 604 by St. Ethelbert, King of Kent. It was destroyed by fire and rebuilt later in that century. The second building, was ransacked by the Vikings in 961. The third and final Saxon church was also destroyed by fire in 1087.

The Normans, energetic builders that they were, launched the most ambitious construction program England had ever seen. The result, Old St. Paul's, erected and amended well into the 14th century, was larger than its present-day progeny. It had a gargantuan tower and steeple (conservative estimates are at 460 to 500 feet), which was the tallest such structure ever completed—and perhaps, as with all such Babel-like towers, doomed to destruction. It was struck by lightning in 1447 and never returned to its original proportions.

The combination of acts of God and acts of man (most notably, the Civil War) eroded the structure and sanctity of the cathedral, so that by the 17th century it was in a shocking state of disrepair. Its nave and porch were used variously as a green and a livestock and ale market, and were the scene of much brawling and thievery. Determined that the cathedral's decline should be arrested, the dean and his chapter in 1663 sought out an up-and-coming professor of astronomy at Oxford, whose talent as an architect was already beginning to be recognized, to submit plans for renovation.

Christopher Wren, 31 at the time, argued that restoration was hopeless and respectfully suggested that the whole thing should be scrapped and a new cathedral built from scratch. The dean rejected this proposal outright, insisting that Wren develop a plan incorporating the existing structure. After three years of trying, Wren finally produced a model to their liking, which was accepted the final week of August 1666. Six days later, a fire broke out in Farriner's baking house. By the time the Great Fire had burned itself out, the cathedral and most of the City of London had been destroyed by the blaze.

Permitted by the fates to proceed with his plan to erect an entirely new edifice, Wren met with trouble at every turn. Having tried and failed twice to produce an acceptable plan, Wren submitted a third model and quite cagily had inserted in his contract a clause granting him license to make "ornamental rather than essential" changes in the accepted model. Obviously given to a broad interpretation of things, among Wren's "ornamental" alterations was the exchange of the spire (echoing the structure of Old St. Paul's) called for in the original plan for an immense Italianate dome.

In the meantime, Wren was knighted and appointed surveyor general, with an annual salary of £200. Nonetheless, the entire project was a headache from beginning to end. Incredible though it seems that such a cathedral could be built in less than 35 years when previously it had taken centuries, the authorities were not impressed with the speed of the operation and docked Wren half his pay. The Portland stone chosen for the building's exterior threatened to run out halfway through the project.

In 1710 Wren's son laid the last stone in the lantern. Wren had made weekly visits over the past 33 years (during which time he designed fifty other churches) to inspect the building's progress. Undoubtedly he heaved a sigh as much of relief as of joy that his cathedral was complete, and hence that his place in history was assured. Eight years later he was sacked as surveyor general and pensioned off to Hampton Court.

You can judge for yourself whether all the trouble of building and preserving the cathedral has been worth it. You can take an hour-and-a-half-long supertour Monday through Saturday at 11 A.M., 11:30 A.M., 2 P.M., or 2:30 P.M. for £3.60. This is a good way to begin, especially because tours are taken to areas otherwise closed to the general public. After the tour, or in lieu of it, if those sorts of things don't appeal, you'll want to spend extra time seeing certain things. There is a small (separate) admission charge to circumnavigate the ambulatory, or descend into the crypt, or climb up to the various levels of the dome.

But before you go dashing off to examine the particulars, do take a moment to observe and absorb St. Paul's in its entirety. Wren—architect, astronomer, historian, mathematician—created a space embodying all the ideas of his age about the legacy of the Classical period—the fascination with balance and order, democracy and symmetry. Try to imagine the room, uncluttered by monuments (which were a late-18th-century addition), with its effulgence of white light and yellow stone. This is not the church of an opiate religion designed to numb the people, but rather a church to awaken and invigorate the worshiper. Chiefly responsible for this effect are Wren's uncluttered design and restricted palette of colors. The church's most elaborate motifs, the mosaics (as with the monuments), were not part of Wren's original design but were added much later.

The most obvious interior feature is of course the **dome,** rising 218 feet from the floor. Immense as it appears, the exterior is actually much larger. The design, in fact, incorporates two domes. The exterior dome of lead-covered wood is designed to blend with the more monumental silhouette outside. The interior dome is constructed within an inner brick cone, which supports the outer-dome timbers and the lantern, 365 feet above the pavement. The interior dome, also brick, was constructed to a smaller size to harmonize with the interior space. The dome's frescoes, depicting events in the life of St. Paul, were executed by Sir James Thornhill.

Thornhill was only one of the many top-of-the-line artists Wren gathered to work on the cathedral. Proceeding toward the chancel you'll notice the choir stalls and organ case carved by Grinling Gibbons, considered to be his best work. The iron gates of the north and south chancel aisles are the work of Jean Tijou. The mosaics are 19th-century additions designed by G. F. Watts, A. Britton, and Alfred Stevens.

This area of the church, known as the **ambulatory,** is well worth the modest admission fee because, as mentioned, it contains some of St. Paul's greatest artistic achievements. It also contains a photo exhibit of Charles and Diana's wedding, which took place here in 1981—you remember. A Henry Moore statue, *Mother and Child* (1984), is on the north chancel, as is the *Role of Modern Martyrs,* remembering those who died since 1850. The page for 1977 reads, "Bantu Stephen Biko—South Africa." At the east end is the **American Memorial Chapel** with a roll of honor listing all U.S. servicemen and women based in Britain who died in World War II. Rounding the corner to the south side, spot the memorial to John Donne, a former dean of the cathedral. This is remarkable for two reasons: The likeness is said to be extremely well executed, copied posthumously by Nicholas Stone from a painting for which Donne agreed to pose in a shroud—while still alive. Secondly, this statue is one of the few objects remaining from Old St. Paul's; it managed to come through the Great Fire with only a scorch.

As you exit the ambulatory, directly to your left is the entrance to the **crypt** (you must pay admission). Smaller and more intimate than the great public space upstairs, the crypt contains tombs and memorials to various luminaries in arts, letters, politics. Immediately upon entering you'll be confronted by the casing of the Duke of Wellington's tomb. Just west rests his contemporary naval counterpart, Lord Nelson, in a sarcophagus originally designed for Cardinal Wolsey but eventually commandeered by Henry VIII, who planned to use it for himself. He changed his mind, however, and it languished about the royal collections for three hundred years, when it was dusted off and trotted out as a suitable receptacle for the admiral's remains.

Beyond Nelson's tomb is Wren's Great Model for St. Paul's, his second design and personal favorite. It's worth an inspection to consider the cathedral you might have been wandering through instead.

At the southeast end of the crypt is Wren's own tomb, whose epitaph was composed by his son: "Lector, si monumentom requiris, circumspice." This roughly translates: "Reader, if you seek his memorial, look around you."

As you climb back up into the cathedral, brace yourself for the final climb—do try to make it if at all possible—up into the dome and its galleries (separate admission charges for each level). Your first stop, 259 steps, is the **Whispering Gallery,** where you can eavesdrop on *sotto voce* conversations across on the opposite side. This is also the best vantage for viewing Thornhill's paintings. The **Stone Gallery,** 543 steps, is next, but its view of the city has been severely limited by postwar building. The **Golden Gallery** at the top of the outer dome rewards your strenuous efforts to reach it by laying the whole of London, 360 degrees, at your feet.

There are prayers and announcements over the public address system on the hour. Organ recitals are on Fridays at 12:30 P.M. Sung services are held weekdays and at 10 A.M. on Saturdays. The crypt and galleries are open 10 A.M. to 4:15 P.M., but closed on Sundays in deference to services held throughout the day. Note that the outside galleries close early and are usually closed for the winter and inclement weather.

Across St. Paul's churchyard from the cathedral is the **City of London Information Centre,** stocked with souvenirs and booklets and staffed by Londoners with an encyclopedic knowledge of the city and the City. There are also good listings of daily events, festivals, and sacred and secular music programs.

A TRINITY OF PUBS

After all this climbing around sacred spaces, you will undoubtedly have worked up a keen thirst. How fortunate that the streets east of the cathedral are full of great little pubs just right for slaking same. The trio we recommend (a half pint at each, perhaps?) is **The Pavillion End,** 24 Watling Street; **Ye Olde Watling,** 29 Watling Street; **The Green Man,** 7 Bucklersbury. The Pavillion End refers to the structure from which the players descend onto the cricket field. This pub has sporting fixtures, murals, and motifs throughout. Ye Olde Watling, whose history is a matter of constant dispute, is one of London's oldest pubs; built of ships' timbers, it once served as Wren's office during construction of the cathedral. The Green Man is a Scots-style pub with tartan swatches on the walls, wood inlays, and leaded glass; large and boisterous.

For takeaway, visit **Duff and Trotter,** 47 Bow Lane, for cheeses, baguettes, quiche, salads, or a ready-made hamper.

Big Business

Farther east from St. Paul's begins the hard-core heart of London's financial district. Some guides suggest that you visit here on a weekend, when the business crowd has decamped to the country, so as to get a better view of the buildings. This misses the point entirely. The point of this place *is* the constant coming and going, so by all means come on a weekday. At the intersection of a web of important streets is the **Bank of England,** the base of which was designed by Sir John Soane in 1788. Unfortunately, Soane's masterful façade has been surmounted by several stories designed by Sir Herbert Baker in 1925.

The Bank of England (est. 1694) was the brainchild of Scotsman William Paterson, who felt the nation's monetary resources ought not be at the mercy of the ebb and flow of successive sovereigns' greed. Paterson developed the concept of national debt and proposed a system of government borrowing from a joint-stock bank. All this is delightfully explained at the newly opened Bank of England Museum, which is open Monday through Saturday 10 A.M. to 6 P.M., Sunday 2 to 6 P.M. till 4 in winter, and closed on weekends. Admission is free.

Across the way is the **Mansion House,** the lord mayor's official in-town digs. Built from 1739 to 1752, its Palladian design is the work of Charles Dance the Elder. The interior is famous for its Egyptian Hall (the banqueting hall) and Ball Room. Admission is by written appointment only: Principal Assistant, Mansion House, Mansion House Place, London EC4. Include alternate dates.

Dominating the eastern front of the intersection is the **Royal Exchange,** home of the London International Financial Futures Exchange (LIFFE). If you've never seen an exchange at work, walk up to the visitors' center, which is open from 11:30 A.M. to 1:45 P.M., Monday through Friday (free). Below the gallery is played a manic melodrama by gentlemen in tatty polyester jackets with the name of their firm on the back, bidding on the vagaries of world monies using an elaborate sign language. It's heated, heavy-duty business.

The exchange was set up in 1569 by Sir Thomas Gresham along the model of the Burse at Antwerp and was originally a market for wholesale and retail goods merchants. Queen Elizabeth was so taken with the hustle and bustle of Gresham's courtyard market that she proclaimed henceforth it was to be known as the Royal Exchange.

The Royal Exchange changed buildings (although always on the same site) and businesses over the years, most notably as a center for the assurance (insurance) trade. When world currencies were floated in 1972, the need for a London futures market arose and it was decided to house it in the current Royal Exchange, completed in 1844 by Sir William Tite.

The **International Stock Exchange of the United Kingdom and the Republic of Ireland Limited** is just down Old Broad Street in a large glass building. Get a Stock Exchange brolly at the shop. The action is pretty tame here compared to LIFFE (and especially tame compared to Wall Street) because most transactions on the London Exchange these days are over-the-counter and made on telephones and computers. There are 35-minute lectures, a film to get you hepped-up to play the market, and computer games to give you the feel of what it's like to be a high roller. Open Monday through Friday, from 9:30 A.M. to 3:30 P.M.; free.

At the corner of Leadenhall and Lime streets you'll spot a steel building seemingly with no skin gleaming in the wan light. This 1986 construction is the home of pub master Edward Lloyd's insurance company. **Lloyd's** coffeehouse was a gathering place for City merchants and as such gained a reputation as a center for reliable shipping information. This developed into the society of underwriters famous for insuring everything from Lord Nelson's tours to Marlene Dietrich's gams to the Concorde.

The steel-cladding-and-glass structure allows you to peer in at the guts of the building, even watch the escalator gears grinding. There is a Disney World-esque information center with scenes explaining the history of Lloyd's and the importance of shipping insurance to the development of Empire.

The visitors' gallery (open during business hours, Monday through Friday; free) is a balcony in the central atrium. On the trading floor is ensconced the Lutine Bell, taken from the HMS *Lutine,* sunk in 1799 with a cargo of gold and silver bullion, the loss of which was paid off by Lloyd's underwriters. The bell was traditionally rung when an overdue ship failed to return to harbor to notify the underwriters that it needed reinsuring. History, adventure on the high seas, modern architecture, million-pound commerce—Lloyd's is a pretty fun place to visit for free.

The latest addition to the city scene is **Broadgate,** a mammoth new development in and around Liverpool Street Station. The complex includes a slew of modern office buildings with surrounding plazas containing shops, restaurants and an outdoor ice-skating rink.

 Tucked behind all these modern monoliths is a splash of olde London, **Leadenhall Market.** The entrances along Gracechurch St. lead into bricked streets covered by a buff and burgundy canopy. The stores, their signs lettered in gilt, are a tad up-market for the working classes who shopped here of yore— some sell champagne and caviar, Norwegian prawns, *corgettes Provençale.* There are several good choices for lunching; try the **Lutine Bell** at Number 35 for gourmet takeaway or sit-down upstairs. After work—closer to 5 o'clock here than in more hectic cities—the double-breasted brokers stand four deep outside the **Lamb Tavern.**

Another hot spot at lunchtime is the passage park behind the Royal Exchange Building. **The Greenhouse** sells wine, port, sherry, and champagne by the glass and bottle, so you can drink it there with simple fare—try the *salsiccia* (Italian sausage) on Wed.—or buy a split and split (champers to take away).

Another ancient and favorite haunt is the **Olde Wine Shades** in tiny Martin Lane off Cannon St. Built in 1663, it is touted as being the only pre-Great-Fire tavern in town. Amid fire on the hod, high-backed benches, and smoke-smudged ceilings, port and sherry are served from tuns behind the bar.

. . . and the Law

With all these bankers, brokers, and bishops scurrying about their business in so small a space, disputes were bound to arise. It's only logical, therefore, that the final group of long-term tenants in the City are lawyers. Their bases of operations are the Central Criminal Court and the Temple.

The Central Criminal Court (better known as **The Old Bailey**), Old Bailey and Newgate streets, stands where the original, notoriously miserable Newgate prison used to be. Conditions there were so shocking that the malodors and pestilence used to seep from the prison into the courtrooms, and judges were obliged to carry nosegays to ward off the effluvium. During spring and summer judges still carry "posies" as a reminder of the days when many among their number succumbed to "gaol fever."

The present building, third to occupy the site, was designed by E. W. Mountford and completed in 1907. An IRA bombing in 1973 has curtailed tours of the building, but you can still sit in on a trial, which is run, as ever, by judges and lawyers in their periwigs and robes (see box "Wills, Wives, and Wrecks: Legal London", in the "Clarkenwell and Holborn" section).

The Temple stands at the extreme west of the City south of Fleet Street and houses two of the five Inns of Court, the Inner Temple and the Middle Temple. "Inn" is merely the name given to a town house used by barristers and students of the law. Today the Temple is a conglomeration of legal chambers built around quads or gardens. A lawyer must become a member of one of the Inns before he or she is permitted to rent chambers therein.

The Temple is a title held over from the Order of the Knights Templar formed for the purposes of protecting pilgrims along the route to Jerusalem after the city was "liberated" from the Moslems in 1099. The Knights Templar built a church here in 1185 and used the land as their headquarters until they grew to be so wealthy and powerful that the king felt threatened, and in 1312 Edward II seized their lands and properties and presented them to the Knights Hospitaler, who subsequently leased out sections to lawyers. The Hospitalers were in turn dispossessed in 1539 by Henry VIII. Finally in 1608, James I granted a freehold charter to lawyers of the Inner and Middle Temples provided that they maintained the existing properties.

Unfortunately, most of the buildings are closed to the public. An important stop, however, is the **Temple Church,** open Monday through Saturday, from 10 A.M. to 4 P.M. and Sunday after services. The official church of lawyers, its curate is outside the jurisdiction of the Bishop of London and is appointed directly by the Crown.

The church is an example of the Transitional style, pointed Gothic arches commingling with the earlier rounded Romanesque. The church is built in two parts; the 1185 round church's floor is fitted with the supine figures of 13th-century knights, and the aisle arcade is worked with grotesque—sometimes merely ludicrous—carved heads. The chancel was built in the 13th century. The church was heavily bombarded during the blitz but has been restored as closely as possible to its original design.

Also in the neighborhood you'll find **Prince Henry's Room,** upstairs at 17 Fleet Street, dedicated to the tireless diarist Samuel Pepys (pronounced "peeps"), who was born nearby. The room is outfitted with Pepys memorabilia and most interestingly with the only pre-Fire Jacobean paneling and plasterwork ceiling in the city. (Open Monday through Friday from 1:45 to 5 P.M., Saturday till 4:30 P.M.; free.)

R. Twinings & Co., 216 Strand, is technically outside the City but close enough by. Below the sign of the golden lion and the pair of Chinese gentlemen, Twinings has been selling teas and coffees since 1706. The air in the shop is heavy with the scent of leaves and beans from around the globe. They sell lovely commemorative tins and gift packages.

Do take a peep in the **Lloyd's Bank Law Courts Branch** at 220 Strand. The entry is all painted tile work, reminiscent of Seville, and the foyer is carved oak and more tiles.

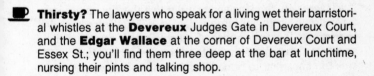

Thirsty? The lawyers who speak for a living wet their barristorial whistles at the **Devereux** Judges Gate in Devereux Court, and the **Edgar Wallace** at the corner of Devereux Court and Essex St.; you'll find them three deep at the bar at lunchtime, nursing their pints and talking shop.

Westminster and Whitehall

This is the London of officialdom: of princes, peers, and pomp—all those things that bring a flush to the cheeks of British subjects, a lump to the throats of the International Order of Anglophiles, and a gleam to the eye of the British Tourist Authority, which thanks its lucky stars that Geoffrey Chaucer had the good sense to be buried here and that Elizabeth Windsor has the good sense to insist on fresh soldiers daily.

The area down by the Thames used to be a sandy marsh called Thorney Island, in deference to its tangle of brambles. A Saxon church was said to have existed here whose consecration was attended by St. Peter himself in spirit form. The first documented structure was a Benedictine abbey built in the mid-eighth century and dedicated to the saint. This abbey was one of the first important outposts from the town of London and was referred to as the western monastery to differentiate it from the churches in the City; hence the name, Westminster.

Edward the Confessor, in lieu of making a promised pilgrimage to St. Peter's in Rome, opted instead for building a monumental abbey to the glory of the saint. Edward grew so attached to the project and the neighborhood that he decided to move the royal palace hither from the City. He died (eight days after the church was consecrated) on January 6, 1066. His son, Harold, was crowned at the abbey, as has been every other English king and queen (with only two exceptions) since. On October 14 of that same year, Harold surrendered the realm to William of Normandy, who was crowned here on Christmas Day.

William's son, William Rufus, turned up his Norman nose at Edward's attempt at palace building and resolved to build his own version of a royal residence, which he called Westminster Hall. Later it became the custom of Parliament to deliberate in the Painted Chamber of the hall, in order to have quick access to the king and in order that the king might keep a royal eye on them. Little is left of William's creation due to fires and the renovations of subsequent monarchs anxious to fit out their palace in the latest style. In 1512 Henry VIII was too impatient to remodel and decamped down the street to a new palace, which became known as White Hall.

Over the nine centuries the area has remained the center of all Britain's institutions of government: federal, in the Houses of Parliament and the prime minister's operation at No. 10 Downing Street; royal, at Her Majesty's London address, Buckingham Palace; corporeal, among the officers stationed at Scotland Yard; and clerical, as the ecclesiastics oversee the workings of all the rest from Westminster Abbey.

In fact, the area is almost exclusively devoted to the business of running Great Britain. For the most part, people arrive

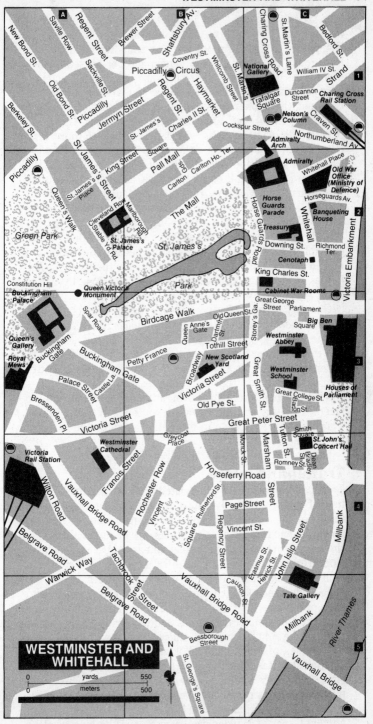

WESTMINSTER AND WHITEHALL

yards 0 — 550
meters 0 — 500

here in the morning, run the nation all day, then head to Hampstead at night. Among the few souls who actually live here round the clock are the Queen and her horses. Unlike other areas of London—where flats and offices, pubs and theaters, are thoroughly shuffled—once you've seen the spectacles and the monuments, you'll probably prefer to leave Westminster to seek entertainment elsewhere. There are several schools of thought regarding how best to tour Westminster and Whitehall, the primary options being to begin at Trafalgar Square and walk south along Whitehall toward the Houses of Parliament; or contrariwise, to begin at Westminster Abbey and walk toward Trafalgar Square. The view as you walk southward is by far superior, and it's better to arrive at the abbey late in the afternoon when the morning tour crowds have somewhat abated. On the other hand, chronologically, Westminster's history began at the abbey and moved thence north and east. Additionally, the morning festivities at Buckingham Palace will place you close by Parliament Square early in the day.

Our suggestion is that you forsake the historic for the aesthetic and enjoy the approach from Trafalgar Square. Besides, by the time the Changing of the Guard is finished so will be half the day, which doesn't leave you nearly enough time to cover the rest of the itinerary. After the ceremony, a better plan is to continue from the palace eastward up the Mall—another elegant promenade—or around the corner to the Queen's Gallery and the Royal Mews (open Wednesday and Thursday only) and then to the Tate Gallery on the banks of the Thames.

Trafalgar Square

Trafalgar Square is best appreciated from the porch of the National Gallery—the putty-putt of the diesel cabs, the grinding thrum of the double-deckers, the counterpoint of German, Japanese, and English as the tourists stream up the steps, the rhythmic chants of the perpetual anti-apartheid vigil outside Good Hope House (the South African embassy), and above it all the distant hum of Heathrow's flight pattern. It's an unimaginable chaos of sound and motion. It charges you with volts of raw energy. Flocks of pigeons fly suicide runs around Nelson's Column. Traffic snarls and untangles on its careen through the Admiralty Arch. And way off down the hill atop the Houses of Parliament the Union Jack whips the cloud-scuttled sky. It is one of London's prime vistas—a great open space in this city of high houses and narrow lanes, a luxurious expanse of openness at the confluence of London's grandest boulevards, with fountains and lions and Nelson aloft on an immense spar of Devonshire granite. It is the kind of place that, no matter how blasé you've become, makes you stop and pinch yourself, "This is it: I'm really here!" It's nice to know you can still be thrilled.

The Traff, or T Square, celebrated Nelson's glorious (albeit fatal for the admiral) victory over Napoleon's fleet in 1805. The land was previously occupied by royal buildings, mews, and stables; and former residents included hawks, falcons, horses, and the parliamentary army and its prisoners. By the 19th century the soldiers and stables had given the area a run-down look, and it was decided that Sir Charles Barry would create a suitably imposing public square securing the far end of Whitehall and the Mall. The work was completed in 1840.

Trafalgar Square became quite literally the hub of London. At the intersection of the Strand and Charing Cross is a sign noting that this is the central point from which all distances throughout the city are measured. It's also the center of festivities. The national Christmas tree is erected here, throngs gather here on New Year's Eve, and every October 21 the Royal Navy holds a ceremony here on the anniversary of the Battle of Trafalgar.

While the square itself is connected to the pomp and circumstance of Whitehall, the buildings surrounding the square have more to do with the art and music of Soho and Covent Garden, and are discussed in that section later.

Down Whitehall

As you begin your journey have a look at the statue of Charles I bestride his charger at the head of the road. This is London's oldest alfresco monument, having been constructed in 1633. It is a most ironic if not tragic positioning of this king, facing down Whitehall toward the Houses of Parliament: ironic because it was Charles's argument over Parliament's right to approve royal appointments that began the Civil War; tragic because Charles's royalist troops were defeated by Cromwell's parliamentarians, and the king was tried for treason and beheaded within plain sight of this statue on the porch of the Banqueting House.

Several blocks beyond the statue are the repositories of Britain's national security. The **Old Admiralty** (1725), on your right, has stood much in the same condition since the days of Nelson himself, and it is from here that the Empire was established and defended. Note the ship, seahorse and anchor motifs. Across the street is the less attractive but no less strategic **Old War Office,** now known as the Ministry of Defence.

Farther on down the road is the headquarters of the **Queen's Life Guard.** The brace of mounted guardsmen, aloft and aloof, patiently permit tourists to pat their steeds and pose for photos, their boyish faces locked in a steely freeze of duty and importance. This is also a good place to see the Changing of the Guard. The Horse Guards mount here every morning in a ceremony much less crowded and, according to many connoisseurs, much more colorful and interesting because you can get much closer. This occurs weekdays at 11 A.M. and Sundays at 10 A.M. At 4 in the afternoon, there is a modest inspection (dismounted) in the courtyard. The equestrian theme is continued down the avenue in a series of statues only slightly more serious and stony than the mounted guards in their sentry boxes.

On the corner of Horse Guards Avenue across Whitehall is the **Banqueting House,** which stands on the site of what was the largest palace in Europe, Whitehall. Whitehall was originally built by Cardinal Wolsey just next door to Henry VIII's lodgings, which paled in comparison. Rancored by his cardinal's uppity building schemes and failure to secure a papal annulment of his first marriage, Henry demoted Wolsey and confiscated his palace. In a piquant reworking of the ruler and his treacherous minister story, *Othello* was first performed before Elizabeth's court at Whitehall Palace. The building burned in 1698; the Banqueting House (and a few other features) are its sole survivors.

The Banqueting House was not part of Wolsey's expansion but was erected within the Tudor palace in 1622 by order of James I. His architect was Inigo Jones, who brought the Palladian style from Italy to London. Just after the new year in 1649, a scaffolding was erected outside the second-floor windows upon which Charles I was to meet his fate with the single blow of an axe that at once severed his head and his countrymen's belief in the divine right of kings. Contemporary engravings of the scene show the streets lined with the populace and the Banqueting House's rooftop lined with celebrities transfixed by the event.

Aside from these associations, the interior is renowned for its grandiose dimensions and most especially for its ceiling and murals by Peter Paul Reubens. Charles commissioned the artist to depict his father, James I, being carried by angels up to his divine rest as reward for all his earthly regal pains. (The Banqueting House is open Tuesday through Saturday from 10 A.M. to 5 P.M., Sunday 2 to 5 P.M.; admission 80 pence.)

The only remnant of the Tudor palace extant and open to the public is Henry VIII's wine cellar, presently encased by the new Ministry of Defence building. Admission is granted only upon written application to the Department of the Environment, Horse Guards Avenue, Whitehall, SW1 London.

Continuing past the **Old Treasury Building,** now the Cabinet Office, you'll come to a police barricade on the other side of which is **Downing Street.** This rather modest-looking row of brick houses was designed on the former site of a brew house by Harvard graduate Sir George Downing, MP. Former residents included James Boswell and Tobias

Smollett. The house at No. 10 has been the official residence of the prime minister since the tenure of Robert Walpole in the early 1730s. Just so she can keep an eye on them, at No. 11 is the official residence of the chancellor of the exchequer (who holds—and sometimes snarls—the nation's purse strings); at No. 12 is the office of the chief government whip, who's in charge of keeping Mrs. Thatcher's supporters in line.

Churchill's Underground

During World War I, zeppelin bombings of London caused Britons to pause and consider the implications of air-based warfare. In 1938 the attacks of Hitler's Luftwaffe on civilian targets in Europe confirmed their worst fears. Luckily for the nation, the farsighted soon-to-be PM Winston Churchill had not waited for aviation history to take its terrible course but had, with others, demanded that a fortified facility be built beneath the civil service buildings next to Parliament Square. It was a brilliant idea destined to prove one of the primary saviors of Britain. On a sunny Saturday afternoon, September 7, 1940, 400 German bombers flew over London and dropped their payloads on a virtually unprepared city.

For the next 57 nights London was attacked by anywhere from 150 to 500 bombers, most intensively on the 15th and 16th of October, when 538 tons of explosives killed or wounded a total of 1,300 people. By May of 1941, 18,800 tons of bombs had been dropped and 40,000 civilians had died. Luckily for London, Hitler shifted his attention and his blitzkrieg to the Soviet Union. But air attacks on London were resumed in the summer of 1944, this time by the incredibly destructive, unmanned V-1 bombs. The primary reason the government and hence the nation was able to go on was that Churchill and his war cabinet and the chiefs of staff could proceed with business as usual from their Cabinet-Room bunker.

Whether you're old enough to have heard the prime minister's original wartime broadcasts from these rooms or not, whether the Second World War is something you don't remember or would prefer to forget, the Cabinet War Rooms are a vital component in London's history. When you're wandering through the reconstructed Wren churches or St. Paul's wondering how it escaped the same fate; when you're touring the cold, postbellum concrete of the Barbican; when you're walking around town trying to figure out what happened to much of London's pre-20th-century architecture, the reasons for it all are nowhere laid out more clearly than here.

From these cramped, stuffy, box-like rooms the prime minister, his cabinet, and generals ran the war. The museum is still run as the installation was run in the forties: the clocks are kept ticking, and the weather-forecast notices are kept up to date. From the Cabinet Room proceed down a long corridor that eventually turns back upon itself and passes through the workaday rooms of the place. The secretary's offices are furnished with original telephones and typewriters, arcane ventilation systems, ancient candle stubs, and a mad snarl of communications wiring. Most interesting are the map rooms, hung with the war's global theaters of operation and still stuck with pins plotting the comings and goings and sometimes the destruction of Britain's lifeline of supplies. There are endless charts and graphs concerned with everything from food prices to U-boat sightings. It gives a lesson in the time-consuming method of running a world war before computers. The War Rooms are open daily from 10 A.M. to 5:15 P.M.; admission is £2.80. Great posters are sold in the gift shop.

On to Parliament

Parliament Square is one of those public places that just seems to have gone wrong. It's always congested, difficult to get across, and full of statues that nobody ever gets a good look at because it's too much trouble to get onto and off the center island where they stand. The square is, in fact, London's first attempt at a roundabout, laid out in 1750 and revamped by Sir Charles Barry in 1868 to provide an impressive open-space foreground for the Palace of Westminster he designed with the assistance of Augustus Pugin. The statues celebrate various heroes of a political or martial nature, but none is nearly as interesting or invigorating as the study of Queen Boadicea riding hell-for-leather off Westminster Bridge in a chariot surrounded by her daughters, executed by Thomas Thorneycroft and unveiled in 1902.

Above the Icenian queen is perennial postcard favorite, **Big Ben**—or, more precisely, the tower housing Big Ben. Big Ben is, in fact, neither the structure nor the clock, but rather the 14-ton Great Bell of Westminster, possibly named for the queen's clockmaker and master of the clockmaker's company, Benjamin Vulliamy, whom Barry chose to design a suitably monumental clock to complement the Palace of Westminster.

Vulliamy's design was rejected, however, and an open competition was held to solicit designs. The public and government were equally riveted by the melodrama surrounding the clock, and one of the primary figures in the debate was Sir Benjamin Hall, chief commissioner of works, who was supposed to have proposed the name Big Ben himself. Another candidate is Benjamin Caunt, a ponderous and popular boxer of the day.

An industrious caster, George Mears, finally took matters into his own hands and formed the present bell from the metal of an earlier defective model. The bell was hung in 1858, and the clock began ticking in 1859 and has proved an extremely reliable timepiece ever since.

The PM and the MPs

One almost hates to describe the glories contained within the neo-Gothic perpendiculars of the **Houses of Parliament,** properly called the New Palace of Westminster, because it is so damnably difficult to get inside. There are several ways of doing it, none of which is simple or surefire, but all of which are well worth the effort if you have the good fortune and tenacity to succeed.

1.   Write directly to a member of Parliament, each of whom is given an allotted number of tickets per day. If you can't get hold of an office address, write to the MP at the House of Commons, Westminster SW1.
2.   Get same-day passes from your own country's embassy or consulate. Most have four such passes available per day. These passes allow you to move to the head of the line but do not guarantee you a seat.
3.   Wait in what may be a long queue outside of the Houses for same-day admittance during sessions. Guides will be provided on request if you have a member of Parliament's permit.

If you're at all confused by these instructions (and who wouldn't be?), the Parliament information number is 219-4272, or switchboard 219-3574.

It used to be that Parliament was open for public tours every Saturday, but unfortunately an IRA assassination attempt forced a clampdown on security. Today, if and when you are allowed entrance, you must go through a series of anti-bomb scanners to check your person and belongings before being ushered inside.

The Central Lobby is bright with the light of a spiky chandelier and a dome of predominantly gold mosaics. There are the larger-than-life-size likenesses of various parliamentary luminaries deployed around the room, perhaps to inspire current members to similar greatness.

West of the lobby is the building's oldest portion, Westminster Hall, built in 1097 by William Rufus, the Conqueror's son. Aside from the sheer size of the place—240 feet long and 70 feet wide—most impressive is the oak hammer-beam roof, added in 1394, which crests at over 90 feet and is decorated with angels aloft. The hall was used for royal banquets, (indoor) jousts, and as a court for the trial of important persons.

The hall is one of the few parts of the building to have survived the fire of 1834. The fire was the result of typical bureaucratic ineptitude. Prior to 1826, the nation's financial books were kept using small wooden tally sticks that recorded various fiscal transactions. When the system was modernized, there was the question of what to do with the leftover sticks—piles of which had been amassed over the years. Some clever soul suggested that they be discreetly burned, and the logical place to do it without its becoming public knowledge was in the very furnace that serviced the palace. This plan being carried out, the fire burned so hot that it could not be contained, and most of the building was consumed in the blaze.

The following year, 1835, the combined efforts of Charles Barry and Augustus Pugin won the competition for designing the new palace, which was to be built in either Elizabethan or Gothic style. The winning design was of a mode called Gothic Perpendicular (for obvious reasons). However, the New Palace of Westminster unfortunately proved to be as vulnerable as the old one when in May of 1941, during a particularly ferocious attack, a direct hit was scored, and the northern section, including the House of Commons, was laid to waste.

The room was reconstructed in a simpler style than the Barry-Pugin original but retaining the face-to-face seating (reminiscent of the old days when the Commons, forced to meet where it could, often sat in the choirs of churches) and the traditional benches of pea-green leather. There have been concessions to modernity. Microphones dangle from the ceiling and monitors glow blue with the news of what the time is, who is speaking, and why.

The atmosphere during the course of a normal debate is remarkably casual. Members loll on the benches, rustling papers, strolling over to their mates for a chat or a joke while a fellow member presents his argument. The action does heat up, though; several years ago an outraged outcry arose over the behavior of one member who, in a particularly florid display of parliamentary pique, grabbed the sacred and ceremonial mace and hurled it to the floor. This egregious breach of decorum caused a much greater furor over abuse of power than eyewitness accounts of coed shenanigans in the House of Commons showers. (One assumes the prime minister was not among the female participants.)

In contrast to the simplicity of the House of Commons is the extravagance of the House of Lords. Lining the walls are the barons originally responsible for Parliament, the 18 lords who "persuaded" King John to sign the Magna Carta at Runnymede in 1215. The room they survey is appointed in opulent golds and reds. In the center is the woolsack, reserved for the Lord Chancellor, which is stuffed with fleeces from all over the kingdom to remind the lords of the importance of shepherds and their trade. At the far end is the throne used by Her Majesty on her annual visit for the State Opening of Parliament, which takes place in November. The sovereign is never permitted to enter the House of Commons.

The Men's Club Run by a Woman

It's 7:30 P.M. at the Strangers' Bar in the Palace of Westminster. The Strangers' is so called because it is the only place inside the building where MPs can entertain their guests. The room is smoky, filled with a haze of animated chatter and middle-aged white men, most of whom are pounding down whisky, neat. They're bickering about the day's business, telling jokes, discussing plans for the impending summer recess—historically allowed Parliament so that the farmers could get back home for the planting and harvesting, and still observed, as one MP puts it, because they "couldn't *possibly* be in London for the summer."

The atmosphere is exactly what you'd expect at the taproom of a men's club, and indeed when queried several members make the analogy themselves. One says, "The Commons is run like a men's club, or a monastery, or a commune. We have to cultivate a good social relationship, even if we don't like each other. It's not like battle lines are drawn; we have to live together. If you don't live together here, you lead a very lonely life."

It is, however, certainly a very exclusive club: 650 members out of 56 million citizens. Currently of the 650, 375 are Conservative, 229 are Labour, and the other 46 are from various parties.

"Strangers" (visitors) are not permitted to order or pay for drinks at the bar, a privilege exclusive to members, so the boys buy us another round and discuss the vicissitudes of life at the Commons. The first complaint regards office arrangements. While pretty to look at, the Palace of Westminster, as a Labour member puts it, was "not designed for work. The best offices go to committee chairmen. Retreads [re-elected members] do better than virgins [first-term members]. If you're new, they give you a locker—where that locker is, Christ knows." A Conservative colleague takes up the litany, "If you're very lucky, they give you a desk in a corridor which you share with twelve other MPs." There are also complaints about the work load. An MP expresses his frustration that the "volume and complexity of the work is too high; it's impossible to be an expert in all of the fields that come up in the course of a debate." And of course there is the matter of pay—the meager amount of money members are paid to run the nation. In 1989 MPs were paid a salary of £24,107 and an office-costs allowance of £22,588.

"It *is* an overblown men's club," the Labour MP smiles ruefully (none of the men apparently note the irony that their club is presently run by a woman). But it's a little more complicated than that: there *is* an exclusivity about the place but it's not the usual aristocratic exclusivity of men's clubs in this class-conscious nation. The Speaker of the House ambles over, and in a cheery, professorial fashion he uncrooks his pinky from around his glass and aims it at several of his colleagues: "He used to be a butcher. He was a lawyer. That one was a stockbroker. This one a coal miner." The Labour MP considers: "It's the smell of it. You're smelling the scent of history."

Westminster Abbey

The abbey you see today through the bobbing heads of the crowds is the result of many tempestuous centuries of building and rebuilding. The first spate of construction was brought about by Edward the Confessor and completed in 1065, just in time for his funeral, a week after its consecration. Edward had chosen a site traditionally associated with churches dedicated to St. Peter, and his new abbey followed suit. After Edward's canonization, there was great cachet in being associated with his abbey, and many princes were generous in their funding for continued work.

The second important period of building was financed by Henry III, who began with a Lady Chapel to serve as a shrine for the sainted Edward. Henry had spent much time in France attending to his principality in Anjou and was duly impressed by the cathedrals he had seen at Rheims and Amiens. Most likely he imported French and French-trained workers to realize his plans for his own cathedral. Working westward, the new abbey consumed the existing structure, which was effectively demolished as progress continued. Although he succeeded in creating a shrine for St. Edward, by the time of his death in 1272, Henry's plans had not been completed, and work was left off while the royal coffers were emptied to finance Edward I's and II's various hammerings of the Scots.

Construction of the nave was resumed again in 1376 under the patronage of Richard II and the supervision of the abbot, who continued along the lines set out by Henry's plans drawn up a hundred years before—which accounted for the abbey's relative unity of style despite the fits and starts of building.

The final major period of building was in the early 16th century under orders of Henry VII. At this time a chapel was built in the Gothic Perpendicular style (compare it to the Palace of Westminster, a credible 19th-century knockoff). By the mid-16th century, three hundred years after the initial work had begun, the abbey was finally completed. The only subsequent alteration of any significance was the addition of the West Towers (1745) designed by Wren and Nicholas Hawksmoor.

The fine Gothic interior of the abbey has been all but obliterated by the proliferation of monuments, which began to be installed the instant the church was completed. Not that this is necessarily a shortcoming; though the entire church cannot be fully appreciated, the variety and importance of the men and women commemorated effectively counterbalances the aesthetic drawbacks caused by their monuments' presence.

There really is so much to see here and so much to understand about the abbey that we strongly urge you to take one of the supertours conducted by vergers. The tours last about an hour and a half and take you to parts of the abbey where you would not be admitted on your own. Supertours run Mon-

1　West Entrance and Bookshop
2　Chapel of St George
3　Belfry Tower
4　Tomb of Unknown Warrior and Memorial for Sir Winston Churchill
5　Organ Loft
6　North Entrance
7　Chapel of St Andrew
8　Chapel of St Michael
9　Chapel of St John the Evangelist
10　Chapel of Abbot Islip
11　Sanctuary
12　High Altar
13　Coronation Chair
14　Chapel of Edward the Confessor – Henry V's Chantry

15　Chapel of St John the Baptist
16　Chapel of St Paul
17　Tomb of Elizabeth I
18　Tomb of Henry III
19　Royal Air Force Chapel
20　Tomb of Mary, Queen of Scots
21　Chapel of St Nicholas
22　Chapel of St Edmund
23　Chapel of St Benedict
24　Poet's Corner
25　Chapel of St Faith
26　Chamber of the Pyx
27　Stairs to Library
28　Jericho Parlour (closed to the public)
29　Jerusalem Chamber (closed to the public)

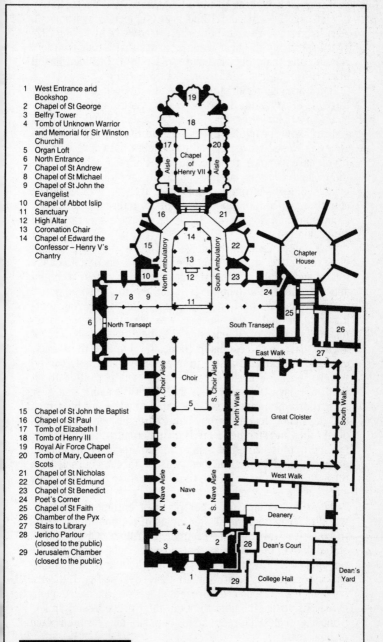

WESTMINSTER ABBEY

| 0 | yards | 33 |
| 0 | meters | 30 |

N ←

day through Friday, at 10 and 11 A.M. and 2 and 3 P.M.; Saturday 10 and 11 A.M. and 12:30 P.M. (subject to availability); admission is £4. You can book tours in advance by calling 222-7110—probably the best way to ensure that a tour is in fact running and that you will have a place in it. Included in the price of the tour is admission to all the sights.

If you are visiting independently, the abbey is open Monday through Friday from 8 A.M. to 6 P.M., Saturday from 9 A.M. to 2:45 P.M.; however, most of the abbey is closed after 4:45 P.M. to allow for evening services. On Sundays most of the abbey is closed to visitors all day except between services. If you have a choice, try to come on a Thursday, the only day the College Garden—at nine hundred years it's probably England's oldest—is open. While it is free to walk into the church, most of the important points of interest—the Choir, Transepts, and Royal Chapels—each charge a separate small admission fee.

One final note: with the noise and haste of crowds scrambling to see the grave of this poet or that monarch, it is easy to lose sight of the fact that this is, first and foremost, a church and not a tourist attraction. If you'd like to get some sense of the original purpose of the building, plan to end your touring right around 5 P.M. so that you can stay for the forty-minute service of Evensong. It's held weekdays except Wednesdays in the exquisite choir, and if you're there early enough, you can find a seat in one of the elaborately carved wooden stalls—where only the clergy was permitted to sit in former days. The service is still much the same as it ever was, the same prayers and the same music sung by a men and boys choir featuring rosy-cheeked eight-year-olds in cardinal robes and starched ruffed collars, craning their necks for the high notes. Whether you're of the Anglican persuasion or not, this is by far the best way to thrust yourself back through the centuries to the time when this church was new and tourists were few.

There is perhaps no other place of entombment in the world that can boast an all-star lineup of postmortal residents to compare with that of Westminster Abbey. Originally, as stated above, the abbey as it stands was built to receive the remains of St. Edward the Confessor, who was to be memorialized here for his saintly rather than royal status. But once one king was buried here a precedent was set, and subsequent monarchs strove mightily to outdo their predecessors in lavishness of scale and preeminence of positioning for their place of final rest.

It wasn't until the reign of Richard II that commoners (albeit august ones) were buried in the abbey. The custom of burying writers here began in 1400 with the entombment of Geoffrey Chaucer. Later this privilege was extended to artists and scientists. Things got so crowded, and since many people preferred to be buried elsewhere, memorials instead of actual graves were included.

Immediately as you enter from the west end you'll come upon the **Tomb of the Unknown Warrior,** who was transported here and buried in earth from the battlefields of France. It is ringed with poppies, a flower of remembrance. Directly to the right is St. George's Chapel, appropriately enough dedicated to warriors. Just to one side of the chapel is a portrait of Richard II, the oldest portrait of an English king drawn from life.

A few bays down across the nave set into the wall just above the floor of the north aisle you'll find a stone marked "O rare Ben Johnson." The poet, who actually spelled his name Jonson, felt that to be buried in the abbey was honor enough and, not wanting to take up more than his share of space, requested that he be buried standing up.

Continuing up the nave, examine the gilt, red, and royal Quire's exterior. The stonework is 13th century, but the screen and stalls were added in 1847. Take a moment to look backward at the set of Waterford chandeliers given on the abbey's 900th anniversary by the brewmasters Guinness. Just beyond the gate is the entrance to the Quire, bordered by the tombs, where coronations take place.

Behind the Quire is the **Chapel of Edward the Confessor,** sometimes called the Chapel of the Kings, owing to the tombs of five of them and three of their consorts that circle the perimeter of the chapel (entrance is around the back). The most popular feature, however, is the coronation chair, carved from oak in 1300, resting on the backs of four lions. You'll notice directly under the seat is a rather ungainly looking rock, which is known as the **Stone of Scone.** The stone, sometimes referred to as the Stone of Destiny, began as an integral part of Scottish coronations, which took place at Scone Palace (hence the name) since the ninth century. Edward I stole the stone and brought it back to Westminster during one of his northern campaigns, and it has remained here ever since. The stone was stolen in 1951 by some Scottish students, who copied it and sent it back to London. One of the culprits alleged later, however, that they had sent the copy to Westminster and returned the real Stone of Scone to its rightful place in Perthshire.

Edward the Confessor's Shrine, the purpose for the abbey, is at the center of the chapel made of Purbeck marble that was a major destination for pilgrims during the Middle Ages. Nearby are the tombs of Henry III—who began the abbey to honor the saint—Henry's son Edward I, and his daughter-in-law, Eleanor of Castile, whose grief-stricken husband had an avenue of crosses set up along the route of her funeral train from Nottingham to London. Walking around the ambulatory you will come upon the stairs leading up to **Henry**

VII's chapel. The tomb of Henry and his queen, Elizabeth of York, holds the most commanding position at the east end. The structure itself is lovely, a more manageable version of memorial than the whole of the abbey. On either side are interred Queen Elizabeth I (north side) and her arch rival and cousin Mary, Queen of Scots (south side), on opposite sides of the matter in death even as they were in life.

Leaving the Henry VII Chapel and returning to the south ambulatory, continue to the transept, where on your left you'll find the **Poets' Corner.** The man who started it all (in many ways), Geoffrey Chaucer, is laid to rest in the east wall. There are more memorials here than actual graves, but writers whose remains actually rest within the abbey walls are Spenser, Jonson, Dryden, Prior, Johnson, Sheridan, Browning, and Tennyson. Monuments have been erected to, among the dozens, Shakespeare, Milton, Keats, Byron, Blake, Coleridge, Wordsworth, Dickens, Austen, the Brontës, Auden, and T. S. Eliot.

To the east of the abbey proper is the cloister, the square arcade around which the monks would walk at their prayers. This is a great vantage point from which to examine the outer structure of the abbey, or have a turn at the Brass Rubbing Centre. As mentioned, the College Garden, fragrant with lavender, is open only on Thursdays. In late summer, there are band concerts held here at noontime. Schedules are available at the Enquiry Desk in the abbey.

. . . And Out of the Mainstream

Around the southern verge of the abbey are a cluster of pretty, quiet little streets, which provide a welcome escape from the packed public spaces of Westminster. As you walk around you can thrill to the quarter-hourly time checks of Big Ben. Here you'll pass the dorms of the **Westminster Abbey School** and at 14 Barton Street the **home of T. E. Lawrence** (of Arabia). Across Great Peter Street you'll see **St. John's** at the center of Smith Square. Originally built as a church, it was badly damaged during the blitz, and instead of returning it to its sacred function it was instead refitted as a concert hall. Schedules are usually listed outside on posters. They have recently opened a gallery and restaurant, The Footstool, downstairs that are open weekdays at lunchtime and evenings when there is a concert scheduled.

Down Dean Bradley St. at the corner of Romney is the **Marquis of Granby Pub.** There are flowers on the ceiling, soft lights, and dining upstairs. You can continue inland on John Islip St. or walk east one block to Millbank, which runs along the Thames. About a half mile along is the Tate Gallery.

The Tate Gallery

Built on the site of a former jail, this gallery, once you've sampled some of its treasures, will completely captivate you, and you'll be reluctant to depart until you've seen every last item in the collection (a project that could take weeks). It takes its name from benefactor and sugar magnate Sir Henry Tate, who put up the original £80,000 needed for its construction in 1897. Along with the cash, he also offered to endow the new gallery with his own fine collection of Victorian painting and sculpture. Other benefactors were the art-dealing Duveens, father and son, who paid for the original wing for the Turners and for the modern collections, respectively. More recently opened is the **Clore Gallery,** a controversial new home for the Turner collection.

Speaking of the Clore, undoubtedly this is the principal reason most people today visit the gallery. In his will, J. M. W. Turner donated a large number of his works to the National Gallery, where they were housed until they were moved here in 1897. The bequest was massive—nearly three hundred paintings and close to twenty thousand watercolors and drawings. Turner insisted that his finished paintings be exhibited en masse, a consummation realized only in 1987 with the opening of the Clore Gallery. Despite the inevitable arguments back and forth over the James Stirling design for the new gallery, unquestionably one of its most fortunate features is its situation beside the Thames, so appropriate to the artist who, throughout his work, used this river—and great bodies of water generally—to explore the effects of light.

All the (justifiable) fuss over the Turners has tended to overshadow the other collections of the Tate, which—were they housed in any other museum—would certainly be considered highlights. The Tate collections focus on two areas: British painting from the 16th to the 20th century; and the modern collection, devoted primarily to contemporary British artists but also including the works of foreign artists. In the British collection you'll find stellar examples of the work of William Hogarth, Thomas Gainsborough, George Stubbs, Sir Joshua Reynolds, George Romney, and William Blake. Especially well-represented among 19th-century artists are the Pre-Raphaelites, including Rossetti, Burne-Jones, and Millais. In contrast to their medieval pictoral style are the more abstract works of contemporaries Sargent and Whistler.

The modern collection is equally strong; it includes Impressionists, Cubists, Surrealists, Expressionists, and Abstract Expressionists. The list—let alone the paintings—will leave you reeling. Favorites in this group include Manet's *Woman with a Cat,* Matisse's *The Snail,* Picasso's *The Three Dancers,* and Rothko's *Maroon* series.

☕ We suggest by all means that you plan to be here at lunchtime to enjoy the treat of eating at the **Tate Gallery Restaurant** (not to be confused with the coffee shop, which isn't nearly so special). It is decorated by a Rex Whistler mural, *Pursuit of Rare Meats.* The food is on the fancy side and not necessarily cheap, but it's worth a visit not only for the wonderful setting but primarily to sample their great wine list. Reservations are urged (834-6754). Lunch only is served from 12 to 3 P.M., Mon.–Sat.

The Tate is open Monday through Saturday from 10 A.M. to 5:50 P.M., Sunday from 2 to 5:50 P.M. Admission is free with the exception of major visiting exhibitions, for which a nominal fee may be charged.

Back in the direction of Parliament Square, just west of it and south of St. James's Park, is an area called Queen Anne's Gate. At No. 36 on the street of that same name is the headquarters of the **National Trust,** a nonprofit organization responsible for the preservation of important places throughout Britain. If you're planning to travel elsewhere in Britain, the Trust (open from 9 A.M. to 5:30 P.M.) will help you with brochures and maps and answer any questions you might have on a particular region.

☕ At the intersection with Dartmouth St. is the **Two Chairmen Pub.** There is a fire on the hearth when necessary and an antique triptych of 18th-century London on the back wall. Spirits are drawn from casks instead of upended bottles.

Of Bearskin Hats and Crimson Uniforms

Before or after you take in the pomp and circumstance, you might like to find out a little bit about the participants in the piece. Along Birdcage Walk is a series of sights devoted to the Guards themselves. The most interesting are at the east end of the street (away from the palace). The Guards Chapel was largely destroyed by bombs in 1944, but miraculously its most exquisite mosaics were saved and installed in their former position behind the altar in the reconstructed church when the new building was built in 1963.

Just next door, opened in 1988 at the cost of some £40 million-plus, is the **Guards Museum** (open Monday through Thursday, Saturday and Sunday 10 A.M. to 3:30 P.M.). Martial music plays as you wander past the displays of wartime memorabilia, including things like the Duke of Marlborough's sword and a lock from the gate at Hougomont Farm, where a pivotal engagement took place during the Battle of Waterloo. Just as you enter are models wearing the full-dress uniform of the guards of each of the five regiments. You can tell the difference between guardsmen by the number of buttons on their jackets, the color and positioning of the plumes on their bearskin hats, and the emblems on their collars.

The Main Event

They're changing guard at Buckingham Palace—
Christopher Robin went down with Alice. Alice is marrying one of the guard.
"A soldier's life is terrible hard,"
says Alice.—*A. A. Milne*

Ever since Mom read these sing-song verses, you were keen to come to London and see the spectacle of the changing of the guard for yourself. If you came when you were still a little tyke, you might not have been able to see much over the heads of the crowd, or you might have been miffed that you had to watch the ceremonies from afar behind the palace's iron gate. These shortcomings have not, however, abated one whit the popularity of the event, which takes place every other morning in winter and daily during the summer at 11:30 A.M. and 10:30 A.M. on Sunday. For a days-on, days-off listing of times, check the board outside the Guard Bookshop just south of the palace on Birdcage Walk. Information is also given on which regiments will be providing the guard and the band for the day's festivities. If you want to get a good parade-route spot, better plan to be there at least an hour early. Keep in mind that the ceremony may be canceled on special state occasions or if the weather's bad.

The Queen's Collections

Frustrating as it may be that the palace itself is not open to the public, you can visit the Queen's Gallery and the Royal Mews, which are located on the south side of the palace grounds along Buckingham Palace Road.

   The Queen's Gallery (open Tuesday through Saturday from 10:30 A.M. to 5 P.M., Sunday from 2 to 5 P.M.) hosts a changing series of exhibitions of objects from the royal collections gathered and arranged around a particular theme.

   Like the gallery, **The Royal Mews** (open Wednesday and Thursday *only,* 2 to 4 P.M.) were designed by John Nash. All the Queen's coaches and the tack for her horses are kept here. The Irish Coach is used for the State Opening of Parliament ceremony; the Glass Coach is for Royal Weddings; and the Gold State Coach is reserved for coronations.

Soho and Covent Garden

The area whose high spirits are just barely contained by Oxford Street, Regent Street, Trafalgar Square, the Strand, and Drury Lane prides itself on the possession of some of London's most sought-after entertainments. This is the place to go when you're hungering for the larger-than-life wallop that only the biggest and best of cities can offer.

Here are London's West End theaters whose exports to Broadway and beyond have made these Edwardian music halls the place to watch for the world's next commercial-theater blockbuster. Twenty-five years since Mary Quant hawked her quirky fashion ideas on Carnaby Street, London's clothiers still find it imperative to rent space for their shapes in shops with a W1 post code. The Covent Garden facelift that swept the Eliza Dolittles out of the neighborhood concurrently swept the beau monde in, and the cafés of Soho are crammed with customers who are far too chic and clever for their own good.

Theaters, boutiques, boîtes, beautiful people . . . the list continues with terrific museums like the National Gallery, the melting-pot feel of Chinatown, and London's primest people-watching in Leicester Square, Covent Garden, and Piccadilly Circus. Your head's sure to be set spinning by the overload of input. It's a bit ironic when you consider the pastoral beginnings of the area. Both Covent Garden and Soho are names that have slipped down through the centuries from days when a very different manner of drama was played out here.

Long before buildings, there were farms and parkland belonging to various religious orders. With the dissolution of churches in 1536, St. Giles's Fields—for thus the area was known in the days when it was the site of a leper hospital—was ceded to Henry VIII, who directed that it should be maintained as a hunting ground for his court. It's present moniker descended from "So-ho!" a call to set off on the chase. Covent Garden is a bastardization (you'll pardon the expression) of Convent Garden, harkening back to the days when the site belonged to the convent (abbey) at Westminster.

Soho has always attracted the Bohemian of one sort or another—from fine artists to striptease "artists," from booksellers to brothel keepers. One of the principal reasons for the historical exotica with which Soho is still imbued has been the subsequential waves of foreigners who have made Soho their home base over the years.

The first bunch of note were Huguenots come over from France to continue their Protestantism in the 18th century. In the 19th, they had integrated with the English population and were replaced by Italian, Greek, and East European Jewish immigrants who were in this century succeeded in turn by Chinese and Indians. And as with most foreign ghettos in

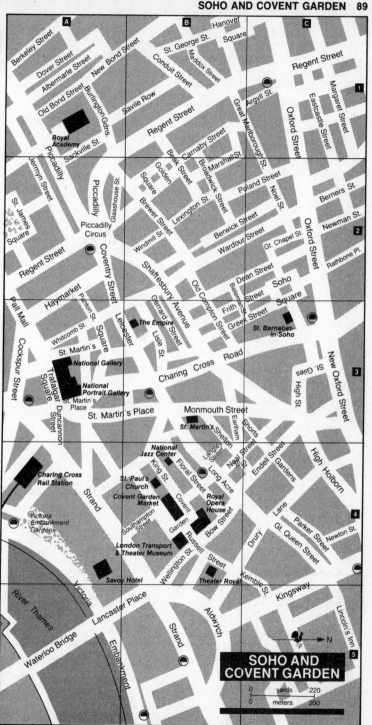

SOHO AND
COVENT GARDEN

big cities, Soho also attracted her share of artists—most particularly actors and painters—who liked the ethnic color and the concomitant low cost of living.

Since there are so many different facets to this neighborhood, it is impossible to devise a walking tour along which you could see everything without having to double back and run off down a stray street; the neighborhood simply cannot be seen in a straight line. Instead we'll start you off at several obvious bases of operations, whence you can see what there is to see within a reasonable on-foot radius. There are the circuses, Oxford and Piccadilly, the squares, Trafalgar and Leicester, and Covent Garden. While you can probably fit in circumnavigations of three or possibly four of these centers, you won't be able to cover them all in one day, especially if you plan—as you really must—to take in the National Gallery and the National Portrait Gallery. So allow yourself a couple of days at least to give Soho the once-over.

The shopping around Oxford Circus and the museums around Trafalgar Square make them morning and afternoon destinations. The shops and cafés around Covent Garden are open later and only begin to really hum (with other than tourists) around 5 or 6 P.M., so make this a late-afternoon/early-evening destination. Leicester Square and Piccadilly Circus are bright and busy well into the night—and they look much better when the cold light of day is long gone—so it's best to come here after dark when the lights are drenching the night sky with their brand of daylight.

Oxford Circus

Oxford Circus holds down the northwest corner of Soho, its easterly radian, Oxford Street, being the northern border and its southerly radian, Regent Street, western. Although the east side of Regent Street could be considered within Soho proper, its shops owe more to upper-crust Mayfair than trendy Soho, so we will include them in the Mayfair section.

Oxford Street

Oxford is that street in all cities where the clothes are cheap and look that way, where the shops try to distract you from the tattiness of their merchandise by bright lights, loud music, and, in some cases, a kick line of mechanical female legs can-canning up a storm in the front window. This in no way dissuades mobs of Londoners from flocking here to pursue their sartorial business. And in no way should it dissuade you either. You may not find anything you're dying to own, but Oxford Street is a scene unto itself and should be seen, if only to make a comparison with similar thoroughfares in your own city. Besides, you just might find a record you're looking for at the shops for **HMV** or **Virgin**—worth a look in to watch the videos—or some raspberry ripple bath bubbles at the **Body Shop.**

Mary and Twiggy and Leather and Chains

It's gratifying to see that Carnaby Street is regaining its position at the cutting edge of fashion that it enjoyed in the sixties when designer Mary Quant launched the careers of Twiggy and the miniskirt in one fell swoop. There is still a store for Quant down at the southern end of what has now become a pedestrian street, and other designers are moving back to capitalize on the street's pop cachet. This is interspersed with shops which sell "fashion" about which the kindest thing one could say is that it is unimaginative. Rock-and-roll T-shirts, studded leather jackets, thigh-high boots, Union Jack briefs, faux-leopard skin-tight skirts—you get the idea. Still, it's fun to mix serious shopping with the tatty pelts and the blaring music, if merely for the kitsch value.

You may find something you'll want to buy in the blocks just east. At 7 Marshall street is the **Craftsmen's Potters Shop,** whose name is indicative of its hand-created ceramics. **Academy Soho** at 15 Newburgh Street features carefully cut, canny clothes, hats, shoes, and jewelry tagged with the name of the up-and-coming designer. Pick up some club passes at the desk. At 1–5 Poland Street **Peter Leonard Assoc.** sells well-designed lighting and furniture mostly in *de rigueur* matte black.

If you want to stop for a nibble check out **Nelsons** at 13 Ganton Street for sandwiches and salads, upstairs or on the sidewalk; and **Phood** at 29 Foubert's Place where emphasis is on gourmet natural.

Music and Movie Mogul Mecca

At Noel and Berwick streets is **Bugle House,** and the gold records on the walls let you know that this is the headquarters for A&M and IRS recording artists' fan clubs. You can get T-shirts and mementos pertinent to Sting, Squeeze, The Bangles, etc. This is merely an introduction to Wardour Street, one block east, where all the major film and record companies have congregated; you'll see the logos of the likes of Paramount, Warner, Rank, and lots of gents in shiny suits. If you're an amateur with professional aspirations in any of these areas, it's a good neighborhood for equipment shops. As for the general public—well, you just never know who might glide up in a limo, hop out, and head up to the boardroom to sign a contract or hold a press conference.

Eastward ho is Soho Square, which architecturally is no great shakes but which has a bit of green in this otherwise overbuilt neighborhood and a wattle-and-daub gardener's bungalow at the center. On the southeastern verge is the House of St. Barnabas on Greek Street.

London Rococo

As it has been since 1862, **St. Barnabas-in-Soho** has provided shelter for destitute women in the elegant surroundings of this 18th-century house. Its rooms, dating from the 1750s, are decorated with original ceilings, mantels, and staircases of the finest quality English Rococo craftsmanship. A portion of *A Tale of Two Cities* was set in its rear courtyard. Since the house is still very much in use, opening times are restricted to Wednesday afternoon and Thursday morning.

LIBATION

Check our restaurant listings for Soho—some of London's best are sequestered along these streets. Or stop at **Ed's Easy Diner** at the junction of Old Compton and Moor St. and slip into a counter seat for shakes and burgers.

At the corner of Bateman and Frith streets is the neighborhood's best pub, the **Dog and Duck.** After work it's wall to wall young business people. There's high-gloss pumpkin paint on the tin ceiling, high-gloss polychrome tiles on the walls, curvilinear woodwork, cut-glass windows. All this gloss makes for a warm bright pub to match its warm bright clientele.

The National Gallery

Along with the Tate and the British Museum, the National Gallery forms London's trinity of transcendent museums. Like the Louvre or the Metropolitan or the Prado, it rather spoils the gallery-goer, spanning the artistic ages with a collection that is not so much large as perfect; each artist is represented by only the finest examples of his or her work.

Hours are Monday through Saturday from 10 A.M. to 6 P.M., Sunday from 2 to 6 P.M. Admission is free. There are guided tours weekdays at 11:30 A.M. and 3 P.M., Saturdays at 2 and 3:30 P.M. Additionally, there are special events daily, lectures and films at 1 P.M. on weekdays, 12 on Saturdays, and audiovisual programs at the Orange Street Theatre, 1 to 5:30 P.M. Tuesday through Saturday. To allay the confusion, pick up a free copy of the month's events at the info desk. There they will also supply you with a map and suggest a tour based on your interests.

The building itself was built from 1832 to 38 to house a national collection begun at the instigation of Sir George Beaumont, who urged His Majesty George IV's government to take advantage of the estate sale of a Russian-born insurance salesman, John Julius Angerstein. After this initial investment, 38 paintings in all, the collection was added to by a spate of purchasing on the part of its first director, Sir Charles Eastlake, in the mid-19th century. Over the years museum purchases, funded by an annual £480,000 government grant, have been accompanied by private donations of works of art that formerly graced Britain's finest homes. When the Tate took on the role of being the showcase for native artists, the National concentrated its efforts on European masters, and here you can certainly see some superb examples of them. The earliest paintings are Italian: Giotto's *Pentecost,* Uccello's *Battle of San Romano.* Later Italian masterpieces include a Leonardo cartoon of the Virgin and Child and the *Madonna of the Rocks,* Michelangelo's *Entombment,* a Raphael study of Pope Julius II, and Titian's *Death of Actaeon.*

There is a gallery full of Rembrandts—somber, sober faces emerging from the umbers and ochers—including a pair of self-portraits and *A Man in a Room.* In contrast, there is a room of voluptuous, dissipated Peter Paul Reubenses, including *Sampson and Delilah* and *The Straw Hat.*

Other Dutch and Flemish masterworks to be seen are Hals, *Young Man Holding a Skull;* Vermeer, *Young Woman Standing at a Virginal;* Van Eyck, *Giovanni Arnolfini and His Wife;* Van Dyck, *Equestrian Portrait of Charles I.*

In the German collection you'll find an Albrecht Dürer portrait of his father, Hans Holbein the Younger's fascinating the *French Ambassadors,* and several Cranach studies of mythological scenes.

French painting is exemplified by relatively newer works, such as Poussin's *Bacchanalian Revel,* several Fragonard fantasies, Degas's *After the Bath,* Seurat's study of *Bathers at Asnières,* and one of Monet's *Irises.*

The Spanish school is somewhat thinly represented by Velázquez's *The Toilet of Venus,* Murillo's *Self Portrait,* and Goya's *Duke of Wellington.*

As mentioned, the Brits have largely decamped to the Tate, but there are plenty of good home-grown paintings left here, including William Hogarth's saucy *Marriage à la Mode,* Joshua Reynolds and Thomas Gainsborough portraits, John Constable's *The Haywain,* and J.M.W. Turner's *Rain, Steam and Speed—The Great Western Railway.*

Of course you'll find great postcards, art books, and journals in the shop.

The **National Gallery Restaurant** is pleasant, and the food is brought to you by Justin De Blank of Sloane Square fame.

Some Old Familiar Faces

Around the corner from the National Gallery on St. Martin's Place is the **National Portrait Gallery.** Often overlooked by those in search of masterpieces of art, this gallery cannot boast the stellar lineup of its neighbor, but it does contain a stellar roster of subjects.

Essentially, the museum is a chronology of the people who have been vital in the creation and promotion of Britain. You can see contemporary portraits of all the characters you've read about and follow their exploits, royal and otherwise, through time. The sitter is vastly more important than the painter here—indeed, many of the tags on Tudor portraits explain that the artist is unknown.

The best way to proceed is to take the elevator up to the top, where you'll find the earliest portraits, and work your way downstairs to the 20th century. All the kings and queens and their relatives are here, as well as statesmen, men of arts and letters—indeed the best pictures tend to be artists' self-portraits—sports figures, warmongers, and peacemakers. It's a good way to get a sense of which artist or prime minister was contemporary with which monarch. And, of course, it reveals as much about jewelers, dressmakers, hairdressers, and swordmakers down through time as it does about their clients, the princes of the realm.

The gallery is open Monday through Friday from 10 A.M. to 5 P.M., Saturday from 10 A.M. to 6 P.M., Sunday from 2 to 6 P.M. Admission to the main gallery is free; occasionally there will be a small charge for a special exhibit. There are gallery talks—usually centering on history and biography rather than art—Tuesday through Friday at 1:10 P.M., Saturday at 3 P.M. Printed schedules are available at the info desk, and daily events are listed on the board in the lobby by the portrait of Mrs. Thatcher.

Sanctuary on the Square

St. Martin-in-the-Fields was originally built in the village of Charing (of Charing Cross fame), which was situated between the City and Westminster. There were several churches previously on the site, the last being completed in the mid-16th century. In 1721 James Gibbs was commissioned to build a new structure incorporating the original bells, dated 1525. Gibbs decided on a Classical exterior and a Baroque interior. The extravagance of the latter has been toned down by coloring its ornate plasterwork with pale creams, buffs, and eggshell with highlights in scarlet and gold. The dark wood pews seem at odds with the splendor of the other architectural features, including a pulpit attributed to Grinling Gibbons. There are free lunchtime concerts Monday and Tuesday at 1:05 P.M., and evening concerts are held twice a month; call 839-1930 for information, or pick up a schedule at the information table. The renowned Academy of St. Martin-in-the-Fields has moved its base to the South Bank Centre but returns here for a week of festivities in July—a terrific opportunity to hear a world-class orchestra in an intimate setting.

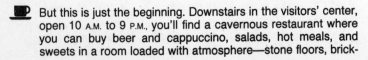

But this is just the beginning. Downstairs in the visitors' center, open 10 A.M. to 9 P.M., you'll find a cavernous restaurant where you can buy beer and cappuccino, salads, hot meals, and sweets in a room loaded with atmosphere—stone floors, brick-vaulted ceiling, candlelight, black camp chairs and tables, to the tune of Sir Neville Mariner et al.

Here is also the new headquarters of the **London Brass Rubbing Centre.** For from 50 pence to £6, you can choose from zodiac signs, knights and their ladies, and beasts, and do it yourself or buy them ready-rubbed for about twice the price. Behind the church outdoors is a crafts market.

Victoria Embankment Gardens

If you walk a little way along the Strand and turn right heading toward the river, you'll come to Embankment Gardens, which has a bandstand at which musical and dramatic events are held during the good-weather months. Programs are placed in the little green boxes by the entrances and posted on the board at the rear.

The gardens are a profusion of bulbs in April, and the trees are lit in the evening to most dramatic effect. Lovers of all types, sizes, and ages cuddle and woo as the pigeons coo and the traffic on the Embankment throbs by.

Stop in at the **Savoy Hotel** with a back entrance at the gardens' eastern edge for breakfast or tea if it's time, and enjoy the view without the noise.

Courtauld Institute Galleries

Past the Savoy Hotel, down the Strand, is Somerset House the street side of which has been converted into the Courtauld Institute Galleries. Formerly situated in Bloomsbury, this is the collection of Samuel Courtauld, a textile industrialist who pioneered the development of such synthetics as rayon. He and Mrs. Courtauld collected all the important Impressionists and donated their holdings to London University. The Institute's collection was aggrandized by the posthumous donation of several other important private collections, including one of Old Master paintings and drawings. The display is remarkably fine and small enough to allow each work to be fully appreciated. Featured are the works of Tintoretto, Bruegel's *Landscape with Flight into Egypt,* a roomful of Rubenses, Van Gogh's *Self-Portrait with a Bandaged Ear,* Degas's *The Card Players,* and Manet's *Bar at the Folies-Bergère.*

Covent Garden

As mentioned, this used to be the garden of the convent of Westminster, and it has always had agricultural associations, most importantly with the fruit and vegetable market that started in the mid-17th century with a few makeshift stalls set up within the square owned by the Earl of Bedford.

By the 19th century the market had grown to be a serious enterprise and source of revenue for the then Dukes of Bedford, and it was decided that a glassed-in structure was needed to contain the crowds and control the traffic that was jamming the streets. Covent Garden had become a cross-class meeting place where those who were terribly upper would come for a picturesque afternoon of slumming it with flower girls and barrow boys.

By the 1960s the market had become an anachronism, and developers saw that the prime real estate could be put to better (i.e., more lucrative) use. By 1974 the flowers, fruits, and vegetables had moved to a new location in Nine Elms, and subsequently the market opened as a collection of shops and eateries crammed with locals and foreigners all day long.

The carnival atmosphere of the 19th-century market is still very much a part of the scene. A man plays a little Stan Getz on a sax while kicking cones for his dog to chase (is this part of the act?). A kilt-clad piper adds his mournful notes to the traffic noises. Mimes, jugglers, break dancers, and comics vie for piazza space and the attention of passersby, who stop, listen, and hopefully drop a copper in their coffer. You can enjoy their antics from the pavement, or stop in for a cuppa or a pinta at one of the many alfresco cafés that spill out of the surrounding restaurants onto the sidewalk.

In the market itself, aside from the permanent-fixture stores—mostly branch offices of big names—stalls are set up that are reminiscent of the former flower and fruit stands. The new tenants sell antiques on Monday, crafts Tuesday through Saturday. The crafts are of quite high quality. A prospective seller must apply to the London Residency Body, which is in charge of seeing that all items are handmade and not imported, and that a variety of items are available.

A Taste of the Old Days

On the western side of the market square is **St. Paul's Church,** where there really is a garden in which you can eat your takeaway. The building is the remaining piece of the original piazza built by Inigo Jones for the Earl of Bedford in 1631. Jones was inspired by the central squares of Italy to build a facsimile of the Palladian style here in London, where this new enclosed courtyard, originally surrounded Venetian-style by a covered arcade, caused quite a stir, thus being the first of the city's great squares.

St. Paul's has long served the theater people who lived in the neighborhood and has been duly dubbed "The Actors' Church." Actors and artists connected with the church include W. S. Gilbert and J. M. W. Turner, both of whom were baptized here; David Garrick, who was a parishioner; and Ellen Terry, whose ashes are deposited in the south wall. Grinling Gibbons is also buried here, and an example of his work, a carved wreath, which originally was incorporated in St. Paul's Cathedral, is preserved by the rear door. Many other folk of a thespian turn are commemorated by plaques in the church, and of a Sunday you might find the lesson being read by a luminary on loan from one of the nearby West End theaters.

Museums at the Market

The **London Transport Museum** is located in a building that formerly served as the flower market. Today actual locomotives and Tube cars and double-deckers are parked where the violets and primroses used to be.

It's a great place for finding out what makes your bus and Tube tick, and what made them tick a century ago. The museum not only discusses the how and why of London transportation but also makes a most persuasive case for the revolutionary sociological changes brought about by the availability of low-cost travel for the masses. In 1864 the Metropolitan Railroad introduced fares for the workingman; heretofore people had to walk to work and obviously were thereby greatly restricted in what and how well they could do.

Some of Britain's best graphic designers have worked for the transportation authority, and therefore the shop has some of London's best postcards, decals, and posters of vintage Underground, BritRail, etc., adverts. Open daily, 10 A.M. to 6 P.M.; £2.50.

The **Theatre Museum** is actually underneath the Transport Museum. At the door is a box office where you can get theater tickets for West End plays with a £2.50 per-seat surcharge. Inside is the box office for the museum.

The collection was formerly housed at the Victoria and Albert Museum but quite wisely was moved here to the heart of the neighborhood that made it all possible. The Harry Beard Room has a great collection of ballet, drama, and pop memorabilia arranged in chronological order in vertical cases slid into the walls. You'll find programs, ticket stubs, and photos pertaining to David Garrick in number 18, Margot Fonteyn in number 238, and the Sex Pistols in number 251.

There are constantly changing exhibitions featuring a historic period of theater, or a style of filmmaking, or a particular actor, or a photographer specializing in celebrity photos. Inexplicably uncrowded, it is one of the best museums in town, through which you can wander at leisure and in peace. There is also a working theater in the building that offers performances, usually evenings at 6:30, and lectures at lunchtime. Check the schedule at the box office. The museum is open Tuesday through Sunday from 11 A.M. to 7 P.M., café till 8 P.M. Closed Mondays. Admission is £2.25.

The Opera House

In 1662 Charles II granted a set of letters patent to two men, dividing between them the rights to build theaters in London.

One set fell into the hands of John Rich, actor and impresario, whose successes at Lincoln's Inn Fields encouraged him to build a new theater at Covent Garden. That was the first in a series of theaters, of which the present one is the third. After a fire destroyed the second theater in 1856, E. M. Barry was commissioned to build a new theater, which was completed in 1858.

What began as a playhouse is now home to the Royal Opera, the Royal Ballet, and the Sadler's Wells Ballet companies. An evening here in the 2,158-seat auditorium should be on everyone's must-do list of London. As the lights in their gold sconces dim and the crimson curtains—with Her Majesty's crest embroidered in gold—part, you will be privy to one of the world's most thrilling and satisfying evenings.

Tickets are of course available at the box office, 48 Floral Street, from 10 A.M. to 8 P.M., Monday through Saturday. You can charge tickets with MasterCard (Access) or Visa by calling 240-1066 or 240-1911. Standing-room tickets, £5, are available on the day of the performance at the discretion of the management.

Cosmo Clothiers and Holdover Hippies

The area surrounding Covent Garden is wall-to-wall with unusual shops and restaurants. One of the best places to explore is Neal Street, just across Long Acre to the north. Pop down Shorts Gardens to **Neal's Yard,** where the sixties are still flourishing and easing into the New Age.

Pick up some natural munchies for the road at the **Wholefood Warehouse** on the corner.

The yard itself is a tiny opening among precious painted buildings, flowerpots, and funky benches made from planters and trash bins. The shops and service centers provide all you need in the way of natural and supernatural care. **Aurora Crystals** has New-Age music, books, crystals—perhaps Shirley MacLaine hung out here during her dalliance with the mystery MP. Upstairs at **Neal's Yard Therapy Rooms** they practice everything from acupuncture to reflexology for whatever ails you, administered by a coop of therapists. Fees range from £16 to £30 for half-an-hour to one-hour sessions.

Or you get your healing to go at **Neal's Yard Remedies,** an herbal apothecary that smells soothing as soon as you walk in. You can buy chamomile and orange flower shampoo, sage and elderflower cleanser, and Dr. Bach's own Rescue Remedy—all in beautiful indigo-blue glass bottles.

Along Neal Street proper are **Rebecca** for women and **Sam Walker** for men, which have collected superb second-hands from ancient England—1940s day dresses, delicious hats, cashmere cardigans, and correct suits. Not cheap.

Ray's Jazz Shop on Monmouth Street where Neal Street intersects with Shaftesbury Avenue is the place for second-hand and new, mainstream and hard-to-find albums and posters. There is also a bulletin board of upcoming events in London's jazz world with good listings of free jazz in pubs.

You can buy your tickets for pop and jazz and sporting events at **Premier Box Office,** flat-ironing the conjunction of Monmouth Street and Shaftesbury. Here is a complete listing of musical events, especially good for shows and concert tickets. They also sell theater and other more middle-of-the-road programs.

Other unusual stops in the Covent Garden sphere include **The Africa Centre** at 38 King Street, a retail store and galleries for paintings and performances. Downstairs is the **Calabash** restaurant. (See the *Restaurants* chapter)

Edward Stanford, 12–14 Long Acre, is for maps, travel, and picture books of subjects around the world—should you wish to extend your journey outside the boundaries of the valuable book you presently hold in your hands.

Paxman, on Langley Street, sells musical instruments—French horns galore, saxes, clarinets, plus scores. It's also just down the street from the **Pineapple Store,** for dance and leisure togs. You can take classes in dance, aerobics, calisthenics, and even get a massage here at the center.

The Sanctuary, at 11 Floral Street is an oasis offering a health club, swim club, beauty salon—everything the city-harried businessperson or traveler could wish to soothe his or her spirits (admissions are £28.50 for the whole day, £19.50 after 5 P.M.).

Contemporary Applied Arts Centre, 43 Earlham Street, sells the best of British artisans in an atmosphere much less hectic than that at Covent Garden.

Leicester Square

Leicester Square (pronounced "Lester") and its down-the-street neighbor, Piccadilly Circus, are the kind of precincts the locals love to hate. Crowded with tourists, bright with the imported plastic and neon of McDonald's and Pizza Hut, Londoners strive manfully to boycott the area and leave the armies of visitors to overrun it at will. Yet somehow, the natives never quite succeed in avoiding this designated no-Londoner's-land. It *is* green, although the grass does tend to get a bit rumpled from overuse. And it *is* a good place to meet, being, as it is, in the center of things. And it is a good place to people-watch while you're waiting for your date.

It began as Leicester Square when the Earls of Leicester acquired it as their London address and built a house on the northern side in 1635. It became quite a chic address among art-world celebrities like Joshua Reynolds, John Singleton Copley, and William Hogarth, who moved in in the late 18th century. Subsequently, the square declined and became the province of music halls, petty thieves, foreigners, and women of questionable character.

Two of London's most famous music halls, the **Alhambra** and the **Empire,** were built here. The former is gone, but the latter remains in all its glory and now divides its space between a movie theater and a disco.

The best reasons to come are the **half-price ticket kiosk** and the glockenspiel at the **Swiss Centre.** The former has same-day returns from most West End theaters and the Barbican and South Bank centers as well. Matinee tickets are sold from noon; evening seats from 2:30 P.M., Monday through Saturday. The queue has been known to stretch around the square, so come early. Tickets are sold on a cash-only basis, and a £1 per-seat service charge will be added.

The glockenspiel chimes on the hour, and so of course is best at midnight or noon, when the business takes a bit longer. Inside the Swiss Centre are shops and cafés—try some ice cream—which are supposed to transport you from London to the Alps—fine, if that's where you'd rather be. If you're not sure, out front on the pavement is a compass indicating the distances to various points around the world.

Perhaps you'd rather be in Shanghai. This is easily arranged by walking a few blocks north to Gerrard Street, the middle kingdom of London's **Chinatown.** The gates at either end of the street will alert you that you've arrived if the crisp tones of Cantonese and the sour scent of bok choy haven't done so already. Lots of Londoners-in-the-know do their grocery shopping here where selection is good and prices are low. They also come here late at night because this is one of the few places where you can get a meal well into the wee hours.

West of the square in Charing Cross Road and most especially on **Cecil Court** and **St. Martin's Lane,** there is a slew of book and print shops, perfect for the browser or the serious collector. A fine print or an illustrated edition of a classic novel can be found at reasonable prices; they make great gifts for the folks back home.

Piccadilly Circus

It is no accident that this second hub of London has at its center a statue to neither a great statesman, nor war hero, but rather to Eros, the god of, well—you know. And, indeed, this piece of London is the center of the city's sensual scene, with its restaurants, theaters, sex shops, and tourist traps. Sitting on the steps of the fountain, the traffic roars, brakes squeal, horns sound, and security guards dash out of a nearby store to nab would-be thieves. The lights run across the big boards with news and ads. Tourists stop to take advantage of photo opportunities, and the biggest hucksters of all, the pigeons, beg and cajole shamelessly.

On the far corner, couldn't miss it if you tried, is the London outlet of **Tower Records.** Inside you can buy concert and sporting-event tickets, as well as records, T-shirts, and, for the homesick, the Sunday (New York or L.A.) *Times.* It's not the best store for browsing: the ongoing videos and annoying overhead strobe lights provide a total assault and force you to make your purchases and scram as fast as possible. Perhaps this was the designer's purpose all along?

A much pleasanter place to shop is the **London Design Centre,** 28 Haymarket. You can find art, architecture and graphic design books and journals at the shop in back. Not just for tourists, the center is a means of connecting interested manufacturers with designers, and provides a referral service.

 There are galleries and a **café** that has salads, quiche, soup, wine, and claret. Open daily.

Indoor Amusements
Lord knows whence the Latino lilt to the title of this place, which is primarily designed to get the tourist off the street and give him a place to spend his stray £s. Not to be flip; some of the attractions are pretty amusing in this complex, which is part amusement gallery, part café conglomeration, part shopping mall. Best to see is the **London Experience,** at which five screens trace London's history from Rome through the plague, the Great Fire and the blitz, with emphasis, as you may have gathered, on the melodrama. The 35-minute multimedia presentation includes film, slides, computer-trafficked images, flames, clouds, strobes, smoke, and a roaring sound system. Good fun. (10 A.M. to 11 P.M. seven days; £2.50.)

Next door at Number One Picadilly, is the pink granite and marble **London Pavilion.** On the top floor is the Rock Circus, brought to you by Madame Tussaud's, where Elvis can be seen jamming with the Beatles and the Boss.

Belgravia, South Kensington, and Chelsea

Looking around at all the street-chic shops and the chic-chic shops, the restaurants and gourmet stores jammed with London's young upwardly mobiles, it's awfully hard to imagine that this neighborhood just south of Hyde Park once resembled more the park itself than the crowd-scuttled streets and rows of town houses—all chopped into flats these days—that you see now.

There are three (at least) distinct neighborhoods packed in between the grass of Hyde Park and the waters of the Thames. Belgravia belonged to the Lords Grosvenor, whose name still graces many of the streets and businesses, and was built by them in the 1820s as a locale for the fashionable to rival the mansions of Mayfair. SW1 post codes still carry the cachet of being some of the toniest properties in London—witness the number of embassies on Belgrave Square—ranged along its gracious streets and around its private gardens.

Just west of this area is Knightsbridge, whose inhabitants bicker over whether it is a neighborhood unto itself or merely the name of the main drag that runs through the area and along which you'll find the redoubtable Harrods. Dropping down from Knightsbridge is Sloane Street, another site of ritual shopping pilgrimages, and the favored stomping grounds of the Sloane Rangers. These peripatetic creatures act more or less like the American preppy (in the same sense that a lobster tastes more or less like a chicken) and reached their highest profile when one of their number, dubbed "Super-Sloane" by the *Sloane Ranger Handbook,* married the Prince of Wales. Naturally they still do exist, but having picked over the subject pretty thoroughly five years ago, the media has grown tired of them and has shifted its attention to the more pressing matter of the burgeoning population of yuppies—some of whom are opportunistic Sloane Rangers.

West of Knightsbridge is South Kensington (South Ken, if you're too busy to finish your phrases). Shopping mania continues here along Brompton Road. But sartorocentricism does give way to a flurry of culture in the collection of concert halls and museums clustered just south of Kensington Gardens at Kensington Gore. These facilities—among them are the Victoria and Albert Museum and the Royal Albert Hall—are all the descendants of the Great Exhibition of 1851 (see box below), the Victorians' pardonably excessive revel in their own imperial might.

South of South Ken is Chelsea, which somehow, despite the maze of buildings, has managed to retain a certain scent of her pastoral origins. Chelsea's favorite shopping streets are

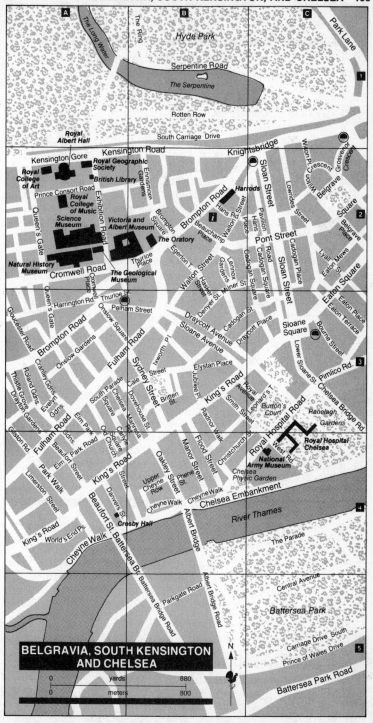

BELGRAVIA, SOUTH KENSINGTON
AND CHELSEA

| 0 | | yards | 880 |
| 0 | | meters | 800 |

The Great Exhibition of 1851

By the middle of the 19th century, Britain had been more or less in charge of the planet for a half century, and London was, therefore, the center of the world. It was deemed necessary that the various national accomplishments contributing to Britain's power and might should be celebrated by some sort of congenially self-congratulatory fête. A committee, headed by Albert, the Prince Consort, was formed, money was raised, a site in Hyde Park was designated, and the commission after much competition and deliberation chose a plan submitted by Joseph Paxton. Paxton had previously designed conservatories, and the structure he proposed as the centerpiece for the exhibition greatly resembled one such, composed of iron and wood but predominantly of glass.

The Crystal Palace, as it was instantly dubbed, was one of the wonders of the world when Queen Victoria herself opened the exhibition on May Day 1851. The building had required £80,000 and two thousand workers for construction. The Exhibition included artworks, machinery, displays of artifacts from distant cultures, the Koh-i-noor diamond, animal specimens—a lot of everything. And it was a smashing success: in the five-and-a-half months it was open, more than six million people from all over the nation and the world had traveled to London to visit the show. Well over £350,000 worth of tickets had been sold. Queen Victoria came dozens of times—an added attraction for the crowds— with her brood in tow.

The Exhibition's stunning success left the organizers with thousands of pounds of profits and with the idea that this sort of exuberant public event should somehow be perpetuated. Eighty acres of land just south of the original site of the Crystal Palace were purchased, and the remaining funds raised by the Exhibition and even some of the objects and art exhibited there provided the seed for the South Kensington museums, galleries, concert halls, and colleges.

among London's most important fashion centers these days. Along Fulham Road is a lineup of stores the constituents of which are constantly trying to anticipate the taste of the well-heeled Londoner. South of Fulham is King's Road, formerly the operating theater for London's punks who inspired designers like Katherine Hamnett and Vivienne Westwood to take their street-tough "fashion" up-market.

Like their antipodes the Sloane Rangers, punks are out of the limelight these days, although you might find a few poly-chrome-pated, nose-pierced lads lolling around Royal Avenue, eager to have you take their photo to include in your collection of sociological anachronisms.

Not to be missed in Chelsea is the Chelsea Royal Hospital, Wren's second masterpiece in London. It's set in peaceful Ranelagh Gardens, which stretch down to the Thames, and is truly one of the city's most underappreciated, and therefore thankfully undercrowded, showpieces.

This then is the area. When you consult your map, you'll see that there is a lot of ground to cover here, but don't be too alarmed; much of it can be seen outdoors on a walking tour. Belgravia, for instance, does not have much to offer in the way of time-consuming activities—unless you're invited to a swinging soiree at the East German embassy—just atmospheric squares and imposing town houses. Shopping in Knightsbridge, South Ken, and Chelsea can take as long as you'd like. Of course, some people like to take an entire day in Harrods alone, but as fun as this grande dame may be, shopping here is not much different from shopping in a department store anywhere else, and if you're looking for a unique experience, better keep to the smaller shops in the street.

The smart thing to do is to plan a morning around museum hopping at the Victoria and Albert and its neighbors, then spend late afternoon exploring the Chelsea Royal Hospital. In between the two you can do a shopping serpentine along Fulham and King's roads.

Prince Albert's Pet Project

The 1851 Exhibition was so phenomenally popular that, despite the expense of mounting it, thousands of pounds in profits were realized. Prince Albert decided that some of this money would be used to fund a group of museums and theaters to continue the spirit of the exhibition and provide space for displaying some of the items that had been collected from all over the Empire.

Royal Albert Hall

The **Hall** runs a very lively one-and-a-half-hour tour of its interior at regular intervals March through September, daily from 10 A.M. to 8 P.M., for £2.50. This includes the hall's art collection, which is otherwise closed to the public.

The idea for the hall was first hit upon in 1853 by Prince Albert, who enlisted Henry Cole to furnish designs. Progress was slow, money was tight, and the Prince Consort died in 1861. It was agreed, however, that plans would go on without him, and in 1867 Queen Victoria agreed to abandon her reclusive mourning for a day in order to officiate at the opening.

The hall today hosts an incredible variety of events, from basketball and championship tennis to pop concerts featuring the likes of Eric Clapton, Shirley Bassey, and Tammy Wynette. The acoustics are still excellent, making the Albert Hall a favorite among classical musicians as well. A standard on London's calendar of annual events is the Royal Choral Society's Good Friday performance of Handel's *Messiah*. Because the group began as The Royal Albert Hall Choral Society, it is a requirement of their charter that they perform this piece every year at Easter. *The Messiah* returns at Christmas for a popular sing-along version. For summertime visitors, the Proms (Promenade concerts, a series of classical music events) are held here from July and are among the most memorable occasions any visitor might hope to enjoy in London. Information on scheduled events can be had by calling the box office at 589-8212. Tickets can be purchased with a major credit card by calling 589-9465.

Collegiate Culture

Albert et al. realized that it was not enough to build repositories for the artistic and musical treasures accumulated; equally important was the matter of fostering new talent. Pursuant to this, a group of colleges devoted to the arts was incorporated into the plan for the Kensington cultural center.

Just west of the Albert Hall is Exhibition Road Gallery, official venue of the **Royal College of Art.** The gallery is open daily from 10 A.M. to 6 P.M.; admission is usually free, although there may be a charge of up to £2.50 for special exhibitions. Emphasis tends to be on contemporary artists, including the annual Graduation Show featuring work of the college's students who have completed their masters in fine arts.

To the rear of the Albert Hall along Prince Consort Road is the **Royal College of Music.** During term time there is a full program of concerts, master classes, and competitions to which the public is invited. The school sponsors free lunchtime concerts Fridays at 1:10 P.M. at St. Mary Abbot's Church in Kensington High Street. For program information for all Royal College events, phone 589-3643, ext. 38. In the basement of the college building itself is a museum, open only during term time, Mondays through Wednesdays 11 A.M. to 4:30 P.M.; admission is 80 pence. It features antique, rare European instruments, specializing in keyboard and wind collections.

Rock Records and Records of Rocks

To the east of the Albert Hall is the **Royal Geographic Society.** For all intents and purposes it is a private club for high adventurers; however, available to the public is the Map Room, a cartophile's nirvana, which contains maps dating back to the Middle Ages.

Obviously strong on Britain, there are also overseas maps of great beauty and interest laid in wooden drawers in the library, although most are stored in the basement waiting to be called up. Outside the library in the lobby is a small exhibition space concerning the recent exploits atop mountains and across deserts of society members. Open Monday through Friday from 10 A.M. to 1 P.M. and 2 P.M. to 5 P.M.; admission is free.

Another unusual facility is the **British Library's National Sound Archive** on Exhibition Road. Open Monday through Friday from 9:30 A.M. to 4:30 P.M., till 8:45 P.M.

Thursday, the archive holds thousands of recordings from the earliest cylinders to the latest CDs. You can make an appointment to use their listening room to replay Parliamentary debates, Bolivian flute music, mating calls of birds, heavy-metal bands, or Bulgarian folk singers. There are two seasons of events, in spring and autumn held at 7:30 P.M., including lectures and A-V presentations pertaining to various aspects of the history of recorded sound. For details call 589-6603.

Exploring the Sciences

Some of the most popular sights at the Exhibition of 1851 were those devoted to the wonders of science and technology. Victorian England's almost fanatic preoccupation with man-made miracles opened the eyes of various entrepreneurs to the possibility of establishing a permanent exhibition displaying the achievements of Homo sapiens. The Science and Geological museums are south along Exhibition Road.

The **Science Museum** (open Monday through Saturday from 10 A.M. to 6 P.M., Sunday from 11 A.M. to 6 P.M.; admission is free) is immense and needs to be as the national museum for science and industry. Among the first exhibits you'll see is one devoted to steam engines, including a reconstruction of Watt's workshop whence came the industrial revolution, whence came the Empire, whence came the Exhibition, whence came the funds for this collection—get it? The museum covers the history of technology from the invention of the wheel to manned space travel. Check out the medical floors at the top of the building; they are extremely interesting and much less noisy than the echo-chamber lower galleries where the school kids are scrambling around shouting at this and that. If you brought kids of your own, take them to the launch pad, where they'll be kept busy with hands-on demonstrator models of various scientific principles—a veritable funhouse of technology that you'll enjoy too.

The **Geological Museum** is available for inspection Monday through Saturday from 10 A.M. to 6 P.M., Sunday from 1 to 6 P.M. (£2 includes a combo ticket for both this and the Natural History Museum). This museum traces the prehistoric life of Britain when it was part of the Old Red Continent. There are cases of glittering gems and the "World's Oldest Rock" displayed in state as augustly as are the sapphires. The more dramatic aspects of geologic change are illustrated by films of volcanoes and an earthquake simulator that re-creates a 1964 quake in Alaska. Standing on the platform as the tremors climb the Richter scale is like bronco riding—hold on!

You can visit the **Natural History Museum** Monday through Saturday from 10 A.M. to 6 P.M., Sunday from 1 to 6 P.M., or if you would like to sneak in a late-afternoon freebie, there is no admission charge if you arrive after 4:30 P.M. during the week, or after 5 P.M. Saturday and Sunday. The Great

Hall as you enter is an impressive 1880s design that is an attraction in its own right. Daily events are listed on the blackboard at the entrance; schedules are available at the info desk to your right. The galleries that are the most popular display the remains of dinosaurs, the origins of man, and a collection of rocks and minerals. In certain galleries you'll find "focus points," manned trolleys for hands-on experience with rocks or animals or flowers. Take a stroll along the museum's arcade of shops before you leave.

The Victoria and Albert Museum

The Victoria and Albert Museum is eclecticism incarnate. The collection is mammoth and encompasses an astonishing range of literally millions of objects. The museum can embrace such a variety of departments because its stated purpose on the occasion of its opening in 1909 was "to encourage and promote a high standard of excellence among the craftsmen, manufacturers and designers of this country." Obviously much can fall under this rubric.

The museum is open Monday through Saturday from 10 A.M. to 5:50 P.M., Sunday from 2:30 to 5:50 P.M., (suggested donation £2) and you'll need every minute to see what you'll want to see. To simplify things, you might like to take a guided introductory tour, which begins at 11:30 A.M. Monday through Saturday, or a tour of the museum's "treasures," which runs at 11 A.M., 12, 2, and 3 P.M. In addition to these regularly scheduled tours, the museum offers a most provocative curriculum of several day- or week-long symposia, so if you plan to be in London over time, it would be well worth your while to consider attending. You can find out more by phoning the Education Department at 938-8638.

Museum director Roy Strong once referred to the V&A as "an extremely capacious handbag," into which Britain could toss just about whatever suited her fancy whether the objects pertained to the original purpose of the museum (an ambiguous purpose at that) or not. The general layout of the museum runs thusly: The main floor is for general-overview collections, items with a common theme deposited in a particular gallery. The upper floors have corresponding galleries for the main-floor rooms, but the exhibits are aimed at those whose interest in the particular style, period, or genre is more scholarly and specific.

What to See on a Tight Schedule. Seeing the V&A in a hurry is almost a contradiction in terms, but here are some highlights: On level six of the Cole Wing is the world's most extensive collection of John Constable's work, donated primarily by his daughter, Isabel. Included among the oils are *Salisbury Cathedral* and *The Hay-Wain.* Study the style sketches, which hold the key to Constable's celebration of the

English landscape and which provide a delightful trip through the British countryside.

The Morris, Gamble, and Poynter rooms are a trio of reconstructions including the work of Pre-Raphaelites William Morris and Sir Edward Burne-Jones; the Gamble Room has a magnificent enameled iron ceiling; the Poynter Room is a Dutch kitchen with painted tile work.

The *St. George Altarpiece* depicts in grisly detail the saint's various triumphs and martyrdoms, highlighting of course his conquest of the dragon. This marvelous work is attributed to Marzal de Sas, who painted it in the early 15th century.

The Raphael Cartoons have nothing to do with Bugs Bunny. Cartone (the Italian) are large-scale works done on a sheaf of paper, usually as a prototype for a tapestry. These cartoons, essentially similar to watercolors, are on loan from the royal collections.

Certainly the most popular gallery is number 40, home of the V&A's costume collection. Window-shop among 16th- to 20th-century garments and accessories—gowns, waistcoats, buckles, buttons, reticules, fans, parasols, corsets, bustles. Modern designers from Azzedine to Zandra are also included.

The **V&A lunchroom** is bright and airy, with blond-wood tables at which you can enjoy a light meal with wine, cider, beer, or tea in the afternoon. The shop is a good place to find gifts supplied by the Crafts Council for your design-conscious friends.

Another thought for lunch in the museum area is the **Sandwich Garden** at 23 Cromwell Place, a storefront café that sells sandwiches on fresh-baked breads, soups, veggie chili, and filled croissants. It is a casual place for a quick bite if you want to avoid the pub crowd.

Italy in London

One building to the east of the Victoria and Albert Museum on Thurloe Place is the **Church of the Oratory of St. Philip Neri,** commonly, albeit incorrectly, referred to as the Brompton Oratory. One of London's finest Catholic churches, the oratory orders were founded in the 16th century by an Italian saint, Philip Neri. The oratory practice was brought to Britain in the 1840s by John Henry Newman, who had returned with his followers from a trip to Rome to study "true" Catholicism.

The Oratory looks more like its Italian than its British brethren, with its elaborate interior of gilt, colored marbles, and mosaics. It was designed by Herbert Gribble, who lived just down the road, in the Italian Renaissance style.

Old-Style Chic

Shopping begins in Knightsbridge, an area surrounding the street of that name. Shops here are the toniest south of the parks. In **Knights Arcade** shop under a dome at stores for Genny, Marc O'Polo, and Penhaligon's perfumers.

A half-mile away from the place, you'll begin to notice a smug succession of shoppers with their telltale green and gold bags. Just to drop a few names, the orange façade of **Harrods** boasts the arms of the Queen, the Duke of Edinburgh, the Queen Mum, and the Prince of Wales in larger-than-life relief. Nearby you'll find strategically located bureaux de change with notoriously bad rates. Use the Knightsbridge branch of American Express, 82 Brompton Road, instead.

Re Harrods: There is not a great difference between it and many other deluxe department stores here in London and the world over, but try telling that to the millions who sweep in, misty-eyed with the thrill, every year. The most interesting and unusual feature of the store are the food halls—the likes of which you will *not* find elsewhere—but don't get glued to the food; the rooms are all tile and Rococo ceilings. Display is as important as produce; check out the hammerhead shark deftly incorporated in the *tableau vivante montage de la mer.*

If you'd like to find many of the same clothes and furnishings as Harrods in a less manic and melodramatic setting, seek refuge down the street at quietly chic **Harvey Nichols.**

Also frightfully up-market are the shops along **Sloane Street** north of Cadogan Gardens. The Europeans have all clustered together along the avenue for protection: Ungaro, Fendi, Krizia, Valentino, YSL, Chanel, Kenzo, the Italians and French displaying a much closer amity than they would otherwise feel. You can get your hair done by Her Majesty's own coiffeurs, Neville-Daniel, should you require a "do" formidable enough to support the weightiest of tiaras.

Just up from the Square is The **General Trading Company,** GHQ for all Sloane Rangers, with in-house catering by Justin de Blank.

Many of Britain's best upmarket designers are to be found on **Beauchamp Place,** just to the west. Bruce Oldfield and the Emanuels are strong Princess Di favorites. Also of interest are Jasper Conran and The Beauchamp Place Shop (two locations).

The Nerve Center

Terence Conran, the tireless, ubiquitous designer, has all of London gushing over his renovation of the **Michelin House** at 81 Fulham Road, an address that has become akin to the first step on the Yellow Brick Road to London's Oz of shopping.

To give Conran his due, it must be admitted that there really is something worth crowing about. The 1911 building, designed by an architect famous solely for his work for the tire company, has been gloriously restored with its stained-glass study of Bibendum overhead. Bibendum, Michelin's tire-

incarnate mascot comes from the Roman, *nunc es bibendum,*
or "now we drink"—a rather unsettling connection with mo-
toring in these breathalyzer days.

On your left as you enter is the **Oyster Bar,** whose aphrodisiacal
wares are excessively overpriced, as are most things in the upstairs restaurant—appropriately named **Bibendum** for the
pudgy, pneumatic guy. Much more fun (reasonable, if not cheap)
is **Grabowski,** a wine bar-cum-gallery behind the funky mosaic
directly across Sloane Ave.

Previously, Sir Terence had an office that directly oversaw
this tease of a building, and so taken was he with the idea of
having his operations inside looking out instead of vice versa
that he bought the place as quickly as he was able and set
up shop in the back. He has collected well-thought-out and
well wrought furnishings from about the globe and serenades
purchasers with thirties pop tunes. Downstairs are more affordable wares and a gourmet department great for hostess
gifts.

Directly across from Sir Terence's is the store for **Katherine Hamnett,** one of the most important London designers
of the last decade, who took street fashion to the couture
world. Next door is **Domus,** with architectural features
somehow reminiscent of Hamnett's architectural fashions.

Le Set, just down Fulham from Michelin House, is the
place for far-out electronics—note the strobe underfootlights
set outside in the pavement. **Oggetti** features Italian new-
wave objects with some affordable smaller items. For unusual
designs, call in at **Anouska Hempel,** down petite Pond
Place, behind the darkened windows. The salesladies are the
height of imperious service, but Lady A. (she married a rich
man with a recent title) does come up with some of London's
more interesting, high-cost creations.

If you're tired of all this mercantilism, take a break down
pedestrian **Thistle Grove,** just north off Fulham, or around
Elm Park and **Evelyn Gardens,** whose pretty brick row
houses have their own floral plots front and back, or up Gils-
ton Road to the **Boltons,** a double-pointed oval with a church
in the center and Chelsea's largest, highest-profile mansions
around the rim.

Down-Market Chic

King's Road is where the world rediscovered black, black
leather, black leather with studs, black leather with studs and
black lace. In the days of The Sex Pistols and The Clash,
bands and fashion were masterminded by Malcolm Maclaren
and Vivienne Westwood, whose shops sold nose-piercing and
ripped T-shirts to Johnny Rotten, Sid Vicious, Joe Strummer,
and their friends and fans. The King's Road entrepreneurs

made clothes that made stars that made their fans want to dress just like the stars—quite a neat trick, really.

As mentioned, the days of punk are fading fast, but among the junky leather and T-shirt shops that are still trying to capitalize on the old days are some places that are still interested in taking risks and setting, instead of following, fashion. Drop in at **Jones** (two stores), **the Shop for Boy, World's End** (featuring designs by Vivienne Westwood), and **Hacketts,** for Savile Row tailoring at off-the-rack prices. These latter two are considerably further west, but keep walking—they're well worth the hike.

Chelsea Royal Hospital

One feature of the neighborhood that will certainly continue to stand the test of time as it has done for over three hundred years is Sir Christopher Wren's magnificent building beside the Thames. A quarter mile down King's Road from Sloane Square is an arcade of trees bordered by some very nice houses and a graveled walkway heading toward the river. Beyond the trees of Royal Avenue is the **Royal Hospital,** truly one of London's most breathtaking vistas to this day.

The hospital is not strictly speaking a facility for nursing the sick but is more along the lines of the French institutions built to house their returned and perhaps ailing soldiers. Indeed, it is quite likely that Charles II, builder and patron of the Chelsea hospital, was inspired to create such a facility by a visit to the Invalides in Paris.

As you approach, doubtlessly you will catch a glimpse of the Chelsea Pensioners, the four-hundred-plus veterans who live here, walking the lawns in their black capes and black stiff caps in winter, strutting their brighter cardinal uniforms in summer.

Within the hospital, the Chapel, Great Hall, and Museum are open Monday through Saturday from 10 A.M. to noon and 2 to 4 P.M. The pensioners' quarters range around either side of the Figure Court, so named for the Founder's Statue, an equestrian of Charles II by Grinling Gibbons, one of the city's finest. Their dining room in the Great Hall is inviting black and white with rows of brass table lamps and another study of Charles triumphant by Antonio Verrio. On a recent visit, their menu included an entrée of roast beef and a dessert of jam roly-poly with jellies.

The chapel apse was painted by Sebastiano Ricci and surmounts a massive carved and inlaid-wood altar radiating from which the sable wood runs along the side walls back to the nave. The place is brightened by hand-worked kneelers denoting pensioners' military affiliations. There is a parade service attended by the residents in full regalia Sundays at 11 A.M. to which the public is welcome.

The museum features pensioner mementos and a case button from the oak tree in which Charles II hid after the Battle of Worcester in 1651 (commemorated with the ceremonial oak wreathes on Oak Apple Day, each May 29). One of the tree's progeny was planted in the garden in 1961.

The hospital enjoys a splendid setting in Ranelagh Gardens, explained and mapped out for you in Sir John Soane's summerhouse. Soane served as the Royal Hospital clerk of works in the early 19th century and added the stables on the western side of the property. Beyond the avenue of elms is the Chelsea Bridge, and beyond that is a power station due to be transformed into a leisure center. It is a heart-warming sight to watch the pensioners walk the gardens and greet with an avuncular glee the toddlers who trundle up to admire their uniforms. The gardens are the site each May of the Chelsea Flower Show, a most rewarding, if claustrophobic, event.

If you've not yet had enough of the military, the **National Army Museum** is just along Royal Hospital Road. (Open Monday through Saturday from 10 A.M. to 5:30 P.M., Sunday from 2 P.M.; admission is free.) This is as much a history museum as a military museum, as must be the case with an island whose past is as bellicose as Britain's is. If you're interested in getting your wars and battles straight—without reading a 12-volume history set—this is a fine place to do it. Not to miss: the skeleton of Napoleon's favorite charger, Marengo, and the American War of Independence model whose designers ironically chose the Siege of Yorktown as their subject.

If you're up for a splurge, stop in at one of London's favorite restaurants, **La Tante Claire,** at 68 Royal Hospital Road. (See the *Restaurants* chapter).

A Secret Garden

Well, practically. A few people know about this wondrous walled garden, the Chelsea Physic Garden (also on Royal Hospital Road), begun in 1673 by apothecaries, making it England's second-oldest botanical garden. It is well worth the extra planning to be here on one of the few days it is open: April through October, Wednesday and Sunday only, from 2 to 5 P.M.; admission charge is £2 (it is open daily from noon during the week of the Chelsea Flower Show).

The garden was laid out by the Society of Apothecaries of London on land they had purchased to use for a boathouse for their launch. Most of the original plantings were brought to the site by river. To this day, the garden is involved in producing therapeutic herbs, and medicinal teaching and research, and is the best place for getting a sense of the atmosphere three hundred years ago when the Thames was lined with some of London's most elegant country manor houses.

Cheyne Walk

The list of former and present residents of the streets named for the Cheyne ("Chay-nee") family, 17th-century lords of the manor, reads like a who was and who is who of British art and literature. George Eliot lived at No. 4 Cheyne Walk, D. G. Rossetti and A. C. Swinburne lived at No. 16, Whistler painted his mother at No. 96 and previously had lived at No. 101, up the way from J. M. W. Turner at No. 119. More recent inhabitants have been glimmer twins Mick Jagger and Keith Richards.

Of special interest is **Chelsea Old Church** (open Monday to Saturday 10 A.M. to 1 P.M., 2 to 5 P.M.; guides available Sundays 1:30 to 5:30 P.M.). Although the church was heavily bombed during the war, some of its original fittings (11th century) still remain, and it boasted some illustrious parishoners including Henry Fielding, Henry Purcell, John Donne, Sir Thomas More, and Britain's only Pope, Nicholas Brakespear (Hadrian IV), who was rector here. For more history, across the little square down Cheyne Walk is Crosby Hall (entry through the annex next door), once the dining room of Thomas More, whose family portrait graces the north wall. Overhead is a hammerbeam ceiling with its stalactites of gilt and painted wood and alcove of oriel window; the 1523 room was transported here in toto from Bishopsgate.

Up from the Albert Bridge on Phene St. is the **Phene Arms,** a pub with a fireplace and a yellow dog inside, patio seating and birds twittering outside. The lunch menu is very good.

Continuing along the river at its great bend is a neighborhood of houseboats for those hoping to beat the noise and high rents of their neighbors on dry land. The area west from here along the river and King's Road is called **World's End** and is becoming quite popular, with shops starting to sprout along the alley at Chelsea Wharf.

St. James's, Mayfair, and the Parks

Perhaps the pleasantness in the pubs, the helpfulness on the Underground, and the down-to-earthiness of the general public has you wondering where went the silly snootiness of yesteryear lovingly portrayed in Wodehouse, Waugh, and Wilde. Have no fear, there is still a small as ever, select as ever group of Brits who embody all the uppityness you seek. And they all live, "work," and play in St. James's and Mayfair.

This is the never-never land of gentlemen's clubs, royal warrants, bespoke tailors, and neighborhood royals-in-residence to keep the uninitiated properly agog. Although the sovereign now lives down the Mall at Buckingham Palace, the Queen Mum's in-town residence is Clarence House in St. James's and foreign envoys to Britain are still styled Ambassadors to the Court of St. James's.

The original inhabitants of the area were not quite so tony or so fortunate. St. James's Hospital was maintained by the abbot of Westminster and was originally devoted to the care of leper women. Henry VIII could not bear to see such a prime patch of real estate "wasted" in this way and bought the property from the resident nuns. Whereon he built a palace which was probably designed by Holbein and was completed in the 1530s, just in time for Henry to move in with his new wife, Anne Boleyn. Henceforth St. James's was the scene of much drama: the planned sort—Ben Jonson's masques were often performed here—and the unplanned sort—scenes of royal rage when a king's mistress was discovered in an act of infidelity (one such incident saw the first Duke of Marlborough leaping from a second-story window).

Unfortunately, the palace is not open to the public. An exception to this rule is made for services in the chapels. The Queen's Chapel, designed by Inigo Jones, is open for Sunday services from Easter through July. The Chapel Royal with its Holbein-attributed ceiling is open for Sunday services the remainder of the year.

With all these crowned heads nearby the area filled up with shops and services to cater to every whim. St. James's was principally developed by Henry Jermyn, Earl of St. Albans, whose name has been bestowed on a street of shirtmakers. Jermyn was allowed to lease the fields surrounding the palace to a variety of builders, who erected what were to instantly become the most sought-after properties in London.

The cachet of St. James's migrated northward to Mayfair, as had the annual spring fete for which it was named. The May Fair was held for the first two weeks of May and was the scene of much jollity and frivolity. As the tenants' blood ran bluer, they were naturally offended by the prospect of the

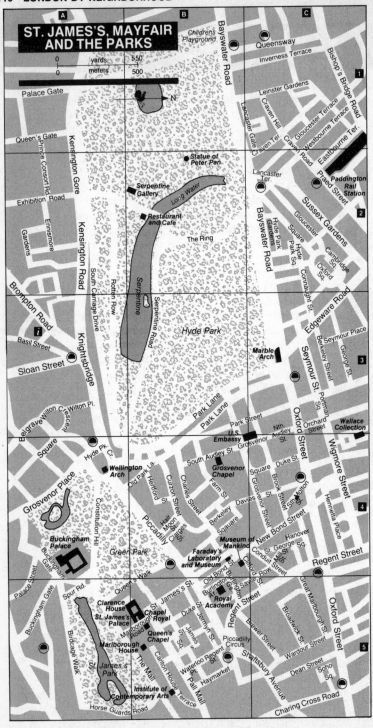

ST. JAMES'S, MAYFAIR AND THE PARKS

populace's overrunning their sanctuary for an annual bout of raucousness; they complained to the king, who was predisposed to take their part rather than that of the people, and the fair was outlawed by the mid-18th century.

Despite this historic downtreading of the lower classes by residents of St. James's and Mayfair, it is still a marvelous place to have a good time. This is most conspicuously owing to the presence of the Royal Parks—Hyde, Green, St. James's, and Kensington Gardens. This tetrad of greenery provides Londoners of all ranks with a cool, spacious playground.

Add to this shopping for London's finest on St. James's, Jermyn, Bond, Regent, and South Molton streets, taking a ritual tea at the Ritz or the Dorchester, roaming through the galleries of the Royal Academy or along Cork Street, and you'll find there is plenty of diversion for the traveler who appreciates the best without necessarily having to pay for it.

The Mall

Probably the best way to begin is to take a leisurely stroll along the esplanade of the Mall. This most Parisian of London boulevards was originally constructed as a course for the game of *palle-malle*—which had formerly been played on the street of that name. But when Pall Mall became busy with shops and traffic, a new alley was constructed by Charles II, who was quite mad about the game and spent many happy hours along the Mall's leafy arcade attended by his ministers and mistresses.

Unfortunately, the days of a purely pedestrian Mall are long gone, and the traffic whizzes by at a furious rate. The best time to stroll is just before the Changing of the Guard, when the street is partially closed to traffic to allow the horses to clop by.

Current Culture

At the eastern end of the Mall is a group of Georgian terraces designed by John Nash of Regent's Park fame. On the Mall level of **Nash House** (No. 12) is the **Institute of Contemporary Arts (ICA)**. The ICA incorporates and celebrates all the modern incarnations of the arts. The bulletin board at the entrance lists the day's events, which range from drama to film to art exhibits to lectures and symposia. There is a 75-pence admission charge to the galleries and special events require additional fees, depending upon the program. The shop stocks funky jewelry, postcards, and a good selection of art books and journals. There is a café/bar servicing the theaters and the three galleries. All tickets are half price on Mondays. The ICA is open 12 to 11 P.M.

The Heart of St. James's

Up the stairs from the ICA are **Carlton Gardens** and the original **Pall Mall.** For those of a tobaccan turn, **Rothmans** is located at No. 65 and there you can buy, of course, cigarettes, and also signature crystal, cuff links, and luggage. Although you cannot enter **St. James's Palace,** you are certainly permitted to skirt its exterior, which is full of Tudor architectural detailing, and perhaps the great clock will sound while you are doing so.

Running up from Pall Mall is St. James's Street, boasting some of London's oldest and finest merchants. **Berry Brothers and Rudd, Ltd.** at No. 3, has been selling wines since the 17th century behind its black, glossy façade. You can still settle in 17th-century chairs while arranging a caseful to be sent wherever in very civilized surroundings. You might want to take a little detour just north of the shop down tiny Pickering Place, which ends in a little courtyard.

Lock and Company, No. 6, is as much a museum of old hats as a store for new ones. Here's where to pick up that perfect felt fedora you've been hankering for, or perhaps a tweed cap or a pith helmet for your next jungle trek. All are served up in large white with black boxes. Opened in 1676, it's the oldest shop in London and possibly in the world.

D. R. Harris, No. 29, self-styled "Purveyors of Toiletries and Medicines to Royalty and the Gentry," will have been in business two hundred years in 1990 and is still run by Harris' descendants. Here you can buy a toothbrush just like the Queen's or a razor like the one Prince Philip uses every morning. Or you can try the famous Crystal Eye Drops Joan Collins swears by, or a bottle of Harris' Original Pick-Me-Up— "Revives in the morning or before meals as an aperitif." They'll ship overseas.

The Clubs

Perhaps you noticed several smart buildings on either side of St. James's Street. **The Carlton, White's, Boodle's,** and **Brooks's** are among the last of a vanishing breed of gentlemen's clubs that flourished during the 18th and 19th centuries. At the close of the 17th century the coffee and chocolate houses of St. James's were famous for their gatherings of men discussing subjects of a political, social, or amorous nature. They tended to be segregated according to political affiliation, the Whigs favoring St. James's and the Tories preferring the Cocoa Tree. A rhyme of the day runs, "About 12 o'clock I go to the Cocoa Tree where I talk treason, then to St. James's Coffee House where I praise the Ministry, thence to White's where I talk gallantry."

Several proprietors thought business might be improved if they took to serving spirits and improved the quality of the food. They were correct. The clubs became the center of fashionable gentlemanly life where all manner of high jinks went on—most particularly gambling. Many an ancient fortune was lost by a noble scion at the piquet tables of Brooks's. There was a report in the papers that a man dropped dead in front of White's and was carried inside, whereupon the members placed bets as to whether he had actually expired. When the surgeon was called to bleed him, the assembled complained that such an act would affect the outcome of their bet.

There was a bit of a controversy at the Carlton—a longtime bastion of conservativism and segregation of the sexes—which as a matter of policy immediately granted membership to all Conservative prime ministers upon election. Since 1979, the Carlton has its first (and only) female member, Mrs. Thatcher. Doubtless many of the gents who still frequent the clubs read *The Economist,* Britain's premier journal on the subject. Its headquarters are here, as is its bookstore, which sells the magazine along with books on style (literary, not sartorial), defense, marketing, and an annual financial outlook for the world.

Jermyn Street

Jermyn Street is known as the premier place for gentlemen's haberdashers. The most famous on the block at 71–72 is the venerable **Turnbull & Asser,** who are responsible for keeping the Prince of Wales in starch and looking smooth. There are cherubs and polychrome bunting to greet you at the door and an army of solemn salesmen ready to initiate you into the mysteries of custom-shirt selection. Two stops for toiletries (ladies as well as gents) are **Czech and Speake** at 39c and **J. Floris** at 88.

All through the square of streets south of Jermyn are many of London's premier vendors of fine art and antiques, if such things appeal to your taste and your wallet.

Craftsmanship of the Modern Variety

If your interests run to textiles and objects produced with care, but with perhaps a bit more flair, at 12 Waterloo Place, the southern stretch of Regent Street, is the **Crafts Council Gallery** (open Tuesday through Saturday from 10 A.M. to 5 P.M., Sunday from 2 to 5 P.M.; admission is free). The council mounts exhibits including textiles, ceramics, tapestries, and woodwork from artists and artisans from around the world.

Piccadilly

Piccadilly sweeps down from the statue of Eros at its circus to the statue of Wellington at Hyde Park Corner. It's also full of fine shops, the most fun of which is certainly **Fortnum & Mason.** With its sage green and gold façade and green and white chandeliered interior, this shop has been supplying London with the finest comestibles and dry goods for years. Here you can find lychees from South Africa, asparagus from Mexico, passion fruit from Kenya. Pick up some F&M gift tins of teas from India, Ceylon, China. Play the standing music box by the truffle counter for 10 pence. The restaurants are perfect for lunch, tea, or an inter-prandial pick-me-up.

Another fun place to shop is the **Burlington Arcade.** Get the Regency feel of browsing along this covered galleria of 39 shops with storefronts downstairs, more space up. You can find cashmere, tobacco, diamonds, handkerchiefs as Beau Brummell undoubtedly did in his day.

Hard by the Burlington Arcade is the **Royal Academy** (R.A.) at the far end of Burlington House Square. Sir Joshua Reynolds, the R.A.'s first president, stands in bronze at its center, brush and palette poised. Founded in 1768 to "promote the arts of design," the Royal Academy serves many functions. It is an art school, a public gallery, and an institution devoted to showcasing new and established talent.

The academy does not have a permanent collection per se, but rather hosts a continuing series of exhibitions that are uniformly superb. The most special event of the year, however, is the Summer Exhibition, which features the work of often young and/or undiscovered artists of an original batch of ten thousand from whose submissions are selected just over one thousand to be displayed at the gallery throughout the summer season.

No matter what the exhibition, it's always worth a look in at the R.A., if only to enjoy the building whose interiors were decorated by Benjamin West and Angelica Kaufmann, among others. The R.A. is open daily from 10 A.M. to 6 P.M. Lunchtime lectures are frequently held on Thursdays at 1 P.M. Admission prices vary according to the exhibits you are interested in visiting. The shop has unusual books, periodicals, art supplies, even R.A. wines and champagne. There is a coffeeshop and also a lovely restaurant (open from 11:30 A.M. to 2:30 P.M.) with a hot and cold buffet.

Art of Your Own
If you prefer to bring art appreciation into your very own home, the north end of the Burlington Arcade runs into Cork Street, a collection of galleries featuring primarily the work of modern artists. **Browse and Darby** concentrates on 20th-century Europeans with an emphasis on British painters. **Redfern** sells Hockney, Miro, Chagall. **Waddington Graphics** has prints, some for as little as £75, by Alex Katz, Milton Avery, Jasper Johns, Jim Dine, Robert Motherwell. Even if you're not in the market for a £10,000 "investment," the street is a modern-art mall perfect for browsing.

The Museum of Mankind
At 6 Burlington Gardens the museum is the Ethnography Department of the British Museum (open Monday through Sat-

urday, 10 A.M. to 5 P.M. 2:30 to 6 P.M., Sunday). It is a fascinating place, with exhibits explicating the food, clothing, shelter, crafts, and religion of the world's distinct peoples. Emphasis tends to be on non-Western societies, especially on their run-ins with Europeans. The bulletin board to the right of the cloakroom displays the day's special events, which usually include films Tuesdays through Fridays. Admission to the museum and its events is free.

If you're feeling a bit peckish, **Morrises Espresso Bar** on Clifford St. between Bond and Cork serves sandwiches, quiche, coffee, and teas in pleasant surroundings.

You'll need this further fortification before you tackle the shops on the streets Bond, Old and New. Along these streets (one actually segues into the next) are all the important European designers: Ungaro, Revillon, Valentino, Loewe. Also here is **Asprey,** correct British furnishers to all kinds of crowned heads and **Smythson's,** famous for the world's most correct stationery.

Savile Row
Just to the east of the Bonds is Savile Row, decorated with more coats of arms than Windsor Castle. Underlings are out polishing the brass, and through the railings you can peer down to the basement workrooms, where the tailors look anything but fashionable in their bifocals with a tape measure as cravat. Savile Row is, of course, the home of posh gentlemen's clothing—although Hardy Ames, the Queen's dressmaker, has a shop at No. 14 in a building once occupied by playwright Richard Brinsley Sheridan, whose fops and dandies certainly patronized the street's tailors. The coats of arms you see attached to the various clothiers are known as royal warrants, indicating that the particular store has been outfitting whichever royal with whatever product for at least three years. By virtue of which service the store has applied for and been granted the privilege to display the client's arms (as part of a very effective publicity scheme) on the premises and any advertising.

Still not sated? Have a pizza at **Condotti,** 6 Mill St. There are magazines by the window seat to relax with if you're alone, or you can gaze at the modern art prints on the walls.

Regent Street
Regent Street was part of John Nash's master plan for an imposing Continental-style avenue between Regent's Park and St. James's Palace, where the Regent (George IV) resided. Although the street doesn't quite cut a straight line as original-

ly intended, the breaks and curves make for interesting strolling. And its high-minded plan has attracted a group of distinctly up-market shops. South from Oxford Circus is **Laura Ashley's** flagship store, with aisles of flowers and ruffles, little girls stuffed into sailor dresses, and boyfriends collapsed resignedly into chairs. Clothes are considerably cheaper here than overseas, especially during sales (January and August). Just down from there is **Dickins & Jones,** a department store so soigné that a pianist by the door serenades you as you make your perfume purchases.

At Long Last, Liberty's

Perhaps one of the best department stores in the world, certainly the best in London, is **Liberty's.** It's most impressive to enter at the main door on Great Marlborough Street into a five-story atrium. Throughout the store you'll enjoy the Tudor-style architecture, which incorporates timbers from two of the British Navy's last sailing ships—whose portraits are displayed just outside the personnel and press offices on the second floor.

Liberty's is famous for its contribution to art nouveau textile design. You can still buy silk scarves and cotton or wool fabric printed with signature swirls, paisleys, and peacock feathers. The Tana Lawn designs of the 1920s are sprinkled with perfect pastel flowers. Liberty's sells its own line of clothing using in-house fabric as well as those of Cacharel and other designers.

After buying a precious smocked dress for the little one at Liberty's, visit **Hamley's,** Her Majesty's own toy merchant. When the Queen needs a Barbie or a Master of the Universe, this is where she calls. Planes zoom overhead and a terrific model railroad chugs around the room. This is a great place to get an official, from-London Paddington Bear.

At the curve in Regent Street known as the Quadrant is **Garrard and Co.,** crown jewelers. Plush carpets muffle any disturbance, and the air is perfumed by sprays of fresh flowers as you select your own regal gems. In the rear are sculptures in gold, amethyst, and diamonds—*caravelles* and magic mountains—large and massively ugly (no accounting for taste).

For the Fashion Conscious

When the mavens of King's Road decided to move operations up-market they came to roost along South Molton Street. They have been joined by other designers whose clothes are decidedly daring. Among the innovators along this pedestrian street are Jean Paul Gaultier at Bazaar, Joseph Bis, Joseph Tricot, and Katherine Hamnett, at whose shop they repaint the wall fabric to fit the fancy of the season.

The best store is **Browns,** strung-together town houses that have been divided up among various designers and feature Britain's current best—Jasper Conran, Rifat Ozbek, and the sharp-as-ever Jean Muir.

Around the mews side of South Molton is **Grays in the Mews,** an amalgam of antiques shops, primarily for jewelry, porcelain, and silver. Down the Garden-of-Eden-motif stairs are medals and uniforms, antique hardware, commemorative mugs, and saucers.

Of Scientists and Shepherds

In the southwest corner of Mayfair there are some rather unique spots to pique your interest. The first is the **Faraday Museum** at 21 Albermarle Street, open Tuesday and Thursday from 1 to 4 P.M.; admission 40 pence. The Royal Institution (of science, responsible for many important discoveries of a practical and theoretical nature) has its basement given over to the laboratory of Michael Faraday, who was a pioneer in electromagnetic experimentation. Faraday's lab is set up as it was when he was given the space to putter in by the Royal Institution in 1791. Many of his experiments have been remounted, often using his original tools. Faraday explored the connection between gravity, electricity, and magnetism and the diaries full of neat and flowing script you'll see on display have diagrams and charts tracing his train of thought. From these experiments Faraday discovered the principles and uses of electromagnetic induction used in electroplating metals, generators, and electrical transformers.

At 17 Half Moon Street is the **Scotch Whiskey House,** a perfect place to drop in if you're a connoisseur, and especially if you're not. Unfortunately, there are no samples, but there is a video explaining the history and procedures of the brew. They will be delighted to advise you on how to best tour the Whiskey Trail of distilleries if you plan to be in Scotland.

If you can't wait that long for a dram, drop in at the **Samuel Pepys Pub** at No. 30 Clarges St. where they have a good selection of single malts (happy hour from 5:30 to 6:30 P.M.) and a piano from 8 on. On the south side of Curzon Street by No. 47 is a little passageway that leads into **Shepherd Market.** Shepherd refers to a person, not a profession; architect Edward Shepherd, who laid out this cozy collection of streets and alleys built on land where the May Fair was traditionally held. It's a quainter, more casual piece of Mayfair, and here at lunchtime **The Grapes** will be packed with local businessmen enjoying a nip and some pub grub.

Of Wallpapers and Walkie-talkies

The western end of Curzon Street intersects with South Audley Street, whose shops sell a curious collection of wares. **Zoffany,** at No. 63, produces an exclusive line of wallpapers and fabrics reproduced from originals in English country houses and the chateaux of France. Now that your house is beautiful, you'll need to protect it. Next door the **Counter Spy Shop** sells alarms and security systems, briefcase phones, bulletproof glass, bomb snuffers, and everything for the undercover agent on the go.

If crime prevention proves ineffective, **Purdey and Son's** at No. 57 is the Queen's own gun and rifle purveyors. Behind the nondescript gold and blue windows are guns galore, hunting gear, and taxidermy samples for inspiration.

Across the street is **Richoux,** perfect for tea time, or any time you feel a twang in your sweet tooth. They have a full menu, but the food isn't half as fab as the sundaes and pastries. Or if you prefer, **Hobbs and Co.** sells gourmet sandwiches and cheeses, port or champagne, which you might like to take away to the benches of the odd-shaped little park behind the Grosvenor Chapel.

The Royal Parks

The welcome refuge of air and space that makes up the Royal Parks has been called the lungs of London; certainly after the fumes and noise and fuss of town it is a most delightful, nay essential, relief to take to the paths of Hyde, Green, St. James's, or Kensington Gardens by foot, bike, or horse.

Their present pastoral ambience belies a most riotous past. Originally fields and forests belonging to various noblemen, the lands of the parks all eventually were acquired through purchase or confiscation by the crown. Predictably, Henry VIII and his court spent many a happy day tally ho-ing after stag, as did subsequent sovereigns into the 17th century, when Hyde Park was open to the public for the first time. Naturally the neighborhood deteriorated rapidly.

Hyde and Green parks were notorious for highwaymen; William III was obliged to string a row of lamps between St. James's and Kensington Palace to discourage their activity—thus making La Route du Roi (eventually mangled into Rotten Row) the first nightlit street in England. St. James's Park, on the other hand, was famous for ladies of the evening, and one might expect to run into several during an after-dark stroll under the trees. The parks were also the favorite settings for duels, and many were fought before the practice was finally outlawed in the 19th century.

The parks today have their distinctive characters. **St. James's** is floral and faunal with bunches of daffodils in spring and lots of waterfowl paddling past the geyseresque fountain. **Green Park** is trees and grass—there is a legend that flowers won't grow here because it was formerly used as a burial ground for the patients at St. James's Hospital (for lepers).

Hyde Park is by far the largest and most diverse. Its eastern end has contoured topography and a random planting of

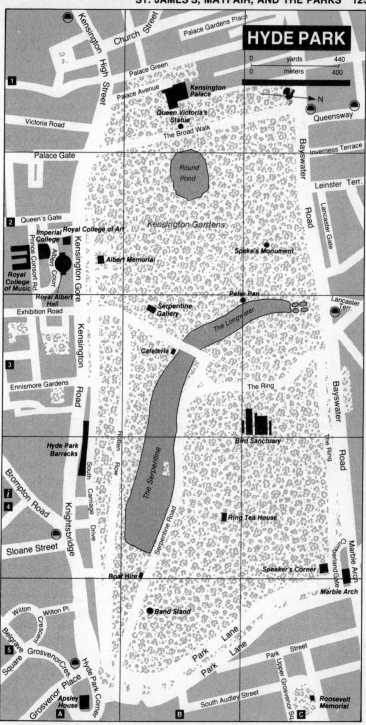

HYDE PARK

| 0 | yards | 440 |
| 0 | meters | 400 |

N

Church Street

Kensington High Street

Palace Gardens Place

Palace Green

Palace Avenue

Kensington Palace

Queen Victoria's Statue

The Broad Walk

Victoria Road

Queensway

Bayswater Road

Inverness Terrace

Palace Gate

Round Pond

Leinster Terr.

Queen's Gate

Imperial College

Royal College of Art

Kensington Gardens

Lancaster Gate

Prince Consort Rd.

Albert Court

Kensington Gore

Albert Memorial

Speke's Monument

Royal College of Music

Royal Albert Hall

Exhibition Road

Peter Pan

Kensington Road

Serpentine Gallery

The Longwater

Lancaster Terr.

Cafeteria

Ennismore Gardens

The Ring

Bayswater Road

The Serpentine

Hyde Park Barracks

Rotten Row

Bird Sanctuary

South Carriage Drive

Brompton Road

Knightsbridge

Serpentine Road

Ring Tea House

Sloane Street

Boat Hire

Speaker's Corner

Cumberland Gate

Marble Arch

The Ring Road

Marble Arch

Wilton Crescent

Wilton Pl.

Band Stand

Belgrave Square

Grosvenor Cres.

Hyde Park Corner

Park Lane

Park Lane

Park Street

Upper Grosvenor Sq.

Grosvenor Place

Apsley House

South Audley Street

Roosevelt Memorial

A   B   C

1 2 3 4 5

trees. The Serpentine lake snakes its way through the center, and beyond it the land flattens out to the more formal tree-lined walkways of **Kensington Gardens.**

Within Hyde Park is the **Serpentine Gallery,** set back from the southeastern shore of the lake. It's open daily from 10 A.M. to 6 P.M., till 4 P.M. in winter; admission is free. If you'd like a bit of culture to go with your nature, wander through the sunlit space, which tends to display the work of modern artists.

The **Serpentine Restaurant** is not worth the money unless you get a window seat. It's better for cocktails. Better still is the **Café Pergola** take-away or outdoor buffet next door. This way you can position yourself according to your desires to watch the boaters, the ducks, and perhaps a game golden retriever sallying into the drink after the latter.

You can rent a boat and enjoy the watery part of the park at the boathouse on the south bank.

At the northwest end of the lake, called **Long Water** now that it has passed into the precincts of Kensington Gardens, are Italian water gardens and huge beds of roses arranged according to color. The statue of Peter Pan is in a clump of shrubberies just down from here. Another favorite spot for kids is the **Children's Playground** in the extreme northwest corner of Kensington Gardens. In it is a venerably gnarled tree trunk studded with elves, imps, and other wee woodfolk. Nearby a sign reminds the little ones *tempus fugit.*

During the summer concerts are held from 3 to 4:30 and 6 to 7:30 P.M. Sundays and bank holiday Mondays from the end of May through August. Programs are usually posted on the large you-are-here maps deployed about the park.

At the Marble Arch corner of the park is a place where all of London is welcome to vent its hostilities. **Speakers Corner** was so designated after a particularly fiery orator preaching anti-government policies was hauled off to prison. The citizenry rose up in protest, and the powers that be thought it prudent to set aside a spot in the city where anyone was permitted to hold forth on any view. Its proximity to the traffic roar of Park Lane insures that not even the most powerful lungs or ideas could possibly be discerned above the din.

Bloomsbury and Marylebone

These precincts have somehow always managed to attract the attention and patronage of an interesting crowd. Like most of London's more extreme margins, they began as farm and hunting land. The reason such a large space as close to central London as Regent's Park remained "unimproved" until the 19th century was that previously the Royals had been jealous about parting with their convenient outlets for sport.

Serious residential building did not reach these northerly parts until the late 17th century, when the 4th Earl of Southampton, dissatisfied with the existing family manse, had it removed and, doubtlessly inspired by Inigo Jones's successful work in Covent Garden, ordered a similar square to be constructed with the new Southampton House as its keystone. Although Covent Garden predated it by nearly fifty years, this was the first London square to be called a square, Bloomsbury Square, a simplification of Blemonds, the family who were the 13th-century owners of the land.

The square was an idea for which London was ready, and many of the Southamptons' neighbors followed suit and had squares built to accompany their great houses. The fashion spread west to Marylebone, again a simplification of a name, this time that of a local parish, St. Mary's by the Bourne (stream). St. Marylebone, as it is correctly called, had a long (and checkered) history of its own. One of the boroughs included within its boundaries was Tyburn, named for one of London's many now diverted or defunct streams. Tyburn is a name fraught with grim connotations for Londoners. For four hundred years, from the late 14th to the late 18th centuries, London's most active and festive gallows (which could accommodate a score of hangings at one go) was set up here. The London hangmen were notoriously disinterested in their duties, the result being that often the condemned's friends were obliged out of compassion to speed the death of their fellow (who would have otherwise been left to squirm pitifully at the end of his rope) by yanking on his legs to finish the business quickly. For his ill-performed task the hangman was granted the clothes of his deceased "clients" and the noose, all of which could be sold at premium prices as macabre souvenirs of the day's festivities. Marble Arch presently stands on the gallows grounds to which Londoners would flock on hanging day. The townspeople were granted a public holiday on such occasions because, it was believed, the execution would serve as a warning. The atmosphere, however, tended to be more like that of a county fair than a terrible event, and Londoners gathered by the tens of thousands to witness a particularly notorious criminal dispatched to meet his maker.

The gruesome spectacles at Tyburn were, thankfully, not characteristic of Marylebone and Bloomsbury as a whole. On the contrary, by the 18th century it had become quite a desirable place to live among the growing numbers of the professional classes. The squares became little village centers unto themselves; from there fanned out a circuit of side streets where shops and market stalls could be set up to service the gentle folk who lived in the town houses.

It was a most gentle, genteel life indeed, a way of maintaining an exurban existence in close proximity to the city. By the late 19th century, the most important of the several generations of artists and philosophers who had chosen this serene atmosphere took up residence in north London and were duly dubbed the Bloomsbury Group. Famous among them, were Virginia and Leonard Woolf. This turn-of-the-century crop of artists and critics believed that the greatest good and happiness to which a human soul could aspire was to be found in lively and learned conversation and in the contemplation of beautiful things. The Bloomsbury Group responded to simple (although never simplistic) pleasures and glorified the innumerable, infinitesimal epiphanies available in day-to-day existence.

To this day, Marylebone and Bloomsbury are among the most tranquil, attractive, cerebral patches of London. The area around Bloomsbury and Russell squares is the traditional habitat of lawyers and professors, the latter of whom practice their trade at the University of London nearby. The university, of course, lends gravity and purpose to the region even as its students inject a bit of fun and energy into what otherwise might become an area drowsy with its own ease.

To keep the intellectuals keen there are some of London's best museums, great and small, tucked away in primarily residential streets. Principal among them, of course, is the incomparable British Museum, home of the Elgin Marbles, the Rosetta Stone, the Diamond Sutra, and various other treasures pirated back to the mother country by British explorers in the name of preservation. Nearby is the Percival David Foundation of Chinese Art, one of the best collections in the city—and in all of Britain—and noted for its porcelains. The Wallace Collection is displayed in a formerly private mansion and includes another eclectic and important group of paintings and ceramics, rare and unusual pieces. Finally, see the small but worthwhile collection of the Foundling Hospital Art Treasures; many objects were donated by the foundation's numerous influential patrons, like Hogarth and Handel.

There are plenty of pursuits of a less serious nature as well: a tour through Madame Tussaud's waxworks, a game of cricket at Lord's—world headquarters of the sport—or perhaps a visit to the London Zoo. The zoo is situated in the north of Regent's Park, easily the area's most obvious and irresistible resource. Designed, along with its ring of Georgian town houses or terraces, by John Nash, Regent's Park recaptures, as the sweet but small squares cannot, the rural past shared by Bloomsbury and Marylebone. Like former residents Francis Bacon, G. B. Shaw, Elizabeth Browning, and Sherlock Holmes, you will be quite captivated by the simple pleasure of padding around the galleries, squares, and green places at a serene and contemplative pace.

The British Museum

The British Museum was begun in 1753 with the art and scientific collections of Sir Hans Sloane, whose will directed they should be sold to the nation at bargain-basement prices. Parliament jumped at the chance and went one better, voting money for an endowment to buy several other important collections. Two years later Montagu House was purchased with funds raised by public lottery. Montagu's previous tenants were the First Duke and Duchess of Montagu. The duke, a former ambassador to Louis XIV, found that his fortunes were in a state of serious decline. He sought about for a rich widow to marry and found one in the person of the Duchess of Albermarle, a woman loaded but totally loony, who insisted that she would only marry royalty. The duke won her hand by convincing her that he was the emperor of China and instructed their servants to treat his new wife with all the deference due an Oriental empress.

In 1757, when the museum first opened, and for the next fifty years, one had to write well in advance for viewing passes and was granted admittance only for a restricted amount of time. Only small groups were permitted to view the collection and were obliged to move along at a brisk pace from room to room. Nevertheless, the museum was extremely popular and was constantly expanding as bequests kept rolling in.

One of the most important donations was George III's 120,800-volume library which, along with existing manuscripts and books, was the seed of the British Library, henceforth incorporated in the museum.

Eventually, Montagu House was bursting at its seams with mummies and books and coins and South Sea artifacts. Architect Robert Smirke built a Greek-style edifice around a courtyard that was later converted into the library's reading room by his brother, Sydney Smirke. The new building, immense as it was, could not accommodate the continued growth of the collections, and portions were divvied up between the Museum of Mankind (see section on "St. James's, Mayfair, and the Parks," above) and the Museum of Natural History (see "Belgravia, South Kensington, and Chelsea," above).

The museum still has ninety—count 'em, ninety—galleries full of treasures brought here by the unflagging zeal of the same people who brought the world the empire upon which the sun never set. The museum is open Monday through Saturday from 10 A.M. to 5 P.M., Sunday from 2:30 to 6 P.M. Admission is free. Gallery tours run daily at 10:30 A.M. and 1:30 P.M.; Sunday 2:45 and 3:30 P.M.; lectures are given daily at 1:15 P.M., except Sunday and Monday. Additionally, there is a perpetual whirl of films, videos, and special events. Pick up a listing leaflet at the information desk, and be sure to consult the information video listing daily features.

An Odyssey Through the Ancient World

The most fascinating aspects of the museum are its holdings devoted to ancient civilizations. It is possible to travel from the galleries of ancient Egypt, where you'll find the Rosetta Stone—which broke the hieroglyphic code by translating ancient Egyptian into ancient Greek—to the Ninevah Galleries, in which are reconstructed Assyrian temples that must have required legions of masons and slaves to complete, and finally to the Duveen rooms, inhabited by the warriors and steeds of the Elgin Marbles, "rescued" from the frieze of the Parthenon in Athens. In a matter of a few hundred yards, you can time-tunnel through the millennia from the primitive theocratic art of the pharaohs to the stylized, stiff monumentalism of the Assyrians, to the form-conscious photorealism of the Cradle of Democracy.

The museum presents many provocative juxtapositionings. Among the British Library collection of documents and manuscripts important to the British people there are two of the remaining copies of the Magna Carta of 1215, complete with the signature of King John, next to which is another, more fabulously famous work by another British John, an original copy of Mr. Lennon and Mr. McCartney's "Yesterday," on loan with several of their manuscripts.

Along with these important documents, do take some time to examine at leisure the group of illuminated manuscripts in the library's galleries. These gilt and painted missals in their miniature, painstaking brilliance are the work of some of the world's greatest artists. Among them are the seventh-century Lindisfarne Gospels brought down from the kingdom of Northumberland, attesting that there were many aspects of that age that were not at all "dark."

The Museum's Neighborhood

Servicing museum-goers, the streets in the area offer great opportunities for anyone interested in books and prints. Across from the museum on Montague and Great Russell streets, and especially on Museum Street, you can refresh yourself with a brisk window-shop. The neighborhood also houses London's best place for price and selection of Scottish goods, **Westaway and Westaway,** (62–65 and 92–93 Great Russell Street). In the Pied Bull Yard down Bury Place, **Jessop Classic Photographica** has antique cameras and equipment. At 105 Great Russell Street is **L. Cornelissen & Son,** art suppliers who make their own pigments and sell all manner of interesting necessities for every medium.

Just west of the museum across Gower Street is **Bedford Square,** one of the best-preserved groups of town houses in London. It was built in 1775–80 by Thomas Leverton, William Scott, and Robert Grews on land owned by the Russell family, the Dukes of Bedford. Bedford Square is the only remaining Georgian square in Bloomsbury that looks today precisely as it did two hundred years ago, unaltered by bombs, fires, or developers. The houses of gray-brown brick attracted tenants of an artistic turn, and many of them are presently occupied by architects and book publishers.

Just beyond Bedford Square is Tottenham Court Road, which in this area is populated by discount electronic stores. If you are looking for British-made equipment—British loudspeakers are exceptionally fine—this is the place to be.

The University of London

The northerly reaches of Bloomsbury are occupied by the **University of London.** Previous to the early 18th century, England's great universities were run by the church and by men. Consequently, aside from being wealthy and bright, one also had to be male and of the Christian (preferably Anglican) faith in order to attend. In 1826 University College was opened to serve some of the rest of the population; women were still denied entrance until 1878. With campuses at several other locations in London, the university's principal buildings, Bloomsbury, were completed in 1936.

Arts at School

The university has been the beneficiary of several great art collectors over the years; many of the finer pieces have been installed in galleries open to view to the public free of charge. Among the University's holdings, of particular interest are the **Petrie Museum of Egyptian Archaeology; the Strang Print Room,** a collection of prints, drawings and etchings including works of the old masters; and the **College Exhibition** tracing the history of University College and the achievements of important alumnae.

Also deserving special note is the **Percival David Foundation of Chinese Art** located nearby at 53 Gordon Square and open Monday through Friday from 10:30 A.M. to 5 P.M. Percival David was a great scholar and collector of things Chinese. A lot of his purchases were made between the world wars, when the objects suddenly became available as the Chinese upper classes, forced to flee the mainland, needed to raise money quickly. The collection begins with ceramics from the Yue Dynasty—over 2,500 years old—and continues through Ming and Ch'ing. A careful academician himself, David's 1950 bequest included a sizable library with the request that the objects all be carefully dated and explained. For connoisseurs or the uninitiated, the foundation provides a marvelous educational as well as aesthetic experience.

Another important asset of the university is the **Blooms- bury Theatre,** at 15 Gordan Street. Student groups and visiting repertory companies perform drama, music, dance, and mime here. Offerings tend to be contemporary and/or experimental works of the highest caliber. The **Bloomsbury Festival,** mid-May to early June, is based here; it brings together a group of stimulating programs of live and cinematic art, exhibitions, and lectures. For information on the theater and to book tickets with a major credit card, call 387-9629.

Around the University

In the university area is another pretty square, **Fitzroy,** which is closed to traffic on three sides and has a circular garden within. Henry Fitzroy, an illegitimate son of Charles II, was granted the land, which was then developed by his great- grandson in 1792 with plans for the south and east sides submitted by Robert Adam. The rest of the square was built forty years later. Although the south side was bombed during the war, it has been rebuilt as the London Foot Hospital, in keeping with the Georgian feel of the place. The neighborhood was a favorite of the Bloomsbury bunch and their descendants. Virginia Woolf and Robert Fry lived and worked here; Whistler, Constable, Verlaine, and Rimbaud lived in the area. Fitzroy Street becomes Charlotte Street, a good place to find restaurants and shops. At the junction of Percy Street is **Janet Fritch,** for clothes and jewelry. This shop concentrates on modern British design, but Paris and Milan are also represented. Clothes are cute but pricey. Across the street, **Chevignon,** decorated with lamps from a Paris *gare,* has a collection of casual French-cut clothes for gentlemen.

On the other side of the university, to the northeast, is Woburn Walk, where the storefronts have been gussied up to their Georgian appearance with a uniform black, white, and gold color scheme. You can get take-away at **Chives** and picnic in Tavistock Sq. (1806–26), whose garden is a peace park with memorials to Hiroshima and Gandhi.

On the north side of the park is the **Jewish Museum,** open Sunday, Tuesday through Friday from 10 A.M. to 4 P.M. Technically, admission is free, but the guard does forcefully encourage a donation. The museum contains historical items stuffed, willy-nilly, in a dreary room. Best for those with a specific interest to pursue.

St. Marylebone for Shopping and Lunching

The sights discussed thus far have been in Bloomsbury; continuing westward WC1 gives way to the W1 addresses of St. Marylebone. **Marylebone High Street** is a good shopping route; better still is smaller, sinuous **Marylebone Lane,** which snakes its way southward to Oxford Street.

Stop in for lunch at No. 35, **Paul Rothe and Son Deli.** They have super-cheap sandwiches to take away or eat at their lo-tech tables; save room for a custard tart.

The most fun shopping street, however, is tiny **St. Christopher's Place** and **Gees Court** just west of Marylebone Lane off Wigmore Street. There is **Mulberry and Co.** (with correct clothes and luggage). **The Changing Room** (casual, constructed clothes), and **Droopy and Browns** (romantic frocks for the ladies).

The Wallace Collection

After a bout of shopping seek refuge in the glorious sanctuary of the Wallace Collection on Manchester Square. The building, Hertford House (1776–88), has served as the Spanish and French embassies but was built as a residence by the Dukes of Manchester and acquired eventually by the Marquesses of Hertford, the first of whom was a patron of Reynolds and who founded a long line of art lovers and collectors.

The Wallace in question was Richard, an illegitimate son of the fourth marquess. Half the family's collection was bequeathed to the nation by Richard's widow; the other half was sold off, much of it ending up in America.

The collection is open Monday through Saturday from 10 A.M. to 5 P.M., Sunday from 2 to 5 P.M. and is free. There is an abundance of riches here and the danger is that many breathtaking treasures, some of which are tiny, will be overlooked. For instance, there is a 16th-century miniature tabernacle, unbelievably intricately carved from wood with figures just millimeters high. There is a large collection of European ceramics from the 15th to the 17th centuries. Upstairs are the painting galleries. Dutch masters are represented by Steen and Rembrandt; the Spanish by Velázquez and Murillo; an entire wing of French, featuring Fragonard, Boucher, and Watteau; and a wing of English—Reynolds, Romney, Gainsborough. There is also a room of European and Persian armors, and French and English porcelain and furnishings. The collection is as large as it is eclectic, so allow yourself a long morning or afternoon to see it thoroughly. Tuesday and Thursday lunchtime lectures run from 1 to 2 P.M.

A Visit to Madame Tussaud's

Marylebone's second museum—certainly more famous than the first—is **Madame Tussaud's,** and connected to the waxworks is the **London Planetarium.** Admission to Madame Tussaud's is £4.50; to the planetarium, £2.50; or you can buy a combo ticket for £5.80. Lines stretch around the block, especially on the weekends and bank holidays, so come early and during the week. (Open daily 10 A.M. to 5:30 P.M.)

Since pre-revolutionary Paris, Madame Tussaud's has been entertaining the masses. Today new figures are made in a workroom at the top of this building, which has stood here for over one hundred years. The tour begins as a history lesson with Pepys at his diary, Mary, Queen of Scots, at her execution, and a petite, barely postpubescent Victoria receiving news of her accession. At the center of the room is the Sleeping Beauty tableau, with a "breathing" princess whose face is made from an original cast Madame Tussaud made of Madame DuBarry.

You can have your photo taken with a livery-clad Benny Hill or a languorous Joan Collins. There is a figure of Marie Gosholtz (Madame Tussaud), who reproduced her hooknosed self in 1842, now situated in the room of famous rulers, where you'll also find an exhausted waxwork tourist, shopping bags in hand, collapsed on a settee from the thrill of it all, and the royal family inexplicably minus Prince Edward.

Downstairs in the Chamber of Horrors—guarded by Hitler—is the original bell from Newgate Prison that tolled at all executions, and Marie Antoinette's ax blade. At Legend's Café, you may want to pass on the food, but don't miss Brando, Elvis, Marilyn, Chaplin, and Bogey. Additionally, you might enjoy the evening laser concerts accompanied by different rock tunes at the planetarium (nightly, £3.75).

Across from Mme. T's is **St. Marylebone Parish Church,** among whose faithful were Sheridan, Byron, Lord Nelson, and the Brownings. The church itself isn't outstanding: Rococo with some Pre-Raphaelite–style paintings and a pair of crystal chandeliers. But if you're in the neighborhood on a Monday at 1:10 P.M., there are free concerts given by the students of the Royal Academy of Music—the large brick building across Marylebone Road—and vesper/organ music at 6:30 P.M.

The Home of Cricket

West down Marylebone (you'll pass Sherlock Holmes's Baker Street), then north on Gloucester Place you'll come to Dorset Square, which was the site of Thomas Lord's (a self-made merchant magnate and sportsman from Yorkshire) original cricket ground, **Dorset Fields,** which has since 1787 been the home of the Marylebone Cricket Club. Continuing up

Gloucester Road, left onto Park Road and left again onto St. John's Wood Road—a good twenty-minute hike—will bring you to Dorset Fields' vast and venerable descendant, **Lord's Cricket Ground.**

Anybody vaguely interested in the sport—or in Things Quintessentially British—should know that Lord's is the official home of the Cricket Council, whence come all rules of sportsmanship and manners for the sport worldwide. Both the Marylebone and the Middlesex County Cricket clubs play matches here April through September. For information about scheduling and tickets, call 289-1611.

If you're a fan, or care to become one, there is the **Cricket Memorial Museum** and a tour of the grounds. The famous Ashes Urn given to the winners of the England vs. Australia Test Matches—cricket's equivalent of baseball's World Series—is here in all its six inches of ceramic glory. Also featured in the tour are the **Royal Tennis Courts,** the **Pavillion's Lawn Room**—one of the most exclusive premises in the world—and a patient explanation of the rules of the game for those who don't know.

Tours of the museum and grounds have been irregularly scheduled and are free; however, there are plans afoot to run them daily and charge admission. For more information, call 289-1611. The **Lord's Shop** sells sweat- and T-shirts, towels, brollies, books, prints, mugs, bats, balls, and rule books.

Emblazoned on all the shop's wares is the symbol of Lord's, Father Time, taken from the weather vane that was built and presented to the grounds by Sir Herbert Baker. No one is quite sure whether this figure was chosen to indicate that cricket is a timeless sport or perhaps that cricket is a sport whose matches seem to last forever.

Regent's Park

If all the acres of perfect lawn at Lord's are a tease for you and you'd like to get onto some grass yourself, Regent's Park is the perfect panacea for all your pastoral needs.

The area of Regent's Park was the forest of Middlesex, grabbed from the Abbess of Barking during the Dissolution of the Monasteries by Henry VIII, who had his eye on the land for royal hunting grounds. The park was sold upon Charles I's execution, and the forest was cut down to provide revenue for the new (non-royal) owners. After the Restoration, the lands returned to the crown and were leased as farmland for the city. In 1811 all the leases came due, and it was decided that better use could be made of the property. John Nash was chosen to develop and landscape the site. He ringed the park with eight terraces—named for the king's brothers—distinct groupings of milk-white to ecru town houses connected behind a unifying Greek-revival façade. Nash's plan incorporated residences, shops, and a farmers' market surrounding a huge area of green, producing the ultimate inner-city suburb. A circumambulation of the park's perimeter is a most satisfying stroll. If you can, plan to do the circuit at dusk, just when they're ringing the closing bells at the zoo, making the coyotes howl. The skylight diminishes and the city lights come up along the arcade of Park Square and Park Crescent just south of the park; it is one of London's prettiest and most romantic promenades.

The park is designed with a pair of concentric rings, the Inner Circle and the Outer Circle. Within the former is Queen Mary's Garden, at its most lovely during tulip time in spring and rose season all summer. Also in the garden is the open-air theater where Shakespeare is performed in a glorious outdoor setting during the summer; check the papers for times and programs. On Easter Monday the annual London Harness Horse Parade is held, and thousands of entrants from Shetland ponies to Clydesdales trot by in full regalia—a terrific spectacle for a spring day.

A New Home for the Tower's Menagerie

At the northern end of the park is the **London Zoo.** The descendant of the Tower of London Menagerie, this is the oldest zoo in the world. It is decidedly not old-fashioned, however; cages have given over to natural-habitat environments. Join the stroller traffic jams or ride the steam train through the animals of Asia. The elephants bathe at 3:45 P.M., and feeding times range from 1:30 to 3 P.M. There are lots of special events on weekends and bank holidays. Open daily 9 A.M. to dusk, winter hours from 10 A.M.; admission is £3.90.

Elsewhere in Bloomsbury and Marylebone

Thomas Coram Foundation: The Art Treasures, north side of Brunswick Square. Having just celebrated its 250th anniversary in 1989, the foundation was set up by a retired sea captain, Thomas Coram, who, though not wealthy himself, managed to raise money to open a foundling hospital to improve conditions for London's huge population of orphans. Coram cleverly enlisted the help of various famous people to get the project off the ground; Hogarth was an original governor and convinced his friends to donate paintings to an annual art show to attract money and attention to the hospital. This show eventually grew into the Royal Academy. Another avid supporter was Handel, whose *Messiah* was given its English-language debut in the hospital's chapel.

The old hospital and school stood on the land now occupied by Coram's Fields Park (which grown-ups are allowed to enter only if accompanied by a child). The foundation's art collection has been preserved in a 1937 building that incorporates the school's staircase, ceiling, and fireplaces. It is not frequented by tourists, despite the fact that there are Hogarths, Gainsboroughs, a Raphael cartoon, Benjamin Wests, and Reynoldses to be seen—but this makes it more pleasant for those who do stop in. It is open Monday through Friday from 10 A.M. to 4 P.M. (admission 50 pence). Get a list of the paintings (20 pence) at the desk because they are not all marked.

Pollock's Toy Museum, 1 Scala Street. Benjamin Pollock was a Victorian toy-theater maker and his museum houses some of his finest creations, along with toys from the Americas, Europe, and the Orient. It is all a bit frustrating to see everything behind glass, but it's great fun to see how kids—and kids-at-heart—amused themselves over the years and around the world. The shop has great do-it-yourself models of buildings, royal wedding rag dolls to sew, reproductions of antique playing cards—the works. (The museum is open Monday through Saturday from 10 A.M. to 5 P.M.; admission is 80 pence, Teddys are admitted free.)

Wigmore Hall, 36 Wigmore Street. The 1901 hall is visually beautiful and acoustically excellent for chamber music, recitals, and similar small-scale musical performances. The room is intimate seating only six hundred, and is richly embellished with marble, alabaster, mahogany, and a soulful cupola painting over the stage. Sundays are especially lively, with Morning Coffee Concerts at 11:30, Sundays at Four (at 4). There are great events nightly, and seats are to be had for a relative song—usually £7 or less. The box office number for info or credit-card bookings is 935-2141.

Clerkenwell and Holborn

Both of these neighborhoods have names associated with London's gone and nearly forgotten water supply. Holburne stream was a tributary of the Fleet River. The Clerkes Well was an underground source used by the worshipful company of parish clerks, a guild whose "craft" was to assist priests in their official tasks and who put on mystery plays around the well during the Middle Ages. The area has seen many changes and gone through various incarnations—from savory to sordid and back again.

Originally this area of central and eastern London, today bounded by City Road in the north and east, Fleet Street (named for another diverted river that ran along here) in the south, and Gray's Inn Road in the west, was popularized by its waters and wells. Its medicinal springs were thought to possess healing properties, and when the City to the south became overcrowded, it was natural that the excess should seep northward. These migrations became especially acute after the Great Plague of 1665 and Great Fire of 1666. In fact, during the former, many City dwellers emigrated hither posthumously and were deposited by the hundreds per day in Bunhill (Bone Hill) Fields and Cripplegate.

The housing built by the (surviving) refugees was makeshift and slatternly, and the area's reputation plummeted from being a haven of fresh green and pure waters outside the City to a province of filth and contagion. Property was, however, cheap, and immigrants from elsewhere in Europe settled here to work at their businesses outside the City, whose guilds did what they could to restrict trade. The plentiful water supply attracted distilleries and breweries, and the area also became famous for producing the finest clocks and watches in Europe.

Continued urbanization during the industrial revolution produced a crisis for the craftsmen. The close quarters and squalid conditions bred more than physiological germs; political extremism was also bred and spred. In the 19th century, Chartism, an early socialist movement, flourished at rallies on Clerkenwell Green—attended by as many opportunistic pickpockets as political zealots. It is also here that Karl Marx and Vladimir Illych Lenin each lived at various times during their careers. The former London Patriotic Club on the Green has been converted to the Marx Memorial Library.

Holborn and Clerkenwell have much to tantalize the traveler who is interested in looking beyond the pretty parks and imposing museums and into the lives of working-class Londoners. There is a wide variety of professions and dispositions to be found here. Three of London's Inns of Court—Staple, Gray's, and Lincoln's—and the Public Record Office Museum, representing the law, are here. Vestiges of the days when the fields and farms were owned by powerful ecclesiastical orders are the Charterhouse, St. John's Gate and Museum, and St. Etheldreda's Cathedral—London's oldest Catholic church. Legacies left behind by former residents are Sir John Soane's Museum, the Dickens House and Museum, and the Old Curiosity Shop where Little Nell plied her pitiful trade.

Clerkenwell is getting bullish on itself: witness the Clerkenwell Heritage Centre at Clerkenwell Road and St. John's Square. It promotes these regions as a unified, important entity within London. Daily walking tours begin here during spring and summer, usually at 2:30 P.M. To be sure they are departing the day you want to go, call 250-1039.

Monks and Knights

If you're planning to proceed on your own, perhaps it would be best to start with two of the neighborhood's most important and interesting, yet least-visited, sights: the Charterhouse and St. John's Gate and Museum. One of the reasons both of these places are not overrun with clicking shutters and squealing school kids is that their hours of opening are very limited. This is also why we suggest visiting them first and planning the rest of your trip to the more accessible destinations around one or both of these centerpieces.

The Charterhouse is seldom open: a one-hour guided tour runs only on Wednesday afternoons at 2:45 P.M. from April through July; it is wise to call ahead to book a place on the tour (253-9503). The Chapel is open for services on Sunday at 9:45 A.M. and 5:45 P.M. It is also difficult to find; the entrance is on Charterhouse Square off Aldersgate Street at the end of Carthusian Street—and even if you ask directions, not many people in the neighborhood can point you to the precise spot, so consult a map when you set out.

The name Charterhouse is a mangling of Chartreuse, the place from which came the Carthusians, the order of monks for whom the place was originally built in 1371. The land was given by Sir Walter de Manny in memory of the victims of a recent bout of plague who were buried in the square. The buildings served as a priory until they were taken over during the Dissolution of the Monasteries, by Henry VIII, who ordered the prior and his monks executed for refusing to recognize him as head of the new (Anglican) church.

The buildings served as mansions for several noble families and eventually were bought by Thomas Sutton, one of Elizabeth's ministers, who in 1611 turned it into a charity school for boys and a home for gentlemen in straitened financial condition. Thus it has remained: eighty pensioners still make this their home—which accounts for the restricted visiting hours. Gentlemen and boys associated with the Charterhouse over the years have been Sir Thomas More, John Wesley, Joseph

The Dissolution of the Monasteries

Henry VIII, primarily remembered for his proclivity to switch spouses, more importantly should be remembered for solidifying and aggrandizing the Tudor monarchy in Britain. One of Henry's primary means of securing power was through transfering power from the church to the state. The first step in this process was Henry's break with Rome over the decision to divorce his first wife, and the concurrent establishment of the Church of England with himself at its head, as mandated by the Act of Supremacy in 1534.

In 1535, under the direction of his minister, Thomas Cromwell, a volume, *Valor Ecclesiasticus,* was presented to Henry, describing in minute detail the wealth of ecclesiastic organizations in the realm. This was the final impetus needed to convince Henry to do what many of his court tacitly supported: confiscate church holdings for himself, and sell off or grant in favor the excess.

The nobility largely approved of the move because many of them already leased monastic lands, and saw this as their chance to own the properties outright. Henry's special allies naturally received the primest plots, and their fealty thus bought and secured. The common folk often had little love for the inhabitants of the monasteries or abbeys, many churchmen and women were foreigners—French or Italian—spoke little English and had little to do with the neighboring communities. Indeed, the medieval monastic life of contemplation and charity had largely disintegrated, and there was no longer the need or tolerance for those who perpetuated the sham of piety monastic life had largely become.

The Dissolution of the Monasteries was effected in two stages between 1538 and 1547. In 1536 a Court of Augmentations was appointed to disband any order whose annual income was less than £200. Cromwell's plan was to "practice" on the smaller, less influential orders in order to increase monies in the royal coffers, and also to gauge public opinion and quell any resistance, before advancing on the wealthy and powerful churches. Brother and sisterhoods were disbanded and occasionally their members were executed for refusing to accept the Act of Supremacy, art treasures were destroyed or sold off, lands were broken up, and churches were partially or totally razed, their stones often serving as building materials for manor houses constructed by the new landowners. By 1547 it is estimated that Henry raked in between £800,000 and 1.5 million, halving again his net worth, and providing much needed funds for his grandiose palace–building schemes and (largely unsuccessful) foreign military campaigns.

Addison, Sir Richard Steele, William Thackeray, and Roger Williams, the founder of Rhode Island.

The path of the tour wends its way through beautiful walled gardens patrolled by legions of cats to keep the city vermin down. The interiors contain some of the only Elizabethan appointments remaining in London (including a charter granted to Sutton, signed by the queen herself). The Great Hall is rich with Tudor wood paneling, charred in the war but splendidly restored. There is furniture from the original monastery throughout, and some of the original Carthusian cells can still be seen. The Chapel walls are from the 14th century and contain a 17th-century memorial to Thomas Sutton. In the Gallery are English-made Tudor tapestries and an original, most unusual Jacobean fireplace. For years residents assumed it was black, but renovation after the bombing revealed that it had in fact been brightly painted with the Royal Coat of Arms, an Annunciation, and a Last Supper.

☕ Before you take your tour here, you might like to take some luncheon in the **Café du Marché,** down a little alley at the far end of Charterhouse Square. Wood-paneled and beamed, it serves French food with an emphasis on the freshest and best meats brought from Smithfield next door.

In the opposite direction, down Charterhouse Street to Aldersgate, **Royal Britain** is one of London's newest, and most popular tourist stops (open daily 9 A.M. to 5:30 P.M.; admission £3.95). Photos, momentos, dioramas, and more celebrate the 51 reigns of British sovereigns.

The Museum of the Order of St. John is located at St. John's Gate—you can't miss it, straddling as it does a pedestrian street below St. John's Square. The museum is open Tuesday, Friday and Saturday from 10 A.M. to 5 P.M. The rest of the buildings (the best part) can only be seen by taking an hour-and-a-half guided tour on open days at 11 A.M. and 2:30 P.M.; suggested donation £1.

The name is today famous in Britain and throughout the world for the St. John's Ambulance Service, one of the first groups to utilize modern transport—first autos and now helicopters—to rescue accident victims speedily and get them to a hospital. Chances are there will be a corpsman on your tour, curious to find out the origins of the organization.

The origins are ancient, beginning with the Military Knights Hospitalar. The tradition of attending the sick began during the Crusades, after which the knights set up hospitals along the routes to the Holy Land and in Jerusalem itself to care for exhausted, wounded, and diseased pilgrims. Eventually the knights established a stronghold in Malta. The order was forced to flee thence when overrun by Süleyman, and much of the furniture displayed in the Gatehouse came from the grand master's palace in Malta.

After the Dissolution of the Monasteries, the monarch used the Gatehouse and its buildings to store his hunting gear and kennel his dogs. Elizabeth gave it over to the Master of the Revels for scene construction and rehearsal space, in which capacity it was probably used by Shakespeare. Later it became a pub and printing house. Presently the Knights

Hospitalar are a royal order of chivalry whose symbol is the Maltese Cross—you'll remember it from Bogey's falcon—an eight-pointed cross first used by the merchants of Amalfi.

In the museum are exhibits based on the history of the Order of St. John and the ambulance service. In the Gatehouse, which crosses St. John Street and its adjoining buildings, are collections of silver, furniture, robes, and medals of the order. Also on the tour is the Church of the Order, with its 12th-century crypt, otherwise closed to the public. **The Clerkenwell Heritage Centre** (open 10 A.M. to 6 P.M. weekdays), which operates area tours, is right on the corner and is stocked with brochures on local events and equipped with a 24-hour video info screen in the front window.

 Ask for directions to **Clerkenwell Green**—scene of many hot-blooded attacks on the established order by the Chartists and later by Karl Marx. Doubtless many radicals wet their pre-oratory whistles at the **Crown Tavern** on the corner of the Green and Clerkenwell Close.

Sadler's Wells Theatre

A hike up St. John Street will take you past City University. Duck into pretty **Northampton Square,** a circular park with a gazebo and plane trees. Three sides are 1810 brown brick buildings, the fourth a modern university structure. A sharp left down Rosebery Avenue will lead to the **Sadler's Wells Theatre.** The box office is at the triangle where St. John and Rosebery intersect. The theater was built by Thomas Sadler, who thought it would be a good sideline for his spa business developing around the medicinal well he discovered on his property in the late 17th century. Sadler's Wells has spawned several important opera, dance, and drama groups, and still features companies important to the international performing-arts scene. Call the box office for info, 278-8916/0855.

Dickens at Home

West of these Clerkenwell locations, Gray's Inn Road begins the legal London of Holborn. But before you dive into adjudications, up John Street, which becomes Doughty Street, at No. 48 is the home of a gentleman who on many occasions spilt some less than kind ink over the legal profession, having himself spent several years keeping a crabbed, correct ledger as a junior clerk at the Gray's Inn firm of Ellis and Blackmore.

The **Dickens House** is open Monday through Saturday from 10 A.M. to 5 P.M.; admission is £1.50. The man who was paid by the word and waxed loquacious thereby lived here for most of his adult life, from 1812–70. It is a modest, unassuming house. If you're not a Dickensian by nature, you may find the exhibits a bit dense and disappointing. There are knickknacks from his life, prints of favorite characters, curtained cases of correspondences, first editions, illustrations, reading-tour texts. The shop has rare and old editions and bits of repro-Victoriana for sale.

On to the Inns

Gray's Inn, rather unremarkable rectangles of buildings built in the 14th through 16th centuries, saw a lot of service during the wars. Members of the local army corps drilled here for the First World War, and the complex was heavily bombed during the Second. The Chapel is rather nondescript, with studies of modern heroes of the church and jurisprudence in stained glass. It is open weekdays from 10 A.M. to 6 P.M.

The most pleasant part of Gray's Inn are its gardens, entrance from Gray's Inn Place, open to the public for alfresco lunching Monday through Friday from 12 to 2:30 P.M.

On the south side of Gray's Inn is the Gatehouse, which lets out onto High Holborn. At No. 49 is **Her Majesty's Stationery Office (HMSO) Book Store:** a gold mine of published editions of the latest (outlandish) budget, the highway code, ordnance survey maps, information on police dog training, manuals of freemanship. For obvious reasons, favorites include immigration acts, the Financial Services Act of 1986, and the Housing Act of 1988.

HMSO also publishes what amounts to an annual yearbook entitled (for instance) *Britain 1990.* This handbook of the nation is a very useful source of finding out the latest facts and figures on the country.

South of High Holborn is another barristorial bastion, **Lincoln's Inn.** Start at the Chief Porter's lodge at the Lincoln's Inn/Serle Street entrance; there are maps, brochures, and postcards to assist you.

The Old Hall and several other buildings in the vicinity were constructed mostly in the late 15th century and are probably the most impressive of all London's five Inns of Court. Later additions were made in the 19th century. The best view of all is probably the upward one with its tangle of Victorian neo-Gothic spires and chimney pots massed in groups of threes and sixes, with different brickwork patterns.

The only part of Lincoln's Inn regularly open to the public is the Chapel (hours: 12 to 2:30 P.M., Monday through Friday). It was built to an Inigo Jones design between 1619 and 1623. It is here that John Donne, preacher to the Honorable Society of Lincoln's Inn, gave the chapel's first sermon to a large and eager crowd. Its bell was captured by the Earl of Essex in Cádiz in 1596 and is tolled whenever a bencher dies.

Treasurers of the Honorable Society from 1680 onward are remembered by nearly three hundred coats of arms set in the stained-glass windows (including the arms of Princess Marga-

Wills, Wives, and Wrecks: Legal London

Practicing lawyers in Great Britain are divided into two groups, solicitors and barristers. Solicitors do much of the nuts-and-bolts work, the kind of work that can be done in an office. Barristers, on the other hand, are permitted to argue cases in court, and consequently tend to get the more complicated (and perhaps glamourous) cases. To become a solicitor or barrister, one must do an undergraduate degree in any field, then do a nine-month law study. This accomplished, the candidate may become a member of the Inns of Court (Middle Temple, Inner Temple, Gray's, Lincoln, or Staple in London) by applying to join. There is a fee charged to become a student member who is required to eat a specified number of dinners at an Inn. There is no formal training for the student member, but rather these dinners provide a course of education with teachers, lecturers, and speakers at meals and other times, enabling the candidate to become part of the life of the Inn.

When the student has joined an Inn and passed his or her bar exam he or she is ready to practice. To become a barrister, one must then serve a year-long apprenticeship with a senior barrister. Barristers are all self-employed. They share the services of a clerk who works for perhaps a dozen or so, acting somewhat like a manager does for a performer, arranging for his client barristers to get a good load of interesting cases. Clerks get paid a percentage of each case commission and are often quite dictatorial when any of their barristers suggest that they might like to vacation in Greece for a few weeks. The lawyers' fees are settled before the case begins, and cannot be renegotiated after a case whether they have won or lost.

Traditions among the Honorable Society of the legal profession run deep. Most obvious is the garb all barristers and judges must wear when in court. The wing collar is known as the "bands," the white wig dates back to the 17th century, and the type of gown denotes one's station in the profession: stuff gowns are for junior members, silk gowns are for senior members. The Supreme Court is a branch of the House of Lords; the attorney general is a political appointment made by the prime minister and is a cabinet post.

ret in 1967). The intricate pecking order of pews is explained on a plaque at the back.

More Matters of Legality

One of London's most important historical collections is housed in the **Public Record Office Museum** on Chancery Lane—a name long associated with overblown bureaucracy. It is here that all the documents important to the history and dear to the hearts of the British people are preserved.

Since the Norman Conquest, Brits, as you might expect, have been most conscientious about collecting and cataloging all their important red-tape activities. Here you can see an original copy of the Magna Carta, the Domesday Book, Guy Fawkes's confession, Shakespeare's will, and transcripts from Mrs. Thatcher's debates. Open Monday through Friday from 10 A.M. to 5 P.M.; admission is free.

A Curious Museum

At No. 13 Lincoln's Inn Fields is **Sir John Soane's Museum,** open Tuesday through Saturday from 10 A.M. to 5 P.M., lecture tours Saturday at 2:30 P.M.; admission is free. Sir John Soane, R.A., lived here from 1813–37, having popped over from next door at No. 12, where he originally lived and which he designed along with this house and No. 14.

Soane was a painter and primarily an architect and a collector of a most unusual sort indeed. His interests were eclectic and so, therefore, are the contents of this house. So fussy was Soane about the arrangement of his household and the sanctity of this monument to himself that he managed to push through a private Act of Parliament that endowed his home as a public museum under the condition that everything would remain just as he had left it.

Throughout the house, Soane cleverly managed to include natural overhead lighting in the design to best show off his collection. Among the illuminated, illuminating treasures are a Reynolds in the dining room, Hogarth drawings in the dressing room, and Hogarth's *Rake's Progress* and *The Election* series in the picture room. Downstairs is a 1370 B.C. sarcophagus encrusted with hieroglyphs inside and out. Turner's *Valley of Aosta* is hung behind a curtain in the anteroom, and Soane's own works grace the breakfast room. The upstairs drawing rooms have works by Veronese and Rubens and another (unmarked) Turner, *Admiral Tromp's Barge.* Soane's personal, quirky collection of books, paintings, sculpture, architectural fragments, fungi samples, notebooks, et al., is indeed fascinating, but you wouldn't want to dust it.

A Curious Shop and Pub

Just south of Lincoln's Inn Fields at 13–14 Portsmouth Street you'll recognize **Dickens's Old Curiosity Shop.** The author's first editions are for sale here at exorbitant prices. Escape the crush of souvenir seekers upstairs, where a case of Dickensiana and junkish antiques are sagging out from under the beams.

If you crave more Dickensian flavor, down the passage at 145 Fleet St. is perennial favorite pub and chop house, **Ye Olde Cheshire Cheese,** circa 1667.

In the chop room is a first edition of Dickens's *A Tale of Two Cities* opened to the page that refers to this establishment. Steaming joints are carried past you, sawdust scrunches underfoot, the church-pew benches have been worn down to a comfortable smoothness. The place is large, so do some exploring.

A Final Inn and a First Church

East down High Holborn is the **Staple Inn,** the last of the Inns of Court. Its most interesting aspect is the row of Tudor frontages along High Holborn; they have been largely restored and now have sweet and smoke shops. But at least they convey some sense of what London looked like when Will Shakespeare and Kit Marlowe were abroad in the streets.

Just past Holborn Circus on Ely Place is **St. Etheldredas,** London's oldest Catholic church (though it served duty for Anglicans after the Reformation, it was brought back to Catholicism in 1874). Holborn was a *via sacra* for Catholic martyrs when they were paraded through the streets to Newgate Prison and/or to execution at Tyburn.

The church was built in 1293 and was almost destroyed by the Great Fire, but the wind changed (parishioners said miraculously) and it was spared. The original crypt with its massive timbers and original ceiling was once a pub.

 It is still possible to have some of your appetite slaked here at the **Pantry,** (open 11 A.M.–2:15 P.M.), which serves cheap, cheap food at lunch: meat pies with two veggies or lasagne to eat in or take away. If you prefer something alcoholic, down twisty Ely Place is **Ye Olde Mitre Tavern,** a neighborhood fixture since the 17th century. Picnic tables hoard every available scrap of sunlight in the tiny alley.

Kensington

The Royal Borough of Kensington received its regal status in 1901 in consideration of the fact that Queen Victoria had been born at Kensington Palace, still occupied by some of the Royals when they are in town. In 1965 Kensington was incorporated with Chelsea, a mammoth merger, which properly included Kensington, Earls Court, South Kensington, and Chelsea. It would be sheer silliness to suggest that one could cover an area so vast and varied as this mega-borough in one go, so we've broken it down into a brace of touring centers, with the logical boundary between them being Kensington High Street.

Similarly, Kensington Palace could rightfully be included in the chapter on the parks, since it borders Kensington Gardens; however, that chapter has a palace in it already, and it is much more convenient to stop in at Kensington Palace while you're touring this western edge of London than to trek all the way across Hyde Park from its eastern border.

It *is* a long way across the parks and gardens; in fact, it used to be such a long journey that Kensington was considered quite out of town. Londoners wrote of taking pleasure trips out of the city to the "freshe ayre and verdure" of Kensington. The area was for many years London's breadbasket. Vegetable gardens flourished on its gentle south-sloping hills. Flowers were sent to brighten Covent Garden, as was hay to feed the livestock at Smithfield and in London's stables. There were large garden markets ranged roughly along the present route of Kensington High Street.

As London grew larger, land within close proximity grew dearer and the farms and gardens of such prime ground as Kensington grew to be a luxury their landlords could no longer afford. Aristocrats frightened by the double blow of the Great Plague and the Great Fire fled from the teeming tinderbox City. Kensington's fields and meadows were gobbled up at a furious rate by the gentry, who built mansions on the cleared land and set up miniature country-estates-by-the-city. Holland House and its park are a perfect, extant example of the gracious, sumptuous living enjoyed by Kensingtonians of the late 17th century.

Needless to say, the days of peacock-guarded mansions did not last forever, and by the early 19th century most of the estates had gone the way of the working farms they had replaced. Between 1801 and 1901 the population grew from 8,600 to over 176,000 souls, all of whom needed to be sheltered and supplied. The luxuriously large landholdings were broken up into smaller and smaller parcels until finally Kensington hill was coursed by neat rows of white or brick town houses built to appeal to the upper-middle-class taste of Victorians, who considered it correct that their streets and squares resemble the fashionable Georgian thoroughfares of town.

Of course some of the Victorians had their own ideas about building and furnishing, and two superb examples of 19th-century interior decorative fancy are preserved, nearly perfect, in Kensington streets. The Linley Sambourne House was owned by a *Punch* cartoonist who collected drawings and photographs with which he populated his pictures and his home. The Leighton House was one man's attempt to make his home his castle. Frederick Lord Leighton's own paintings and those of his Pre-Raphaelite cronies adorn the walls.

These Victorians were genetically disposed to shopping, and many of the stores along Kensington High and Kensington Church streets have been catering to the neighborhood's bourgeois-gone-bohemian tastes for generations. The best living example of this is, of course, the famous Saturday market at Portobello Road. People have been known to find fine silver and furniture among the stash for bargain prices—although the market's burgeoning popularity is making "finds" extremely rare these days.

To escape the bartering mania, there is Holland Park, certainly the city's most delicious dollop of green. It has everything: hills, meadows, woodland, fields of daffodils, beds of roses, a 17th-century manor house, an Inigo Jones gateway, an open-air theater, and plenty of in-house birds and bees.

Kensington Palace

A good place to begin your peregrinations is at Kensington Palace, the only palace in London of which a major portion is open for public inspection. It is, relative to other palaces you may have seen on the Continent or elsewhere in Britain, surprisingly understated. John Evelyn pronounced the house "very noble tho not greate"—an epithet quite appropriate to the place. Being a royal residence, it is not exactly modest; however, for those grown weary of ceilings dripping with cherubs and walls Rococoed with gilding, Kensington Palace should provide welcome relief.

Perhaps it is more homey because it was not always a palace but actually began as a private residence. It was built in the early 17th century for Sir George Coppin. During the reign of William and Mary, the Earl of Nottingham purchased it for £14,000—a most princely sum in those days, so the house must have been fine indeed—and called his new home Nottingham House. However, the sovereigns were dissatisfied with the palace at Whitehall, which they found at turns damp and claustrophobic, and were delighted by the prospect of a palace with ample grounds for an ambitious garden. In 1689 William and Mary bought Nottingham House, hired Christopher Wren to turn the Jacobean country house into

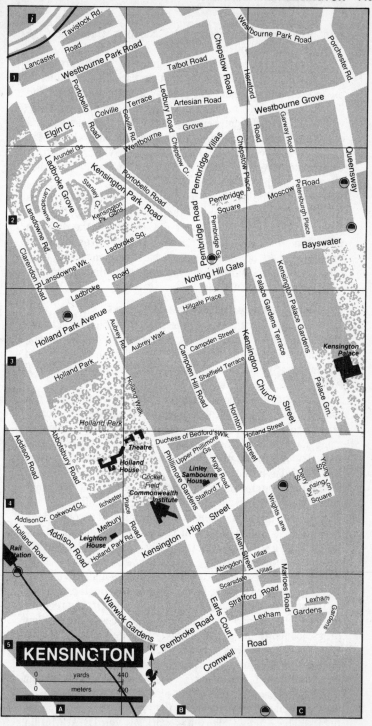

a modern palace, and contracted Nicholas Hawksmoor to oversee construction.

Until the reign of George III, Kensington was the preferred palace of British monarchs, who made various alterations to the interior and grounds. The palace then fell out of favor and was used by lesser members of the royal family until 1819, when the Duke of Kent, recently married to Princess Victoria of Saxe-Coburg, moved in with his pregnant wife, who in May of that year gave birth to a daughter, also Victoria. Victoria was raised here but moved to Buckingham Palace upon her accession to the throne.

Portions of the palace were opened to the public early this century and were the home of the London Museum, the contents of which were moved to the new building at the Barbican Centre in 1982. Presently Princess Margaret lives in part of the palace, as do occasionally Charles, Diana, and their brood—hence the surveillance cameras stationed at strategic breaks in the garden walls.

Dresses and Daintinesses of Court . . .

There is quite a lot to see at the palace: private royal apartments, an exhibit explaining court protocol, and a terrific collection of finery that ladies and gentlemen wore when presented at court. The exhibits are open from 9 A.M. to 5 P.M., from 1 P.M. on Sunday. Admission is £2.60.

By way of explanation, the first exhibit one comes upon discusses the painstaking rules of proper etiquette when being presented at court. There are panels explaining all the niceties and a soundtrack of Baroque music to give a sense of fanfare. Now that one knows what to do, one must know what to wear, and the dress collection is truly a treat for anyone remotely interested in pomp, history, fashion, or textiles. A 1750s gown with farthingale far wider than the wearer was tall makes one wonder how she sat let alone danced or made it through doorways; this is not explained in the etiquette section. Menswear of the 18th century was equally sumptuous and, thankfully, more form-fitting.

Low light preserves the costumes' fabrics and also actually creates a very nice gaslit effect. Working through hoopskirts and bustles to the 20th century, last but not least, just recently installed and already a firm favorite is Princess Di's wedding dress, loaned to the exhibit so you can see up close the fairytale fantasy gown you saw on TV.

The tour continues up Wren's square spiral stairs, which he installed with low risers so the Royals wouldn't get out of breath. Again the rooms are of reasonable proportions—smaller, quieter, cosier in scale than many other state apartments. The King's Gallery has work by Van Dyck, Murillo, and Rubens. Also charming are Victoria's dolls and dollhouse.

Outside you might like to join the boys in their tweed tams sunning themselves on the porch of the Orangery, built in the 1790s by Wren's staff. Or perhaps take a turn around the formal gardens; most are gated, but you can certainly enjoy the view over the hedges.

Pretty Streets and a Sky Garden

Just west of the palace, one of the first streets you come to, running north-south, is Kensington Palace Gardens, a quiet avenue of dappled light lined with palatial homes of its own. Several are embassies, therefore the police presence.

Running parallel to this street is Palace Gardens Terrace, which runs into Brunswick Gardens, all rows of lily-white town houses with pretty postage-stamp-sized gardens, all impeccably maintained. One block west again is Kensington Church Street, whose northerly end is full of antiques shops. The southern boundary of Kensington Church is Kensington High Street, another place for shopping. The most fun place to shop along the High is **Hyper Hyper.** Hyper Hyper, big as a barn, is a showcase for London's fast-rising stars of fashion. This is the best place in town to find soon-to-be household names; they set up stalls, market style, and sell their wares at reasonable prices.

Down Derry Street is **Kensington Square,** built in 1665 for aristocrats who wanted to escape the rigors of William and Mary's court at Kensington Palace. Numbers 11 and 12 date from that time, the rest primarily from the 18th century. Householders have included the philosopher John Stuart Mill and the actress Mrs. Patrick Campbell.

If you prefer your greenery in an elevated state, back up Derry Street in the building numbered 99 Kensington High Street take the lift to the top, where basks the **Roof Garden** with palms, fountains, and pink flamingos (live ones, although the pink shade looks like it might run in the rain). The gardens are open from 9 A.M. to 5 P.M. (if there is no private function going on) for a rooftop escape to a Mediterranean villa. It is all here because the fire department refused to allow Derry and Tom's Department Store (now defunct) to build an extra floor. To circumvent the ruling, it was decided to build a garden instead.

At the center of the garden is the Garden Club, a restaurant and nightclub available for private parties, but open to the public only for a sylvan Sun. brunch. At 122 Palace Gardens Terrace is **The Ark** looking much like a houseboat in a tiny brick townhouse and an extension. This restaurant has lace curtains, wood tables and a daily changing menu of simple, light dishes.

Down on the ground, back on the High, is a modern building with 48 flags snapping smartly out front. These banners represent the 48 member nations of the Commonwealth, the loosely joined group of nations that is the modern-day version of the British Empire. The **Commonwealth Institute**—for so this modern structure with its hyperboloid roof is called— was opened in 1962 to promote the association of nations and pride in same. The Commonwealth is explained and denoted on a wall map in the entrance that pinpoints each of the member countries. There is a terrific shop with music, books, crafts, posters, maps, and toys from the far reaches of the world. In a huge interior space under the roof of Zambian copper, the member nations have set up exhibits highlighting their strengths and resources—it's a bit like a world's fair under one roof. There is also an information center with a library of books, periodicals, and a collection of phone books for those of you who want to call home to Sydney but have forgotten the number. Out back is an art gallery showing special exhibits of Commonwealth artwork. Finally there is a casual café serving samples of Commonwealth countries' cuisines. (Open Monday through Saturday from 10 A.M. to 5:30 P.M., Sunday from 2 to 5 P.M.; admission is free.)

A Slice of Victoriana

Bracketing the Institute are two houses dating from the days when the Commonwealth was the Empire. Eastward on Kensington High Street, turn up Argyll Road and a quick left down Stafford Terrace. Number 18 is the **Linley Sambourne House.** Open from March through October, Wednesday from 10 A.M. to 4 P.M. and Sunday from 2 to 5 P.M., so be sure to schedule yourself accordingly. Admission is £1.50.

Your impression will be of entering a pleasant private home. There are no large signs directing you to the door. You must ring the bell and then be greeted by a guide who will show you into the drawing room to begin your tour. The house's 19th-century owner, Edward Linley Sambourne, drew satirical cartoons for *Punch* magazine. He filled his home with photographs and paintings he created or collected to use as inspiration for his own work, many examples of which are also hung around the house.

This is the only Victorian house in its original form in London. Sambourne's granddaughter Anne lived here till the end of her life and changed very little in the house. All the wallpaper, furniture, plumbing, and pictures remain untouched, as they appeared in 1875, right down to the walking sticks in the entry. The heavy, overstuffed furniture in the overstuffed rooms preserves precisely the flavor of life for the artistic Kensingtonian of the Age of Empire.

To the west, turn right off Kensington High Street onto Melbury Road and left on Holland Park Road. At No. 12 is **Leighton House,** the legacy of a second Victorian artist,

Frederick Lord Leighton, painter and one-time president of the Royal Academy. Obviously concerned with making a bold aesthetic statement, Leighton worked with architect George Aitchison to create a residence the likes of which had not been seen before.

Their crowning achievement is the Arab Room, where a dome ceiling blossoms down to walls of mosaics, intricately and exquisitely painted tiles and carved screens, and a fountain tinkling prettily within.

In other rooms of the house Leighton hung his pictures along with some painted by Sir Edward Burne-Jones and J. W. Waterhouse. Exhibits relating to Victorian or painterly themes are often mounted in some of the unused rooms upstairs. Outside is a sculpture garden and lawn studded with daffodils and bluebells in the spring. The house is open Monday through Saturday from 11 A.M. to 5 P.M.; admission is free.

Leighton House is also the home of the Kensington and Chelsea Music Society. Many Thursday evenings at 7:30 concerts featuring chamber, vocal, and piano music are held in the upstairs studio. Tickets are £3.50 and can be reserved by phoning 602-3316. The combination of art and music makes for a most enjoyable evening.

Holland Park

Holland Park is easily the prettiest park in central London. Its hillside topography and thick planting of trees and shrubs is the closest you'll come to finding the countryside in the city. **Holland House** and its grounds are the last of a lost era when Kensington was a town of country gentlemen's estates. This particular one dates from the early 17th century, when Sir Walter Cope had a house built on the property. Cope's Castle, as the Jacobean mansion was called, was inherited by Sir Walter's son-in-law, Henry Rich, Earl of Holland, and thence was referred to as Holland House. The next famous inhabitant of the house was publisher and essayist Joseph Addison, who married a Holland widow, Charlotte. The house passed through several more generations who made several more additions and renovations, but unfortunately all their work came to naught when it was bombed and gutted in 1940. The London City Council bought it in 1952 and restored the east wing and opened it as a youth hostel. Another portion of the house was transformed into the **Open Air Theatre.**

The park covers nearly 55 acres and preserves some of its original splendors in the 17th-century gateway attributed to Inigo Jones, a Dutch Garden full of tulips, the ballroom (which has been turned into a restaurant), an iris garden, a rose walk, the former ice house (now an exhibition space), 28 acres of woodlands called the Wildernesse, and several tennis courts. During the summer, the Open Air Theatre mounts productions of operas and Shakespeare, and other spectacles. Check the arts section of the daily papers for listings.

To Market, to Market

London's most famous alfresco shopping is at the **Portobello Antiques Market.** Portobello Road is best reached from Notting Hill Gate. Right by the Underground station, on the north side of the street, is Pembridge Road, a left-hand fork off of which is Portobello Road. If you come for the Saturday market, you can't get lost, because you'll notice the streams of people heading in that direction.

By the late 19th century Portobello Road was lined with shops and had become the market center of Kensington. Today on any Saturday, the streets are just jammed with would-be bargain spotters rummaging through the old silver, jewelry, furniture, clothing, and knickknacks. Chances are, you won't be buying, but the crush and the atmosphere is great fun and worth spending a Saturday morning on.

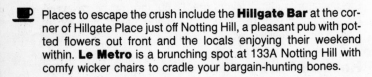

Places to escape the crush include the **Hillgate Bar** at the corner of Hillgate Place just off Notting Hill, a pleasant pub with potted flowers out front and the locals enjoying their weekend within. **Le Metro** is a brunching spot at 133A Notting Hill with comfy wicker chairs to cradle your bargain-hunting bones.

The South Bank

The regions south of the Thames had for some time been viewed as *terra incognita* by generations of visitors to London. No doubt about it, compared to the river's northern shore, the things to see and do to the south were few and far between. It's had the unfortunate reputation of being a bombed-out, badly rebuilt working-class neighborhood with little color and less elegance. This is all changing. Southwark (pronounced "suthuck" by the locals) was hit hard during the blitz, and money for rebuilding has been slow in coming. But inevitably, as space on the other side of the Thames is filling up, developers are looking back across at the South Bank as a logical place to deposit London's burgeoning population of yuppies so they can walk to work across Southwark or London Bridge to their jobs in the City. To amuse these new arrivals, a huge complex of stores, restaurants, and offices, called Hays Wharf, has just opened east of London Bridge. Hays Wharf does for southside London what the South Street Seaport did for New York and Quincy Market did for Boston— revitalized a neighborhood needlessly neglected. Of course there are those who sniff in indignation at the office towers blocking out everyone else's river view, but for the most part the new buildings have injected some cash and energy into an area sorely short of both.

Hays Wharf joins another complex of new buildings designed to take advantage of underutilized space. Farther west at the river's great bend southward is the South Bank Centre, a most festive home of the arts that includes the Royal National Theatre Company's theaters, the National Film Theatre, the Hayward Gallery, Royal Festival Hall, the Museum of the Moving Image, and several other stages and galleries.

But to dwell upon these recent additions is to give the impression that the South Bank's history is relatively recent. Nothing could be further from the truth.

> Bifil that in that seson on a day,
> In Southwerk at the Tabard as I lay
> Redy to wenden on my pilgrymage
> To Caunterbury with ful devout corage, ...
> "General Prologue," *The Canterbury Tales*

When Geoffrey Chaucer began his poetic junket in 1386 he, like many pilgrims, drank a quaff to a safe trip at one of the many taverns for which Southwark was famous. Southwark was also the home of brothels, breweries, prisons, and theaters. The most famous of this last group came to be the Globe, which was home to the Chamberlain's Men, a company whose principal asset was their playwright, son of a Cotswold glovemaker, William Shakespeare. The Globe was only one of a slew of theaters that favored the 16th century public with

highbrow entertainment like *King Lear* but also some less ce-
rebrally taxing fare such as bearbaiting, cockfighting, bullbait-
ing, and dogfighting.

Although the Puritans in a fit of righteous indignation had
the theaters destroyed in the mid-17th century, Southwark,
and its neighboring borough Rotherhithe, are still great places
to go for a pint. All along the bank are wonderful pubs with
great views and outdoor decks upon which you can enjoy the
aquatic traffic plying Father Thames.

Ranged along the southern shore of the Thames are three
boroughs: from east to west, Southwark, Bankside, and Lambeth. There are three centers of interesting sights along the
riverbank. Beginning in the east, by Tower and London brid-
ges are The Design Centre, the H.M.S. *Belfast*, Hays Dock,
and the *Kathleen & May* schooner. West of London Bridge
are Southwark Cathedral, Borough Market, the Operating
Theatre of Old St. Thomas's Hospital, and the Shakespeare
Globe Museum. The next conglomeration of sights is farther
west, just over Waterloo Bridge, where you'll find the South
Bank Centre and the Old and Young Vic theaters.

The route we favor follows the bank of the river, with a
short detour inland to take in some interesting spots around
the Cathedral. If you begin at the Design Centre in the east
and walk westward to the South Bank Centre, stopping along
the way, this journey could easily take a day or more. You
can break off at any point but the Thames-side stroll, with its
views of all the major monuments on the north side of the
river, is well worth the effort in and of itself. We have ended
the tour at the South Bank Centre, but if you are game, by
all means continue westward to the view of the Houses of
Parliament and recross the river at Lambeth Bridge.

As for the Thames-side pubs, some will be along your
route; two notable exceptions are The Mayflower and The
Angel to the east in Rotherhithe. These places are great for
lazy Sunday afternoon lunches, so you can catch them then
(see "Pubs," at the end of the section).

Waterside Diversions

East of Tower Bridge along Shad Thames is the **Design Museum at Butler's Wharf.** Brainchild of Sir Terence Conran,
of Michelin House fame, this sparkling new installation show-
cases the works of important designers in fields as diverse
as education, fashion and advertising. Phone 403-6933 for
opening times and info.

Parked just west of Tower Bridge is the **H.M.S. *Belfast*,**
a 1938 cruiser that you can climb aboard and scramble around
from 10 A.M. to 5:20 P.M., till 4 in winter for £3. The exhibitions within its hold are best appreciated by those especially
interested in naval history.

The Hays Wharf installations are being built and opened piece by piece, and when it's all finished it will be a mini city unto itself. Of interest to the visitor is the **Hays Galleria,** a Milan-styled atrium with an overarching of glass, an unobstructed view to the river, and a sculpture depicting a humongous, improbable battleship. The galleria is full of up-market shops ranged around the high-gloss polished floors; offices line the atrium up above.

The **Horniman** is a pleasant restaurant overlooking the water for those who prefer a pubby atmosphere. **Quintessence** on the other side of the gallery is a bit more genteel. Both are populated by business folk at lunchtime.

Next door is the **Cottons Centre,** with another riveroverlook atrium replete with palm trees, waterfalls, and plenty of polished-granite floor space to accommodate exhibitions and cocktail parties for the nabobs.

The Bestial and the Celestial

Across Tooley Street is the **London Dungeon,** open every day from 10 A.M. to 5:30 P.M., till 4:30 in winter (£4.50 admission). Under the guise of displaying a historical record of man's inhumanity to man, the dungeon has incredibly grisly tableaux depicting such favorite miseries as plague, torture, cannibalism, and a particularly gurgling, gushing, decapitated Mary, Queen of Scots. Don't bring the kids (or yourself) if you're prone to nightmares.

If you'd prefer to get away from it all, just next door is **Space Adventure** (open daily from 10:30 A.M. to 5:45 P.M.; £3.50). Visitors travel with Doctor Who, blast off in Starship 3001, and may even learn a thing or two about the extraterrestrial world if they're not careful.

Inland Diversions

From the west end of Tooley Street, take a leftward jag down the High Street to check out some land-locked sights. A Roman villa once stood on this site that was later to support a nunnery in 606. The official name of **Southwark Cathedral** is the Cathedral Church of St. Savior and St. Mary Overie ("over the river"). It has gone through many incarnations and many renovations.

There are a few vestiges of a 12th-century Norman priory within the 13th-century Gothic St. Mary Overie, which was begun in 1220, making it the first Gothic church in London and the only significant Gothic building in London besides Westminister Abbey. Because the church has been subject to fires, roof cave-ins, and the pleasure and displeasure of various monarchs, much of the Gothic construction has been replaced or obscured.

The nave was completely rebuilt in the 1890s, after the 15th-century roof collapsed. Luckily, however, a dozen carved bosses from the original ceiling were recovered and are displayed in the church. Also of note are the choir and retrochoir; although they are much restored, it is still possible to discern the fine 13th-century workmanship. The altar screen was executed in 1520.

Being in the neighborhood of the theaters, many players and playwrights attended services here and were often chastised by the vicar for their scurrilous profession. Commemorating one of their number is an installation to Shakespeare (several of whose relatives are buried in the church). Above the alabaster figure of the recumbent bard is a stained-glass window—replaced after German bombings and unveiled by Dame Sybil Thorndike—featuring a cast of characters: Bottom, Caliban, Malvolio, Lear, Lady Macbeth—some you probably never expected to find in church.

Of interest to scholarly types is the Harvard Chapel north by the transept, donated by Harvard University alumni in memory of their founder, who was baptized here in 1607.

There are organ recitals on Mondays and on Wednesdays at 1:10 P.M. Check the schedule by the info desk.

Just south of the cathedral, under the BritRail trestle, is the **Borough Market.** If you happen to be here before midmorning, you can catch the jaunty, agricultural atmosphere of the greengrocers and florists. Proceedings are presided over by a congenial dalmation who keeps an eye on the fruit and cress vendors.

Make a left down St. Thomas Street where you'll see a turret at the rear of a church and climb the spiral stairs to **The Operating Theatre of Old St. Thomas's Hospital** (open Monday, Wednesday and Friday from 12:30 P.M. to 4; admission £1). In the roofspace above the church is a marvelous beamed attic containing a small museum of 18th and 19th century medicine. Next door is the actual hall where surgery was performed on the poor women of London (wealthy people had operations at home on the kitchen table). The room is set up as it would have been during the 1800s including bank seats surrounding the operating space so that trainees could watch the master surgeons at work.

THE GEORGE, A GEM

Down a little alley at 77 Borough High St. is one of the few National Trust properties in London, the **George Inn.** Luckily, the inn has not become a look-but-don't-touch fossil but is still doing delightfully what it was always meant to do, provide customers with cheer and libations.

The George was built in 1676 on a site that has probably offered hospitality to travelers since the Middle Ages. It is the only galleried inn left in London, a picturesque pair of wood-railed porches running—and sagging—along the length of its façade.

A good meal can be had for £6–£8 on picnic tables set out in the courtyard or on the sturdy ones inside, upstairs and down. Check out the largish 18th-century clock in the barroom. In 1797 Parliament levied a tax on watches, so clever tavernkeepers installed clocks in their pubs to encourage folks to drop by to check on the time, and perhaps stop for a pint while they were at it. Some of London's most fun events are the performances of Shakespeare held in the courtyard in summer.

The Schooner and the Clink

Returning back to the riverside, just beyond the western end of the cathedral you'll spot the spars of the *Kathleen & May,* a coastal trading schooner of the type that used to frequent the wharves of Southwark and Bankside when much of London's intranational trade was conducted over water instead of over land. Built in 1900 the *Kathleen & May* is sadly the sole survivor of what used to be a huge fleet of ships that scuttled along the coasts of Britain and returned laden with coal, cement, gunpowder, etc. These ships were based on the fore-and-aft rigged ships favored by blockade runners in the American Revolution. Quick, light, and responsive at helm, the qualities that made these vessels good for Yankee gun smugglers also made them perfect for sailing along the rugged, irregular coast of Britain, so English shipyards copied the New England design.

On board you can poke around the decks and visit the exhibition with a video telling the ship's story and panels explaining the routes and importance of the coastal trade. Open daily from 10 A.M. to 4 P.M., Sunday from 10 A.M. to 6 P.M.; £1.

Just across is the **Southwark Heritage Information Centre** (open 9 A.M. to 5 P.M.), chockablock with brochures and information.

Under a high-arched bridge and high stone walls runs **Clink Street,** named in honor of the dismal Clink Prison— whence the expression "in the clink"—which stood here until it was burned in an anti-Roman Catholic riot in 1780. Note the rose windows, all that remains of Winchester Palace, home of Bishops till 1626.

If you continue around the bend toward the river you will find a pleasant stretch of walkway that flows by the waterside for a little way.

Just shy of Southwark Bridge is the **Anchor Bankside,** a pub and restaurant with an outdoor barbecue patio right on the water. It is tourist-traveled but nonetheless a most pleasant place of respite along the way. The present building was erected in the late 18th century after a fire had destroyed the original a hundred years earlier.

Proceed along the river over Southwark Bridge till you come to Bear Gardens, a street on your left just beyond the first row of buildings. At No. 1 Bear Gardens, you'll find **The Bear Gardens Museum of the Shakespearean Stage.** On the site of the last bearbaiting ring in operation (1662–82), the Bear Gardens were frequented by Samuel Pepys and Ben Jonson, some of whose plays were performed nearby.

Bearbaiting was one of the 16th and 17th centuries' top attractions. The "sport" consisted of the contest between a bear chained to a post and a pack of British bulldogs who fought the bear to the death. The onlookers would bet on the outcome, either for the dogs or the bear. The same bloody sort of scheme was also applicable to bulls who were beset by dogs in a fight to the finish.

The museum traces Elizabethan and Jacobean theater with models and relics and text. The small theater hosts dramatic and musical workshop performances. Open Tuesday through Saturday from 10 A.M. to 5:30 P.M., Sunday from 2 to 6 P.M., closed Monday; admission is £1.

Returning to the riverside path and continuing westward, there's an exciting project underway. All the construction you see and hear is eventually to result in an exact full-scale replica of the Globe Theatre, just a few hundred yards from the original site. The **International Shakespeare Globe Centre** will include a second theater based on a 1616 Inigo Jones design, a new museum of Elizabethan stage history, a pub, and a restaurant.

On or about April 23rd of each year there is an annual fete celebrating Shakespeare's birthday, including a special service at Southwark Cathedral and a carnival along Bankside with ox-roasting, ale-drinking, street theater, and revelry.

A Thames-Side Stroll

Farther west along the river the river walk continues, on the land side of which you'll pass what is purported to be **Christopher Wren's house.** If you turn round to see the vista, you'll understand how this rumor got started. Stop for a photo opportunity so you can keep a permanent eye on St. Paul's as Wren might have done from the front windows. You'll then walk past an immense windowless structure, the **Bankside Power Station;** completed in 1964, it is now a monument to human wastefulness, having been shut down in 1981.

Along the route there are plaques of the skyline across the river with labels for the major features to help you figure out just what it is you're seeing.

 At the end of the walkway is another waterside pub, **Founders Arms,** a modern glass structure with a pleasant patio and fine view, just out the back door of the Bankside Gallery.

The **Bankside Gallery's** official address is 48 Hopton Street, and its official function is to serve as exhibition space for the Royal Society of Painters in Water Colours and the Royal Society of Painter-Etchers and Engravers. It's open Tuesday through Saturday from 10 A.M. to 5 P.M., till 8 on Tuesday, Sunday from 1 to 5 P.M.; £1. The small, pleasant gallery of course features the work of members but also of young and promising artists; it also has a good shop.

More Art on the Water

In 1951, spiritually and financially depressed by the aftermath of World War II, as London was still digging itself out from under the rubble, some game souls sought to boost the city's morale by staging a Festival of Britain. It was also a good excuse for some organized fund-raising to finance some badly needed concert space after several halls had been destroyed by the blitz. One of the centerpieces for the festival was **Royal Festival Hall,** to be built in a bombed-out riverside neighborhood. Phone 928-8800 for the box office; 240-7200 to book with a major credit card.

After the festival in 1951, it was decided that the whole area would be given over to a comprehensive center for all of the arts, fine and performing, and as such proved a prototype for many other such planned cultural centers around the world.

Royal Festival Hall has become the home of the London Philharmonic and also plays host to visiting classical and pop musicians. **Queen Elizabeth Hall** and the **Purcell Room** are smaller venues more suited to chamber music, New Age music, recitals, folk music, and some theater pieces. For general information and schedules, phone 928-3002. The **National Film Theatre** (928-3232) produces festivals of cinematic achievement built around the work of a particular director, performer, period, or theme. The **National Theatre Company** has three venues in the complex: the **Cottesloe,** in-the-round seating for four hundred; the **Lyttelton,** a proscenium theater with 890 seats; and the **Olivier,** with a thrust stage into the audience of 1,160. For information and schedules, phone the information desk, 633-0880. To buy tickets with any major credit card, phone 928-2252.

Not merely in the evening but all day long the **South Bank Centre** provides primo artistic diversion. The complex opens at 10 A.M. and there is lunchtime music daily at 12:30, commuter jazz Friday evenings at 5:15. Those are just the official offerings on the network of esplanades; you're also likely to find buskers singing, fiddling, telling jokes, pantomiming, and generally cutting up.

During the day you can explore the **Hayward Gallery,** open Monday through Wednesday from 10 A.M. to 8 P.M., Thursday through Saturday from 10 A.M. to 6 P.M., Sunday from 12 to 6 P.M.; admission is £4.00. The gallery specializes in contemporary painting and photography.

New to the South Bank is the **Museum of the Moving Image,** or MOMI (open Tuesday through Saturday, 10 A.M. to 8 P.M., Sunday from 10 A.M. to 6 P.M.; admission £3.25). From the first magic lantern show to MTV, anything and everything having to do with film is examined in an original and diverting way, from movies, costumes, stills and sets, to actors who mingle with delighted patrons. Not to miss.

The **South Bank Crafts Centre** is located on the ground level tucked in the east side of Waterloo Bridge. Here you can find ceramics, jewelry, weaving, and woodworking on Tuesdays through Sundays. Many of the artisans have workshops on the premises and give informal demonstrations.

One of the most fascinating things here is a backstage tour of the National Theatre. Guides will take you into the guts of the operation to show you what really makes the curtain and the lights go up. The visits last about an hour and a quarter, begin at 10:15 A.M., and run at regular intervals Monday through Saturday; admission is £2.50. Schedules are sometimes juggled to accommodate special events, so it's best to call in advance to check (633-0880).

And if all this weren't enough, there are bookstores and cafés and terraces and the Jubilee Gardens next door for picnics. During special festivals tents are set up in the gardens for free summer concerts, and barges pull up along the water's edge from which are shot massive rounds of fireworks. In all, this is a most exciting place to be.

. . . and More Theater

The National Theatre grew out of a company that originally performed in a theater close by these impressive new surroundings. Standing firm amid urban teardowns and traffic is the Chippendale-topped façade of the **Old Vic.** It was founded by Emma Cons, for whom the gardens opposite are named, a pupil of the Victorian critic John Ruskin. The Old Vic is still very much in operation at Waterloo Road and the Cut. The company tends to produce updated versions of classics or debut new pieces. For information, phone 928-7616. To make a credit-card reservation, phone 261-1821.

At No. 66 the Cut is the **Young Vic,** a cinderblock box of a building wherein are performed contemporary, riskier productions. The theater is pleasantly small and tickets are cheap—less than £10. For information, phone 928-6363. To make credit-card reservations, phone 379-4444.

 This neighborhood is a wasteland for restaurants. One very special exception is **South of the Border** on Joan St., a left turn off the Cut east of the Young Vic. The border in question is the Pacific equator, and this restaurant features Indonesian and

South Pacific specialties. There are straw chairs, flowers, and funky art to give you that down-under feeling. Try a jug of one of the chef's special drinks.

PUBS

While we're on the subject of imbibing, as mentioned before, there are a few terrific pubs not directly on your parade route. They are a long way from anywhere on foot. You might like to try the trip by bike, but bring a map along; otherwise, play it safe and take a taxi. As mentioned, Sun. lunch is a very good idea.

The Angel, 26 Rotherhithe St. This began as a tavern run by monks. There are still the remains of trap doors used by smugglers. There is a cask-shaped bar and ship's lantern to carry on the nautical theme. Along the stairs are prints and photos of local relevance. The upstairs dining room is surprisingly elegant, with table mats, linen napkins, and a terrific view.

The Mayflower, 117 Rotherhithe High St. This tavern is an 18th-century building originally named the Spread Eagle and Crown. The name was changed to Mayflower in deference to the ship that sailed the Pilgrims to Massachusetts. Captain Christopher Jones had sailed his ship into port at Rotherhithe and was enjoying a jar with the lads when he learned that his mission was to transport some conscientious objectors to the New World. It was from Jones's ship that the tavern took its present name. To celebrate the trans-Atlantic connection, the Mayflower is the only pub in London licensed to sell both U.K. and U.S. postage stamps.

The Goose and Firkin, Borough and Southwark Bridge roads. Unlike the other two, this pub is not on the Thames, but it is remarkable because it is the home of London's only home-brewed ales. In the basement is Bruce's Brewery, which puts forth several selections including: Goose—weak; Borough—medium; and Dog Bolter—dangerous or, as the barman says, "It's not good, it's GREAT. Do be careful with it, though, especially with attractive young ladies." There are wood floors and benches and a collection of private-brewery coasters tacked up behind the bar. There is usually live music Tues. through Sat.

8

SHOPPING

We know that for some travelers shopping can be the raison d'être for the entire trip. Like all major European cities, London is a terrific place to shop; whether you come home laden with parcels or spend several ecstatic hours a day window-shopping, London should have those consumer juices flowing in no time.

Shopping in a big city should be an event, not like running to the grocer's for a quart of milk or to the mall to see if they have any T-shirts on sale. Big-city shopping is as important and intrinsic to London as are the British Museum and the National Theatre. In our shopping section, therefore, we include stores and neighborhoods unlike those you can find at home. We list only a few department and chain stores because shopping at such places is pretty much the same the world over. There's no point in spending pots of money to fly across the ocean to shop in a store that's essentially the same as one in your town that you could reach on a gallon's worth of gas.

We also include shops that sell items that you can't find elsewhere in the world—items native and exclusive to Britain. With the pound as high as it is against other currencies, it simply does not make sense to come to London to buy French perfume or Italian shoes. You can find such items at more favorable rates of exchange at home. These listings concentrate on things British—the best of British designers, tailors, shoemakers; luxurious English soaps and toiletries; country-house chintz fabrics and fine antiques—for which London is duly celebrated.

Most major department stores and boutiques accept credit cards or traveler's checks. If possible, using a credit card is the best way to pay for any item. If you pay in cash, the money changes hands immediately. If you pay by credit card, the money remains in your bank account earning interest for you that much longer. Additionally, credit cards are obliged to give you the best rate of exchange on the day of your purchase; you will not be able to get so favorable a rate if you are changing money on your own.

V.A.T.

One almost hesitates to mention V.A.T. (Value Added Tax); the process for reclaiming money on any purchases you might have made is annoying and time-consuming (one assumes it was made to be that way in order to discourage as many people as possible from bothering to cash in).

Not every shop operates a V.A.T. scheme, and the ones that do usually require a minimum purchase (£50) to qualify. When you make a purchase, they will give you a V.A.T. form for you to fill out along with a stamped, self-addressed envelope. When you leave Britain, you must carry your purchase on the plane with you so that you may produce it for British customs along with your V.A.T. form. They will stamp the form, then you must mail it (from the airport, so the stamp will be good) back to the addressee (the store where you purchased it). The store will then send a refund to your home address. Usually the refund will be in pounds sterling, so you will then have to exchange the check at your bank, and lose more money on it. As you can see, the whole program is more trouble than it's worth, unless you spend a lot of money in one store.

We have divided the shopping section into categories according to type of item. As you may have noticed, many shops were included in the *London by Neighborhood* chapter. Some of those shops appear here as well. The rest are in the quick reference list at the end. In the case of shops with several branches in London, we have listed the flagship store.

To the right of each store name, you'll find the name of the neighborhood it's located in, followed in most cases by a key to the atlas. For example, to locate Aquascutum on the map, you would turn to page 5 of the atlas and find where the coordinates 3 and C meet.

CLOTHING

Clothes in London divide themselves easily into two categories: the traditional "correct English" look you'll find on Savile Row and the Bond streets, and the new wave of British designers who take their cue from modern architecture and street fashion.

One of the best-known names in this latter category is Vivienne Westwood, whose taste runs from biker babe to Barbie doll, and who helped pioneer several waves of punk ten years ago. Katherine Hamnett is a fan of close-to-the-body knit dressing in muted (usually black) shades. Rifat Ozbek brings his Middle Eastern sensibility to well-cut, adventurous, structured designs. Joseph (Bis, Tricot, or Pour la Maison) is a huge fan of knitwear in layers and monochromes. Jean Muir actually is one of the Old Guard, having been designing for decades; however, Muir's take on fabrics and shapes is always experimental, innovative. Zandra Rhodes has also been around for a while, but her frothy, billowy styles remain eye-catching.

TRADITIONAL ENGLISH CLOTHING

Aquascutum   MAYFAIR; P. 5, 3C
100 Regent St., tel. 734-6090
Raincoats and smart clothing to go underneath in the best of fabrics and understated palettes.

Burberrys
SOHO; P. 5, 3D
18–22 Haymarket, tel. 930-3343
Rain gear in the beige, black, red, white plaid. Clothes with a bit of the sportsman's scent about them.

Droopy and Browns
MARYLEBONE; P. 2, 3B
16–17 St. Christopher's Place, tel. 935-3198
Frilly, silly, fun party dresses for debs and pretenders.

Fenwick of Bond Street
MAYFAIR; P. 5, 3C
63 New Bond St., tel. 629-9161
Department store for correct, if not wildly daring, designers for the executive man or woman who is such.

Hardy Ames
MAYFAIR; P. 5, 3C
14 Savile Row, tel. 734-2436
The Queen's dressmaker. Look at her photos. 'Nuf said.

Jasper Conran
SOUTH KENSINGTON; P. 4, 5A
37 Beauchamp Place, tel. 589-4243
Could also be listed with the moderns. Clothes that allow even executives to be "interesting."

Laura Ashley
MAYFAIR; P. 2, 3C
256–258 Regent St., tel. 734-5824
Floral prints, flounces, sailor dresses. Has any woman on the planet not seen or worn one?

Liberty's
MAYFAIR; P. 2, 3C
210–220 Regent St., tel. 734-1234
Delicious cotton prints in paisley and tiny florals. Dresses for women and suits for men. Terrific clothes for little girls.

Marc O'Polo
COVENT GARDEN; P. 5, 3D
3–7 Southampton St., tel. 831-1501
Simple, comfortable sportswear for men and women.

Naturally British
COVENT GARDEN; P. 2, 3D
13 New Row, tel. 240-0551
Homemade, but not housebound. Unusual and one-of-a-kind clothes and gifts.

Paul Smith
COVENT GARDEN; P. 2, 3D
41–44 Floral St., tel. 379-7133
This is a cross between the old and the new—old ideas like suits and ties given new twists like color and fun. Not for the timid.

The Scotch House
SOUTH KENSINGTON; P. 4, 4B
2 Brompton Rd., tel. 581-2151
Mission control for north-of-the-border favorites like tweed, tartan, and cashmere.

Tommy Nutter
MAYFAIR; P. 5, 3C
19 Savile Row, tel. 734-0831
A casual name on a formal street. Men's tailoring done with style and expertise.

Turnbull & Asser
71–72 Jermyn St., tel. 839-5133
The Prince of Wales's shirtmakers draw on years' experience
at pleasing the most demanding of clientele.

THE MODERNS

Academy
188A King's Rd., tel. 352-0507
Showcase for the best young British designers whose work and
prices are climbing the ladder to fashion success.

Arkitect
No. 1 Langley Court, tel. 240-5071
Traditional clothes gone haywire. Jackets in chartreuse silk,
skirts with darts in weird places. For men and women.

Boy
153 King's Rd., tel. 351-1115
Funky, punky clothes with the logo printed larger-than-life on everything.

Brown's
South Molton St., tel. 491-7833
Row houses full of the best of British and Continental upscale
avant-garde. Plenty of traditional-style clothing as well.

Christopher New
52 Dean St., tel. 734-5363
Not-too-far-out clothes for the trendy traditionalist. Has seen
them come and go and managed to keep them coming.

Ice Station
294 Pentonville Rd., tel. 278-0230
Not on the usual beaten track, with an inventory of offbeat
clothes from new British designers. Check out the art gallery
downstairs.

Joseph Bis
166 Sloane St., tel. 235-6117
Along with **Joseph Pour la Maison** 16 Sloane St., tel. 235-
9868 and **Joseph Tricot,** 16 South Molton St., tel. 408-2031,
are the brainchildren of Joseph Ettedgui, whose taste favors
body-conscious cuts and knits in basic colors.

Katherine Hamnett
264 Brompton Rd., tel. 584-1136
King's Rd. gone uptown and up-price. Minis, jeans, T-shirts in
good sturdy fabrics at more-than-sturdy prices.

World's End
430 King's Rd., tel. 352-6551
And you'll figure you've got there by the time you trek out here,
but it's worth the hike if you're into raffish, outré fashion from
Vivienne Westwood.

Workers For Freedom
4 Lower John St., tel. 734-3767

High-minded name for high-quality goods whose prices are not overly high. Men's and women's wear for casual living.

Zandra Rhodes

MAYFAIR; P. 5, 3C

14A Grafton St., tel. 499-6695
An established name in an establishment neighborhood, yet there's nothing old-ladyish about Ms. Rhodes's fluid, sheer, floral creations for women.

DEPARTMENT STORES

Dickins & Jones

MAYFAIR; P. 2, 3C

224–244 Regent St., tel. 734-7070
Soigné surroundings for top European designers.

Harrods

BELGRAVIA; P. 4, 4B

Old Brompton Rd., tel. 730-1234
The world-famous. Food halls are better than fashion. Still, if you tell your friends you skipped shopping here, what will they think?

Harvey Nichols

BELGRAVIA; P. 4, 4B

Old Brompton Rd., tel. 235-5000
Variety of featured designers from sedate to sexy. Down the street from you-know-who and often less claustrophobic.

Liberty's

MAYFAIR; P. 2, 3C

200 Regent St.
(see "Traditional English Clothing," above)

Selfridges

MARYLEBONE; P. 1, 3B

400 Oxford St., tel. 629-1234
Started by an American, best for menswear and one-stop shopping for the ladies. Miss Selfridge for the younger set.

BARGAIN

The Constant Sale Shop

CHELSEA; P. 4, 5A

56 Fulham Rd., tel. 589-1458
A bargain-basement feel in fashionable Fulham. Haute couture, prix bases.

Hyper Hyper

KENSINGTON

34 Kensington High St., tel. 937-6964
Huge venue for young designers on the move who sell their soon-to-be-celebrated wares from market stalls. Terrific fun.

Monsoon

MARYLEBRONE; P. 1, 3C

67 South Molton St., tel. 499-3987
Indian cotton prints gussied up to appeal to the young romantic. Cheaper than anything else on the block.

A Shop Called Sale

COVENT GARDEN; P. 2, 3D

28 Bedfordbury, tel. 240-9730
Silly name, but to the point. Designer clothes for men and women at great savings.

Thomas Pink

THE CITY; P. 3, 3G

16 Cullum St., tel. 929-1405
A discount store for those dressing for the City nearby. High-minded clothes, low-brow prices.

Warehouse
27 Duke St., tel. 486-5270
Constantly changing displays of fashions for the savvy woman with a sense of humor. Not having long-term stock keeps prices down.

Zap
413 Mare St., tel. 985-2491
You should probably call for directions, because this isn't exactly on the route of the traditional tourist, but it is a great place for menswear that's for the conservative or the adventurous, at most reasonable prices.

FURNISHINGS

People have been coming to London in droves for years to outfit their homes like the English country houses they've seen on *Masterpiece Theatre.* London abounds in stores with all the swags and chintz your heart could desire. And most importantly, you can buy direct from the supplier here, whereas abroad you must have a decorator order for you—and pay the ensuing extra charges. Unfortunately, though, modern British design lags way behind that of the Continent, and most contemporary furniture fashion is imported.

Colefax & Fowler
39 Brook St., tel. 493-2231
The perfect place to pick up traditional English fabrics and wall coverings.

The Conran Shop
81 Fulham Rd., tel. 589-7401
Terence's dreamchild in the Michelin Building. A place to be seen at as well as to shop for designer furniture and accessories from around the world.

Designers Guild
King's Rd., tel. 351-5775
Guild is the surname of the owner, who prefers a modern twist to traditional fabrics and papers, accessories and furniture.

Freuds
198 Shaftesbury Ave., tel. 831-1071
Furniture and accessories for the modern home with a great sense of style and originality.

Halcyon Days
14 Brook St., tel. 629-8811
Sells the most precious, delicately painted enamel snuffboxes, cigarette lighters, jewelry cases to all the Royals.

Liberty's
200 Regent St., tel. 734-1234
Longtime purveyors of sumptuous home-furnishing fabrics in signature nouveau designs.

Ogetti
CHELSEA; P. 4, 5A
133 Fulham Rd., tel. 581-8088
Hyper-designed furniture and accessories. Is it an object or an *objet*? Good for gifts.

Sanderson
MARYLEBONE; P. 2, 2C
52 Berners St., tel. 636-7800
An old favorite for old-fashioned style and solicitousness in wall coverings and matching fabrics.

Watts & Co.
WESTMINSTER; P. 5, 5D
7 Tufton St., tel. 222-7169
Authentic fabrics and papers (Watts has been making them for 200 years). Where to go for the real thing, not a nouveau.

Zoffany
MAYFAIR; P. 4, 3B
63 South Audley St., tel. 629-9262
Wallpapers and fabrics copied from actual English country houses and French chateaux.

ANTIQUES

Unlike other types, antiques shops tend to be clustered in various areas of the city. The best places to find the finest are Pimlico Rd. and Bond St., Old and New. Just-under-top-drawer selections can be found in South Ken and Chelsea, and along Kensington Church St. Bargain hunters can try their luck around Portobello Rd. and Camden Passage in Islington. Red-letter days for antiquers come in April for the Chelsea Antiques Fair held at Chelsea Old Town Hall; in June at the Fine Art & Antiques Fair at the Olympia Exhibition Centre; and twice in Sept., again at Chelsea Old Town Hall, and at the Burlington House Fair at the Royal Academy.

Bennison
BELGRAVIA; P. 4, 5B
91 Pimlico Rd., tel. 730-3370
The finest in 18th- and 19th-century furniture at appropriately elevated prices.

George Johnson Ltd.
KENSINGTON
120 Kensington Park Rd., tel. 229-3119
17th- and 18th-century fine hardwood furniture and clocks.

H. C. Baxter and Sons
CHELSEA; P. 4, 6A
191–95 Fulham Rd., tel. 352-9826
Collections of 18th-century English furniture.

Harvey and Co.
MAYFAIR; P. 5, 3C
5 Old Bond St., tel. 499-8385
A new address for this family-run business dealing in mid-17th to mid-19th-century antiques.

Hoff Antiques Limited
KENSINGTON
66A Kensington Church St., tel. 229-5516
English and Continental antiques and porcelain.

Mallett and Son
MAYFAIR; P. 2, 3C
40 New Bond St., tel. 499-7411
The finest of English art and antiques at the highest of prices.

Norman Adams Ltd.
BELGRAVIA; P. 4, 4B
8–10 Hans Rd., tel. 589-5266
Across from Harrods; Sheraton furniture to chandeliers.

Stair & Co Ltd.
MAYFAIR; P. 4, 3B
120 Mount St., tel. 499-1784
This international firm stocks the toniest antiques and accessories.

AUCTIONEERS

If you like the thrill of contest and possibly the thrill of buying an overlooked masterpiece for a song (although this is indeed rare these days), try the active shopping at:

Bonhams
SOUTH KENSINGTON; P. 4, 4A
Montpelier Galleries, Montpelier St., tel. 584-9161

Christie's
ST. JAMES'S; P. 5, 4C
CHELSEA; P. 4, 5A
8 King St., tel. 839-9060
and 85 Old Brompton Rd., tel. 581-7611

Phillips
MAYFAIR; P. 5, 3C
Blenstock House, 7 Blenheim St., tel. 629-7702

Sotheby's
MAYFAIR; P. 2, 3C
34–35 New Bond St., tel. 493-8080

COSMETICS AND TOILETRIES

One of the best gifts you can give to a friend or to yourself from London is an exclusive cosmetic preparation, a luxurious natural sponge, a boar's bristle shaving brush, or a mahogany-handled razor from one of the city's purveyors of delectables for the bath. Our recommendations:

The Body Shop
SOHO; P. 2, 3C
32–34 Great Marlborough St., tel. 437-5237
One of many stores in London that sell cosmetics for moderns in flavors like rain and raspberry ripple. Not tested on animals.

Crabtree and Evelyn
KENSINGTON
6 Kensington Church St., tel. 937-9335
Again, one in a chain of stores (this time worldwide) that sell to sweet young things who want to stay that way.

Czech and Speake
ST JAMES'S; P. 5, 3C
39C Jermyn St., tel. 439-0216
Traditional chemists whose Number 88 has been scented on the best of men for years.

D. R. Harris & Co. Ltd.
ST. JAMES'S; P. 5, 4C
29 St. James's St., tel. 930-3915

Since 1790 Daniel and Henry's shop has been selling lavender water, bewitching soap, and the Original Pick-Me-Up to the gentry. Specializing in handmade and natural products 200 years before it became fashionable.

J. Floris
ST. JAMES'S; P. 5, 3C

89 Jermyn St., tel. 930-2885
Take away the best of British floral scents in soaps, shampoos, colognes in a royal-and-gold Floris bag.

Neal's Yard Apothecary
COVENT GARDEN P. 2, 3D

Neal's Yard, tel. 379-7222
Natural and holistic preparations sold in beautiful blue-glass flagons.

Penhaligon
COVENT GARDEN; P. 2, 3D

41 Wellington St., tel. 836-2150
More British floweriness at this traditional shop, which will wrap up gift packages most willingly.

QUICK INDEX TO SHOPS

Following is an index to stores which have been discussed elsewhere in this guide.

Academy Soho　　SOHO; P. 2, 3C
13 Newburgh St.; tel. 439-3225

The Africa Centre　　COVENT GARDEN; P. 2, 3C
38 King St.; tel. 836-1973

Anouska Hempel　　CHELSEA; P. 4, 5A
2 Pond Pl.; tel. 589-4191

Aurora Crystals　　COVENT GARDEN; P. 2, 3D
Neal's Yard; tel. 379-0818

Berry Brothers and Rudd, Ltd.　　ST. JAMES'S; P. 5, 4C
3 St. James's St.; tel. 839-9033

Bluebird Records　　MARYLEBONE; P. 1, 2A
376–78 Edgeware Rd.; tel. 723-9090

The Book Boat　　GREENWICH
Cutty Sark Gardens, Greenwich; tel. 853-4383

Browse and Darby　　MAYFAIR; P. 5, 3C
19 Cork St., Burlington Arcade; tel. 437-0750

Bruce Oldfield　　KNIGHTSBRIDGE; P. 4, 5A
41 Beauchamp Pl.; tel. 581-8934

Bugle House　　SOHO P. 2, 2C
Noel and Berwick Sts.; tel. 439-2282

The Changing Room　　MARYLEBONE; P. 1, 3B
10 Gees Ct., St. Christopher's Pl.; tel. 408-1596

Chevignon　　BLOOMSBURY; P. 2, 2C
One Charlotte St.; tel. 436-1280

**Contemporary Applied Arts
Centre**   COVENT GARDEN; P. 2, 3D
43 Earlham St.; tel. 836-6993

Counter Spy Shop   MAYFAIR; P. 4, 3B
62 South Audley St.; tel. 408-0287

Craftsmen's Potters Shop   SOHO; P. 2, 3C
7 Marshall St.; tel. 437-7605

Design Council   SOHO; P. 5, 3D
28 Haymarket; tel. 839-8000

Dickens's Old Curiosity Shop   HOLBORN; P. 2, 3E
13–14 Portsmouth St.; tel. 405-9891

Domus   CHELSEA; P. 4, 5A
266 Brompton Rd.; tel. 589-9457

Edward Stanford   COVENT GARDEN; P. 2, 3D
12–14 Long Acre; tel. 836-1321

Fortnum & Mason   ST. JAMES'S; P. 5, 3C
181 Piccadilly; tel. 734-8040

Garrard and Co., Crown Jewellers   MAYFAIR; P. 5, 3G
112 Regent St.; tel. 734-7020

Grays in the Mews   MAYFAIR; P. 1, 3C
1–7 Davis St.; tel. 493-7861

Hackett Clothiers   CHELSEA
656 New King's Rd; tel. 731-2790

Hamley's   MAYFAIR; P. 2, 3C
188–96 Regent St.; tel. 734-3161

**Her Majesty's Stationery Office
Book Store**   HOLBORN; P. 2, 2E
49 High Holborn; tel. 873-0011

HMV   SOHO; P. 2, 3C
150 Oxford St.; tel. 631-3423 and 363 Oxford St.; tel. 629-1240

Janet Fitch   BLOOMSBURY; P. 2, 2C
2 Percy St.; tel. 636-5631

Jessop Classic Photographica   BLOOMSBURY; P. 2, 2D
67 Great Russell St; tel. 831-3640

Jones   CHELSEA; P. 4, 5B
King's Rd.; tel. 352-6899

Le Set   CHELSEA; P. 4, 6A
115 Fulham Rd.; tel. 581-3676

Lock & Company   ST. JAMES'S; P. 5, 4C
6 St. James's St.; tel. 930-8874

Mulberry Co.   MARYLEBONE; P. 1, 3B
11–12 Gee's Ct.; tel. 493-2546

Neville-Daniel Sloane St. Ltd.   CHELSEA; P. 4, 5B
175 Sloane St.; tel. 235-6683

Paxman Musical Instruments   COVENT GARDEN; P. 2, 3D
Long Acre; tel. 240-3642

Peter Leonard Assoc.   SOHO; P. 2, 3C
1–5 Poland St.; tel. 734-6945

Pineapple Store   COVENT GARDEN; P. 2, 3D
7 Langley St.; tel. 836-4004

Purdey and Son's   MAYFAIR; P. 4, 3B
57 South Audley St.; tel. 499-1801

Ray's Jazz Shop   COVENT GARDEN; P. 2, 3D
180 Shaftesbury Ave.; tel. 240-3969

Rebecca   COVENT GARDEN; P. 2, 3D
66 Neal St.; tel. 379-4958

Rothmans   ST. JAMES'S; P. 5, 4D
4 Pall Mall; tel. 930-6937

Rough Trade   KENSINGTON
130 Talbot Rd.; tel. 229-8541

Sam Walker   COVENT GARDEN; P. 2, 3D
41 Neal St.; tel. 240-7800

The Shop for Boy   CHELSEA; P. 4, 6A
153 King's Rd.; tel. 351-1115

The South Bank Crafts Centre   SOUTH BANK; P. 5, 4E
Waterloo Bridge; tel. 921-0850

Tower Records   SOHO; P. 5, 3D
1 Picadilly Circus; tel. 439-2500

R. Twining & Co.   THE CITY; P. 5, 3D
216 The Strand; tel. 353-3511

Virgin Mega Store   SOHO; P. 2, 2D
14–16 Oxford St.; tel. 636-1771

Waddington Graphics   MAYFAIR; P. 5, 3C
4 Cork St., Burlington Arcade; tel. 439-1866

Westaway & Westaway   BLOOMSBURY; P. 2, 2D
62–65, 92–93 Great Russell St.; tel. 405-4479/636-1718

9

RESTAURANTS

Rules, London's oldest restaurant, has been serving pretty much without interruption since it opened as oyster bar in 1798. So if you ate there last time you visited London, you can look forward to eating there again in 1990. London has several such historic restaurants, yet from the point of view of eating out it's by no means quaint or old-fashioned. The British capital is up there among the world's top five gastronomic capitals, with over 30 international cuisines now represented, so change is what you should expect. And if a restaurant you loved on your 1989 visit is still open in 1990 the chances are that it will have changed.

Expect diversity, too, when you're planning on eating out in London. You can select from just about any national, regional, or hybrid cuisine. And you can select any price level, paying from £3 for three courses—plus the cost of a can of beer you take in—to over £100 for a gourmet meal by a leading chef, served with fine wines.

At its best, food in London can be great at all price levels, but planning is the key word for successful eating out whatever your budget. In London you really have to know where to eat—and that's an understatement. If you don't and your luck or your instinct fails you, mealtimes can become a study in culinary mediocrity, sullen service, and even dubious hygiene—in all the price brackets, right up to the highest. Discerning Londoners themselves avoid their city's worst eating places by using a restaurant guide. Egon Ronay's *Lucas Guide* and others list only the best and most celebrated restaurants in Great Britian; *The Time Out Guide to Eating Out in London* is the only one devoted exclusively to London restaurants of all types and prices.

The eating places covered on these pages are merely a selection, made to appeal to as diverse a collection of people as possible. We have chosen the most famous London restaurants; in some cases these are the most expensive; in others they're the most fashionable; but in most they are the restaurants with the most famous chefs. We have confined our choice of restaurants to the more central districts, and to those that tourists visit: Covent Garden, Soho, Piccadilly, Chelsea, Knightsbridge. However, an important aspect of our selection has been to insure that we cover as many as possible of London's 20-plus ethnic cuisines, and for this you need to travel out—to Brixton and north to Stroud Green for Afro-Caribbean restaurants; to Camden for the newest tapas bar; East to Brick Lane for genuine Asian cooking. We've also tried to include the best of what is really English: a good fish-and-chips shop; a few good places for breakfast; the best-value hotel carvery for roast beef; a genuine, decent London café; even an old-fashioned East End pie 'n' mash shop.

Our restaurant guide is divided into two sections: general information on eating in London followed by The Selections—our list of best bets. The first pages give you guidance on how to choose a restaurant in London—where to eat, what the best cuisines are, chefs to watch for. Throughout these pages are a round-up of restaurant choices, some that made our selections list and some just worth mentioning. In the case of the latter, pertinent information is given for each such establishment as it comes up. The restaurants on our selections list with addresses, telephone numbers, reviews, opening hours, prices, and credit cards accepted are toward the end of the chapter.

DISTRICTS TO EAT IN

If you had no restaurant guide and wanted to know what district to head for where you'd be pretty sure of finding a good place to eat, the answer would be: Covent Garden or Soho in the West End. Covent Garden, the center of London's theaterland, was until a few years ago the capital's fruit and vegetable market. The market has since moved, and the lovely Victorian iron and glass buildings that housed it have been converted into shops and restaurants. You can sit in the sun at one of the tables out on the Piazza and watch street entertainers perform in front of St. Paul's (The Actors') Church.

In the streets around are many excellent restaurants: **The Calabash** in the Africa Centre, where you can try dishes from all over the African continent, for example, or **Joe Allen,** one of London's premier American restaurants. Next door to Joe Allen is **Orso,** the superb, fashionable Italo-American restaurant opened by Joe Allen.

Up on Shorts Gardens is Neal's Yard, a pretty courtyard full of vegetarian and whole-food shops, cafés, and restaurants. **Neal's Yard Tea Rooms** consists of a downstairs take-away counter where you buy homey vegetarian food to eat in the little tearoom upstairs. (6 Neal's Yard, WC2; tel. 836-5199; open 10:30 A.M.–7:30 P.M. Mon., Tue., Thur., Fri.; 10:30 A.M.–5 P.M. Wed.; 10:30 A.M.–4:30 P.M. Sat.)

And in the little complex of streets full of secondhand and antiquarian booksellers off St. Martin's Lane and Charing Cross Rd. you'll find **Chez Solange,** one of the area's oldest French restaurants and an essential pre-theater venue.

Soho, which starts on the west side of Charing Cross Rd., has always been the most adventurous part of the capital. In the 17th century it was London's westernmost frontier, a successful speculative property venture settled by the fashionable and aristocratic who were spearheading a breakout from the confining walls of the crowded, dirty City. The gentry moved on west, and Soho became a focus of foreign immigration—first from France, later from everywhere: ". . . Untidy, full of Greeks, Ishmaelites, cats, Italians, tomatoes, restaurants, organs, coloured stuffs, queer names, people looking out of upper windows . . ." wrote John Galsworthy of Soho in *The Forsyte Saga.*

It has retained some of its original character. The French are best represented by **Maison Bertaux** at No. 28 Greek St. (the Shaftesbury Ave. end). This redolent patisserie, now 118 years old, still employs the same number of people in the same labor-intensive, on-site bakery as in Victorian times. Only the best, freshest butter and cream are used in Bertaux's delectable croissants, brioches, buns, and tarts—as you'll discover if you try them in the little upstairs café. (tel. 437-6007; open 9 A.M.–7 P.M. Mon.–Sat.; 9:30 A.M.–1 P.M. and 3–7 P.M. Sun.; no credit cards).

You find the Italians with their delis and restaurants in and around Old Compton Street—an excellent place for cheap eats. When you despair of finding a cup of good coffee in London, take refuge in **Bar Italia** at 22 Frith St. (tel. 437-4520; open 7 A.M.–midnight Mon.–Sat.; 8 A.M.–midnight Sun.; no credit cards). It's tiny, usually crammed, and impossible to get into when there's a soccer game on the video, but it's worth all this for the best cappuccino in town. For cheap eats go to the **Lorelei,** a minuscule, very basic café which for some 33 years now has been serving the best Italian pizza in town. Find it at 21 Bateman St. (tel. 734 0954; open noon–midnight Mon.–Sat.; no credit cards).

The Greeks have moved northward to Charlotte St., W1 (across Oxford St., in Fitzrovia), where you can find Greek restaurants in abundance. Most notable for the party atmosphere is the **Apollonia,** on nearby Percy St., which puts on live Greek music and encourages customers to dance and smash plates every night. Best for the price is the **Venus Kebab House,** at 2 Charlotte St., a corner restaurant with tables out on the sidewalk in summer (tel. 636-4324; lunch noon–3:30 P.M. Mon.–Sat.; dinner 5:30–11:30 P.M. Mon.–Sat.; average £10; credit card, V). Best for food is **The White Tower,** on Percy St., a quaint, charming, and (rare in London these days) old-fashioned restaurant.

Right through the 19th century up until two or three years ago Soho was the sleazy part of London, unequivocally the red-light district, with peep shows and strip clubs taking every available space for rent. Thanks to a dedicated cleanup campaign on the part of residents, business interests, and the municipal authority (Westminster Council) most of its pornographic clientele has been squeezed out in favor of enthusiastic new businesses—Soho now has a settlement of young, up-and-coming fashion designers whose shops you should visit.

The effect of the new local regime on the restaurant trade in this, its historical center in London, has been electrifying. There are now more restaurants than ever in Soho and they're becoming more eclectic. You can sample duck tea-smoked on the premises and spicy seafood at the excellent **Si Chuen** on Old Compton St., an escapee from Chinatown just across Shaftesbury Ave.; or delicate, spicy Vietnamese food at the **Saigon** on

Frith St. and in a host of new restaurants in and around Chinatown.

Americans feeling homesick might indulge in nostalgia at
Ed's Easy Diner (12 Moor St.; tel. 439-1955; open 11:30 A.M.–
midnight Mon.–Thur.; 11:30 A.M.–1 A.M. Fri., Sat.; 11:30 A.M.–11 P.M.
Sun.; average £8; no credit cards). This gleaming reconstruction
of a fifties' American diner stands in such a prime position on
Moor St. you just can't miss it. True to style it has dime (5 pence)
jukebox selectors on the counter and a burger/chili menu.

RESTAURANTS TO BE SEEN IN

It's fair to say that London's most fashionable restaurants—the
restaurants the glitterati go to be seen in—are now in and
around Soho, specifically on Frith St., W1. The oldest of these
is **L'Escargot,** on Greek St., which has been fashionable since
it was taken over and reopened by restaurateur Nick Lander.
Downstairs is a brasserie, the main attraction between 6–7 P.M.
because you can buy drinks without accompanying food; but the
restaurant upstairs is also very much patronized by media people and politicians. Various stars—from young English chef Martin Lam to Jancis Robinson, the wife of Nick Lander and creator
of the restaurant's outstanding wine list, and more recently the
beloved Elena, who officiates at the front of house—have
helped to keep this restaurant in the limelight for some five or
six years. Nick Lander was forced to retire but the rest of the
team work on.

Way over the West side of Soho, behind Piccadilly Circus, is
the stylish **Sutherlands,** opened only this year by Gary Hollihead, currently London's most fêted new chef. If food is your
passion you must book ahead from abroad to be sure of being
able to enjoy his colorful, definitely-flavored, thoroughly modern
cooking.

You should have no trouble booking into either of the above
two restaurants since both have ample seating, but if your visit
to London is to be short you must write well ahead to book a
table at **Alastair Little,** on Frith St. Prices of meals cooked
by this celebrated, self-taught chef are high, at £30 or more (including pricey wines), but the food exhibits life and imagination.

London's trendiest restaurants are not all in Soho. The opportunity to buy one of the capital's most beautiful buildings—the
Michelin Building at the junction of Knightsbridge, South Kensington, and Chelsea—inspired designer Terence Conran to
open his new restaurant. The Michelin Building is now beautifully
restored and more than a year later **Bibendum** is still one of
the capital's trendiest places to eat. The chef is the revered
Simon Hopkinson, who cooks basic French food. Book about
a fortnight in advance.

Also one year into the see-and-be-seen stakes is **Kensington Place,** a glass-fronted restaurant on Kensington Church
St. Run by Nick Smallwood and Simon Slater, who have together been responsible for a good many of London's most fashionable restaurants in the past, this restaurant had no chance to
fail. The decor is modern; the chef is award-winning Rowley
Leigh, a former Roux Brothers' trainee; the menu is eclectic. The

time to go is lunchtime, when the kitchen is quietest and the food at its best; the pudding to have is baked tamarillos.

CHEFS YOU SHOULD KNOW ABOUT

Considering the proximity to France, it is to their credit that British chefs, freed by modern electronic gadgetry from the need for huge brigades and a rigorous training system, have jettisoned the influences of the mother country and gone out on their own. In the U.K. the result has been a liberating one. Over the last five years or so London has seen the emergence of a new generation of inspired chef/patrons, some of them brilliant, some self-taught, few trained in the techniques of classic French cuisine, all anxious to develop their own style. Various names have been given to this new cooking: "new British" is one; "modern European" another. Eclectic and progressive is what everyone agrees it is.

Chefs you should not only know about but whose cooking you should try while in London include such luminaries as Alastair Little, Simon Hopkinson, and others mentioned earlier. Equally fashionable is chef/patron Sally Clarke, who serves her innovative brand of West Coast food at **Clarke's** in Kensington Church St., W8. Another woman chef, Carla Tomasi, operates from **Frith's,** on fashionable Frith St. in Soho, a pretty little restaurant with a tiny garden and wonderful food you eat to the accompaniment of live classical music on Fridays and Saturdays.

Last year's *enfant terrible* of British gastronomy, Marco White of **Harvey's,** south of the river in untrendy Tooting, is now settling into stardom more graciously. This young chef, still in his twenties, won a Michelin star within a year of opening his little restaurant. His cooking is complex, interesting, and expensive. You'll have to book *at least one month ahead* to sample it—and you'll be safest if you write some weeks ahead from abroad.

If you book into **Chez Nico,** Nico Landenis's new restaurant on Great Portland Street, you will have to be prepared to toe the line since Nico is notoriously boorish toward customers who, in his view, do not appreciate good food and wines. Book *at least two weeks ahead;* be prepared to forgo martini in favor of a well-selected wine; and for heaven's sake don't smoke between courses. Allow Nico and his wife and daughter, who run the restaurant, to look after you in the way they feel is appropriate and you'll have a meal you'll always remember.

Though his cooking is modern, Pierre Koffman, holder of two Michelin stars, bases his techniques on classic cuisine. He runs the kitchens at **Tante Claire,** in Chelsea, a pretty, airy restaurant run with formality, so a jacket and tie are required at dinner. Staunchest supporters of classic French cookery are the Roux Brothers. **Le Gavroche** in Mayfair is run by Albert Roux, the capital's only chef with three Michelin stars. (You must book at least a week in advance and a jacket and tie are de rigueur.) His brother Michel runs the **Waterside Inn** (just 40 minutes out of London along the M4), a beautiful restaurant overlooking the Thames. Both restaurants are phenomenally expensive but offer excellent value prix fixe lunches. If you intend to spend a

Sunday in London, think in advance about lunch at the Water-side Inn.

CUISINES IN THE NEWS

Not all fashionable food in London is French or modern British—in fact, French food is currently rather out of the news. Highest in the cuisine charts are Spanish, Lebanese, Thai, Vietnamese, and Indonesian. London is proud of its latest Spanish restaurant, **Guernica,** and its young chef who trained in Santander in the *nueva cocina vasca* (new Basque cooking). Have the squid cooked in its own ink. Tapas bars are still opening at quite a rate. There is a good one in Waterloo conveniently near the South Bank Arts Centre—**Meson Don Felipe** (53 The Cut, Waterloo; tel. 920 3237; lunch noon–3 P.M., dinner 5:30–11 P.M. Mon–Fri.; Sat., dinner only 6.30–11 P.M.; average £9; MC, V); near Euston Station—**El Parador** (245 Evershold St; tel. 387 2789; open noon–3 P.M. Mon–Fri., Sun.; 6–11 P.M. Mon–Sat.; MC, V); and out in Notting Hill Gate—**Meson Doña Ana** (37 Kensington Park Rd.; tel. 243-0666; lunch noon–3 P.M.; dinner 5:30–11 P.M. Mon.–Fri.; noon–11 P.M. Sat.; MC, V). All are busy at lunchtime and quieter in the evenings, except on weekends, when they tend to attract a rather loud, young clientele.

Now experiencing something of a renaissance in London is Italian food, partly due—it must be said—to the efforts of Joe Allen (proprietor of **Orso**) and of Enzo Apicella, a veteran Italian-born London restaurateur, owner of the **Pizzeria Condotti** (off Regent Street), cartoonist, and art buff. The most exciting Italian restaurant event this year was the opening of the **River Café** beside the Thames at Hammersmith, a restaurant in a different league from other Italian restaurants in London. The style is rustic; menus change daily and use seasonal ingredients.

The Lebanese restaurant of choice is **Al Sultan** in Mayfair (52 Hertford St.; tel. 408-1155; Underground Hyde Park Corner; open noon–midnight daily; average £16), a new, elegant place serving a bright, trendy crowd. But if you genuinely love Middle Eastern food, don't stop there. Head for Edgware Rd., where the Arab community is based, and walk into almost any restaurant or juice bar along there.

Southeast Asian restaurants win the award for the fastest growth in numbers in recent years—from about 10 in 1985 to over 100 at the end of 1989. Of all the restaurants serving the cooking of the Straits (of Malacca), by far the best is the delightful new **Butterfields,** a wine bar/restaurant hidden away in the basement of church premises in Margaret St., behind Oxford Circus. Half the kitchen produces Malaysian dishes, the other Tex-Mex—an unusual combination, but both taste pretty good to us.

For Thai food, arguably the most authentic place in town is the **Bahn Thai,** located in the building on Frith St. in Soho, in which John Logie Baird first demonstrated television.

It's some time now since American restaurants have been a topic of food gossip in London, but this year Londoners are oh, so proud of everything about the slick new **Mitchell & O'Brien**—the long, lean thirties looks, the dim lighting, the deli, the long bar, and the authentic pastrami on rye. As we write

Mitchells is very much a place to be seen. Find it, if you get homesick, down a little alley running between Wardour St. and Dean St. in Soho.

One French restaurant that has managed to stay fashionable through the trends towards ethnic eating is **L'Artiste Assoifé** in Notting Hill—but it's the eccentric decor as much as the food which is the attraction here.

EATING ETHNIC

London is big and rambling enough for immigrant communities to have their own areas full of character, as New York does. Some, like Southall with its heavily Asian population, are far from the center but still worth a visit. Southall (a short train ride west from Paddington Station) is a colorful mixture of shops selling beautiful sari fabric and Asian dresses; and of the unimaginable collection of stalls that makes up Liberty Market (open every day), selling herbs, spices, clothes, embroidery, and other Oriental knickknacks. There are dozens of Indian restaurants and take-aways in Southall. There's another Indian community in Wembley and the remains of an old one right at the Warren St. end of Whitfield St. Make a point of finding **Anwar's** up there at 64 Grafton Way (tel. 387-6664), near Warren St. Underground (open 10 A.M.–10 P.M. daily). In this wonderful café/take-away everything is fresh and so cheap it's hard to spend £5.

In fact, London is full of Indian restaurants and you don't have to walk far to find a good one. Currently the best is the **Jamdani,** on Charlotte St., opened by chef Amin Ali, who has been responsible for a whole chain of excellent Bengali restaurants across central London. Jamdani is notable for its stark decor and its eclectic menu, which incorporates dishes from all over India. There are little clusters of vegetarian Indian restaurants on Westbourne Grove (Notting Hill Gate Underground/bus 31) and in Drummond St. (Euston Tube/BR or Warren St. Tube).

Notable in Brixton, with its marvelous daily market (at the junction of Brixton Station Rd. and Electric Ave.), full of stalls selling West Indian vegetables, textiles, and music (be cautious at night, however) is **Taste of Africa,** where the food is as hot as it should be.

London's Chinatown is just south of Soho in a pedestrian area centered on Gerrard St. If you want to eat after midnight you can confidently head here, knowing there will be somewhere open if you want to dine at 5 A.M. Gerrard St. and Wardour St. are lined with restaurants serving Cantonese, Sichuan, and Peking food, but in fact, the better ones are discreetly tucked away on Lisle St. (parallel to Gerrard St. and just to the south): **Mr. Kong,** the **New Diamond,** the **Fung Shing,** and the tiny **Poons** are the best Chinese restaurants in Chinatown.

There are few kosher or Israeli restaurants around central London (most are around Finchley Rd. and in Golders Green), with one noble exception: **Grahame's Seafare,** a superb fish and chips restaurant on Poland St. in Soho, where you can ask for your fish to be deep-fried in kosher batter (made from matzo meal) or ordinary batter.

EATING BRITISH

Steer clear of any restaurant with a name prefaced with "Ye Olde"; any with the adjective "traditional" in its description; any menu entitled "Bill of Fayre"; and any meal held in what passes for a banqueting hall. You can find outstanding British cooking—both the old-fashioned homely sort and the progressive modern variety—in many London restaurants, but we've never heard anyone describe the food in these bogus English heritage places as good.

Far better to try dishes resulting from genuine historical research at the few more modest yet more famous British restaurants in London. Dishes such as Elizabethan lamb at the charming **Veronica's** in Bayswater; gindle wakes, a medieval poultry dish, in the recently reopened **Tate Gallery restaurant** (accompanied, of course, by something from the Tate's incomparable wine list); pot-roasted wood pigeon at the new **Jasons Court,** opposite Bond St.; or one of the venison dishes in the hallowed dining-rooms of the venerable **Rules.**

What most visitors love about English food is the roast beef. So do the English, and most restaurants oblige by abandoning their daily menus and individual cooking styles and serving up a roast on Sunday lunchtime. The elegant **Launceston Place** in West Kensington puts a modern British interpretation on two traditional British roasts and a fish dish in a marvelous value prix fixe Sunday lunch.

The London restaurant most famous for its roast beef is **Simpson's Grand Divan Tavern,** where the roasts seemed to us on a recent visit pretty close to perfect. This rather grand restaurant requires formal dress—jacket and tie for men—even at lunch-time, and it tends to be pricey. Our tip for a roast served in the correct atmosphere at a reasonable price would be either the **St. James's Restaurant** on the fourth floor of Fortnum & Mason's department store on Piccadilly—or a hotel carvery. The **Hotel Russell** has a marvelous old carvery (Russell Sq.; tel. 837 6470; lunch 12:30–2:30 P.M., dinner 6–10 P.M., daily). In this type of family restaurant you pay a set price of between £10 and £13 for unlimited returns to counters of starters and a choice of roasts with all the trimmings; dessert, cheese and coffee. Children under five are usually admitted free and those aged 5–14 for half price.

Some of London's oldest restaurants are the fish restaurants and bars. The taste for fish and chips is an acquired one. Most Americans find them greasy, but that's mainly because in the cheaper places they often are. It's worth searching out good ones—such as the kosher **Grahame's** in Soho.

Peculiar and very English are the little eel, pie, and mash shops of turn-of-the-century London. The family owners of these quaint old cafés buy their eels and beef each day at dawn. They prepare the food themselves, serving the jellied or stewed eels and meat pies with mashed potatoes and liqor (parsley sauce). If you want to see one go to **F. Cooke's** (41 Kingsland High St.; tel. 254-2878; Dalston/Kingsland BR; open 10am–8pm Mon., Thur.; 10am–6pm Tue., Wed., 10am–pm Fri, Sat). You may not love the food, but it's nourishing and cheap at an average of £1.50 a plateful.

FOR BREAKFAST, LUNCH, OR TEA

Breakfast tends to be served in restaurants and brasseries from 7 A.M.–11 A.M. or noon. The little streetside cafés (fondly called "caffs") serve fry-ups (fried egg, bacon, sausage, etc.) all day. The oldest and most authentic serve bubble-and-squeak (potatoes and cabbage cooked, mashed together, then fried) and black pudding. The good ones are easy to pick out—they're clean. The cleanest is probably **Andrews,** Gray's Inn Road in Holborn (open 7 A.M.–6 P.M. Mon.–Fri.; unlicensed; no credit cards).

The record for London's most gigantic breakfast has been held unbroken for some years now by the **Fox & Anchor** in the City (115 Charterhouse St., EC1; tel. 253-4838; breakfast served 6:30–11 A.M. Mon.–Fri.). The Fox is a market pub and so has a license to serve alcoholic drinks early in the morning for the benefit of the market porters, so you can order champagne with your mixed grill (£8.50). Brunch, usually served on the weekends between 10:30 A.M. and 2 P.M., is becoming increasingly popular in London, especially for family meals out. The best is reputed to be at **Mitchell & O'Brien.**

Lunch is served usually from 12:30 P.M. to about 3 P.M.—and because the licensing hours have been extended, in many restaurants you will be able to drink through the afternoon if you want to. In central London, as in all big cities, the cafés and restaurants are packed with office workers at lunchtime. Out in the suburbs, however, the opposite is the case, and it would be sensible to contrive to be visiting away-from-the-center museums and other places of interest around lunchtime. If you are in town you'll find that many national monuments have excellent cafés and restaurants. The counter-service café at the **National Gallery** (Trafalgar Square; tel. 930-5210; open Oct.–June 10 A.M.–5 P.M. Mon.–Sat.; 2–5 P.M. Sun.; July–Sept. 10 A.M.–5 P.M. Mon., Tue., Thur.–Sat.; 10 A.M.–7 P.M. Wed.; 2–5 P.M. Sun.; average £6) is run by Justin De Blank, who also runs the excellent café and restaurant in the **British Museum** (open noon–4:15 P.M. Mon.–Sat.; 12:30–5:15 P.M. Sun.; no credit cards and the café in the **General Trading Company Store** on Sloane St. (tel. 730 6400; open 9 A.M. 5:30 P.M. Mon., Tues., Thur.–Sat.; 9 A.M.–7 P.M. Wed.; average £9; no credit cards). The international-style food is varied, very reasonably priced, and good quality; the restaurants are pleasant and spacious. The most impressive of the museum restaurants is the **Tate Gallery Restaurant,** decorated with a mural by Whistler. The food here is British and the wine list is exceptional. The café of the **Museum of London** (London Wall, open 10 A.M.–5 P.M. Tue.–Sat.; noon–5 P.M. Sun.) is half outdoors, half indoors and overlooks a garden. The short menu of sandwiches and snacks makes for a pleasant light lunch or afternoon tea. Don't fail to visit the museum.

Tea is an institution that can now rarely be enjoyed by the British, who must work or be struggling home through rush hour at the appointed time. Tourists should take full advantage. The

Customs and Etiquette

It is sensible to book for any meal at a London restaurant, especially lunch in central London and dinner from Thursday to Monday. Always book for the more expensive, better-known restaurants. You may occasionally be asked to confirm reservations for dinner in writing, or to pay a deposit, especially for parties of six or more. This is a move by restaurateurs to try to combat the increasing number of no-shows, who leave their restaurants half empty at peak dining hours, and it deserves to be treated with some sympathy.

Overbooking by the restaurant staff is unfortunately becoming more common: it's annoying to arrive punctually for your booking only to be told there's no table. A booking is a contract and you're entitled to a table, so most restaurant managers will make you comfortable while they try to sort out the problem. By the same token, if you don't turn up on time they are entitled to give your table to someone else, but in practice most will hold a booking for ten minutes or so.

The menu must be displayed outside or just inside a restaurant. There is often a minimum charge. (You cannot eat the main course in one restaurant and your dessert in another.) All charges, including cover charge, minimum charge, and service, must be written on the menu. Prices must include purchase tax (value added tax, or V.A.T.; it is not added on to the bill at the end). A verbal or written description of the composition of a dish must be accurate, and wines must be accurately labeled.

If you eat a meal you genuinely think is awful you are obliged by law to pay a fair price for it. In a dispute you should tell the restaurant manager the reasons why you feel dissatisfied and try to come to an agreement about what is a fair price; if you can't do this you should pay what you think the meal is worth (taking the standard of the restaurant and the listed price of your meal into account). The management has to accept the payment or take legal proceedings.

If the bill lists a service charge but you don't think the service worth paying for, you are entitled to deduct the charge from the bill, but you must inform the manager of your intentions and your reasons beforehand. In all cases of dispute you must leave your name and address. Such disputes are civil matters vis-à-vis the law, and the restaurant management cannot call in the police. Most instances of customer dissatisfaction are dealt with quickly and easily on the spot and will not reach such an extreme.

You don't have to vacate your table if new customers arrive before you have finished you meal, unless you have agreed to a time limit.

Should an accident occur and a waiter drops food or drink on your clothes, the restaurant management should offer to pay for the cleaning and deduct the amount from the bill, or ask for a receipt to be sent to them and pay in full.

best places for afternoon tea are the hotels: The **Park Room** at the Hyde Park Hotel, with its view over Hyde Park, is a superb place for a cream tea (or, indeed, breakfast). And tea (and breakfast) at the **Ritz** near Green Park Underground station (Piccadilly, tel. 493-8181; Green Park Underground); English (£10.75) and Continental (£7.75) breakfasts are served from 7:30–10:30 A.M. Mon.–Sat. and 8:30–10:30 A.M. Sun.; afternoon teas (£10.50) are served from 3:15 P.M.–4:15 P.M. daily. Both are luxurious experiences for which you should book.

The **St. James's Restaurant,** up on the fourth floor of Fortnum & Mason, Piccadilly, is one of the few places in London still serving high tea: more substantial than afternoon tea but much lighter than dinner. The menu offers a wonderful choice for both breakfast and for afternoon or high tea (which is accompanied by "Classical Tea Music"). Service is polite and efficient as in Fortnum's two other restaurants (**The Fountain** and **The Patio,** where breakfast, afternoon, and high tea are also served).

🖳 THE SELECTIONS

London restaurants change rapidly so you should call ahead to check pertinent information. In the listings below the times given are first and last orders. Most restaurants close an hour to an hour and a half after last orders. The prices are strictly average prices of a three-course meal without wine; you could spend 25 percent more or less depending on what you order. Tipping is usual in London restaurants: 10 percent of the bill in the smaller, cheaper restaurants; 15 percent in the more expensive establishments. The following credit-card abbreviations are used: AE for American Express; MC for MasterCard; V for Visa; CB for Carte Blanche; DC for Diners Club. Keep in mind that not all restaurants accept traveler's checks. To the right of each entry you'll find location information: the restaurant's general location and a reference key to the map of London in the atlas section. Some of London's better restaurants are not within the parameters of our street atlas; in these cases only a neighborhood name is given. In all cases a tube stop or bus numbers are given with the restaurant's address.

Ajimura
COVENT GARDEN; P. 2, 3D

51 Shelton St. (tel. 240-0178). Covent Garden Underground. A picturesque and informal little Japanese restaurant, notable for especially cheap lunches (£6.50) and pre-theater dinners (served 6:30–7:30 P.M.). Ajimura is also noted for sushi. The menu is carefully translated, and the staff either are or speak English. Lunch noon–3 P.M. Mon.–Fri. Dinner 6–11 P.M. Mon.–Sat., 6–10:30 P.M. Sun. **Average £15.** Credit Cards: AE, DC, MC, V.

Alastair Little
SOHO; P. 2, 3D

49 Frith St. (tel. 734-5183). Piccadilly Circus Underground. A small, unpretentious restaurant—you can see right into the kitchen—run by a young, ingenious, self-taught chef who changes his menu twice a day and the emphasis of his cooking as often as the spirit moves him. Alastair has a well-deserved reputation for being good with offal and with fish. His Frith Street

restaurant is one of London's most fashionable. Lunch 12:30–2:30 P.M. Mon.–Fri.; dinner 7–11 P.M. Mon.–Fri. till 11:15 P.M. Sat. **Average £30.** No credit cards.

Apollonia   FITZROVIA; P. 2, 2C
17A Percy St. (tel. 636-4140). Tottenham Court Rd. Underground.
One of Charlotte St.'s many Greek restaurants, selected as one of the best for a plate-smashing, party ambience at night. The ground-floor dining room is a calm place in which to try some decent Greek food and Keo beer; downstairs there is dancing (on dance floor and table), bouzouki playing, singing, and plate-smashing until the early hours. Lunch noon–3 P.M., dinner 6 P.M.–1 A.M., Mon.–Sat. **Average £11.** Credit Cards: AE, DC, MC, V.

L'Arlequin   BATTERSEA
123 Queenstown Rd. (tel. 622-0555). Queenstown Rd. BritRail station.
People for whom nouvelle cuisine can never be passé will love chef Christian Delteil's fine cooking, exquisitely arranged. Like the pastel-painted restaurant dotted with exquisite displays of flowers, the food at L'Arlequin is simple in preparation and beautifully presented. It's expensive but the £16.50 set lunch is a bargain. Lunch 12:30–2 P.M., dinner 7.30–10 P.M., Mon.–Fri. **Average £31. Prix-fixe lunch £16.50.** Credit Cards: AE, DC, MC, V.

L'Artiste Assoiffé   NOTTING HILL
122 Kensington Park Rd. (tel. 727-4714). Notting Hill Gate Underground.
An old-established restaurant, one of a fine tradition of eccentric London eating places. Artiste Assoiffé occupies a residential house on a corner near Notting Hill Gate. The food is French though light and served in portions so large the nouvelle cuisine is not an apt description. More interesting is the decor: This quaint old place is scattered with bric-a-brac collected from junk shops, old buses, and even fair grounds. There's a roaring fire in winter, in summer you can dine out on the terrace. Lunch noon–3 P.M. Sat. only. Dinner 7:30–11 P.M. Mon.–Sat. **Average £15.** Credit cards: AE, MC, V.

Bahn Thai   SOHO; P. 2, 3D
21A Frith St. (tel. 437-8504). Piccadilly Circus Underground.
One of London's oldest Thai restaurants and one of its best. The restaurant, run by an English-Thai couple, is in trendy Frith St. in Soho. The downstairs room is crowded and noisy; the softly decorated, green room upstairs has a hushed, meditative atmosphere. The food is superb (the emphasis here is on seafood) and authentic—but the chef will spice down your curry if you ask when you order. Lunch noon–2:45 P.M. Mon.–Sat.; 12:30–2:30 P.M. Sun. Dinner 6–11:15 P.M. Mon.–Sat.; 6:30–10:30 P.M. Sun. **Average £15.** Credit Cards: AE, MC, V.

Bibendum   SOUTH KENSINGTON; P. 4, 5A
Michelin House, 81 Fulham Rd., SW3 (tel. 581-5817). South Kensington Underground.
British design baron Terence Conran effected a coup when he bought the lovely old Michelin Building at the interface between

Knightsbridge, South Kensington, and Chelsea, restored it, and opened Conran (his new lifestyle shop) and Bibendum in it. Bibendum is beautiful, its clientele is stylish and fashionable, and the food is superb. The chef is the hallowed Simon Hopkinson, renowned for his classically balanced modern French food. Needless to say, you'll have to book to eat here, well in advance. Lunch 12:30–2:30 P.M. Mon.–Fri.; 12:30–3 P.M. Sat. Dinner 7–11.30 P.M. daily. **Average £45 dinner, £19.50 lunch.** Credit Cards: MC, V.

Braganza
SOHO; P. 2, 3D

56 Frith St. (tel. 437-5412). Piccadilly Circus Underground.
A restaurant/brasserie complex, the work of famous restaurant designers Fitch & Co., who have used sculpture in the decor to great effect. When it opened this was the place to be seen in in London and it is still popular. The ground-floor brasserie is busiest; on the second and third floors are spacious dining rooms decorated with frescoes. The food is good: French with Californian inspiration. The wine list is eclectic. Open 11:30 A.M.–11:30 P.M. Mon.-Fri.; 6–11:30 P.M. Sat. **Average £6** brasserie. Credit Cards: AE, DC, MC, V.

Butterfields
OXFORD CIRCUS; P. 2, 3C

84 Margaret St. (tel. 636-8394). Oxford Circus Underground.
In the basement of a building belonging to the exceptionally beautiful Victorian Gothic church over the road is an airy wine bar and restaurant serving the rather unusual combination of Tex/Mex and Straits food. It works well. The Tex/Mex portions are appropriately large and the cooking good. The indefatigable Terry Tan is in charge of the Straits side of the kitchen, turning out Malaysian, Indonesian, and Singaporean dishes prepared with due care and attention to the authenticity of the herbing and spicing. If you're unfamiliar with the cooking of the Straits (of Malacca), Terry has helpfully left copies of his many informative books on the subject lying around. Lunch noon–3 P.M., dinner 5–9 P.M., Mon.–Fri. **Average £15.** Credit Cards: MC, V.

Calabash
COVENT GARDEN; P. 2, 3D

The Africa Centre, 38 King St. (tel. 836-1976). Covent Garden Underground.
This dark, atmospheric restaurant in the basement of the Africa Centre does well the difficult job of representing African cooking. The menu lists dishes from all points of the pan-African compass; respect is paid to Caribbean cooking. The food is consequently varied and very nicely cooked—but the service is an exercise in patience. Lunch 12:30 A.M.–3 P.M. Mon.–Fri. Dinner 6–10:30 P.M. Mon.–Sat. **Average £12.** Credit Cards: AE, DC, MC, V.

Chez Nico
GREAT PORTLAND ST.; P. 2, 2C

35 Great Portland St. (tel. 436-8846). Great Portland Street Underground.
Hot off the wires as we go to press is the news of another Nico Ladenis move. Lately, this chef has not been able to stay put, thus forcing his pilgrims to purchase *London Streetfinders*. Origi-

nally he had just one lauded restaurant in Battersea, Chez Nico. Then he left his sous chef in charge and moved out of town. Last year he moved back to London, closed it, and opened Simply Nico in a back street in Victoria. Now he's renamed that Very Simply Nico, left his sous chef in charge, and has opened Chez Nico Mark II in Great Portland Street. But this is Nico Ladenis, so we don't have even to see it to recommend his new restaurant unreservedly, or to predict that you will have to book ahead of your stay if you want to eat there. Do heed our warnings in the "Chefs You Should Know About" section, and have a wonderful meal.

Chez Solange
COVENT GARDEN; P. 5, 3D

35 Cranbourn St. (tel. 836-0542). Leicester Square Underground.

The French proprietor can remember when Chez Solange was one of only two restaurants in Covent Garden and he catered then, as he does now, to a mainly thespian clientele. A trip to the theater is hardly complete without a meal here. Restaurants serving traditional French food are disappearing in London; this is one of the few, and the menu ranges from simple omelettes to dishes of great complexity. Eat in the restaurant, the brasserie behind it with tables out on St. Martin's Court, or in the downstairs wine bar. Open noon–2 A.M. Mon.-Sat. (last orders 12:15 A.M.). **Average £20. Set lunch and pre-theater menu £13.50.** Credit Cards: AE, DC, MC, V.

Clarke's
WEST KENSINGTON

124 Kensington Church St. (tel. 221-9225). High St. Kensington or Notting Hill Gate Underground.

As a result of her period of pupilage under Alice Waters, the kind of food Sally Clarke cooks is an interesting blend of what Londoners now call "new British" or "modern European," with Californian overtones: colorful salads, perfectly composed pizzas. Her food is simple, with gourmet touches and accompanied by California wines. Sit downstairs, where you can watch Sally at work in her kitchen. Lunch 12:30–2 P.M., dinner 7:30–10 P.M., Mon.-Fri. **Set lunches £14, £16. Set dinner £25; supper** (10–11 P.M.) **£25.** Credit Cards: MC, V.

L'Escargot
SOHO; P. 2, 3D

48 Greek St. (tel. 437-2679). Tottenham Court Rd. Underground.

A former Soho landmark, the brainchild of Nick Lander and his wife Jancis Robinson, who writes the superb wine list, L'Escargot has long been one of the most fashionable places to be seen in London. Not least of its attractions is the discreet Elena Salvoni at the front of the house in the first-floor dining room, who may no longer be young but who is still the darling of the media world. Downstairs is a popular brasserie and upstairs is the restaurant. Lunch 12:30–2:15 P.M. Mon.–Fri. Dinner 6:30–11:15 P.M. Mon.–Sat. Brasserie: Lunch 12:15–3 P.M. Mon.–Fri. Dinner 5:30–11:15 P.M. Mon.–Fri., 6–11:55 P.M. Sat. **Average £20.** Credit Cards: AE, DC, MC, V.

Frith's

14 Frith St. (tel. 439-3370). Tottenham Court Rd. Underground.
Carla Tomasi is chef-proprietor of this pretty Soho restaurant,
where she serves a monthly changing menu of simply cooked
meats and fish, plus wonderful things for vegetarians. Her cooking exhibits diverse influences—from France, Italy, and Southeast Asia. Her breads and cheese board are all frequently
praised, and her wine list is well chosen. Lunch noon–2:30 P.M.
Mon.–Fri. Dinner 6:30–11:30 P.M. Mon.–Sat. **Average £25–30**
(drinks and wines are also expensive). Credit Cards: MC, V.

Fung Shing

15 Lisle St. (tel. 437-1539). Piccadilly Circus Underground.
Cantonese gourmet food is served in elegant, comfortable surroundings here. The menu is varied and imaginative, the food
flawlessly cooked. Booking is usually necessary. Open
noon–11:30 P.M. daily. **Average £15.** Credit Cards: AE, DC, MC,
V.

Le Gavroche

43 Upper Brook St. (tel. 408-0881). Marble Arch Underground.
Albert Roux is justifiably revered as the first chef in Britain to
have won three Michelin stars. His restaurant is not a place to
come to see or to be seen. The clientele is not necessarily famous but consists mainly of well-off people who want to spend
money on gourmet food. There's a very good-value set lunch
for under £30, but if you eat à la carte be prepared to spend up
to £100. The wine list is more like a book than a list and the
markup is high. Lunch noon–2 P.M., dinner 7–11 P.M. Mon.–Fri. **Average £50-£100 à la carte.** Credit Cards: AE, DC, MC, V.

Grahame's Seafare

38 Poland St. (tel. 437-3788/0975). Oxford Circus Underground.
London's gourmet fish and chips restaurant is a kosher establishment and one of its attractions is that you can get fish fried
in crisp matzo meal. The range is wide—from salmon to rock
salmon—and prices are high, though portions are massive. The
takeaway counter is inside the rather old-fashioned, green-
upholstered restaurant. Open noon–2:45 P.M. Mon.; noon–2:45
P.M., 5:30–8:45 P.M. Tue.–Thur., Sat.; noon–2:45 P.M., 5:30–7:30 P.M.
Fri. **Average £10.** Credit Card: V.

Guernica

21A Foley St. (tel. 580-0623). Oxford Circus or Great Portland
Street Underground.
Traditional Spanish dishes are given a new, light twist in the new
style of Basque cooking currently sweeping through Spain. This,
the first serious Spanish restaurant to open in Britain since before World War II, boasts a notable Basque chef, Denat Arroya-
be, who trained in the kitchens of one of the Basque country's
leading restaurants. Lunch noon–3 P.M. Mon.–Fri. Dinner 7–11
P.M. Mon.–Sat. **Average £18. Set lunch £12.** Credit Cards: AE,
DC, MC, V.

Harvey's

2 Bellevue Rd. (tel. 672-0114). Clapham Common Underground.

Within a year of opening his own restaurant in London's outback south of the river, Marco Pierre White became the youngest chef to be awarded a Michelin star. Food pilgrims trek out there in such numbers that you must book about a month in advance for dinner. The enfant terrible of English gastronomy produces an Italian-influenced cuisine, of which his *tagliatelle* of oysters is a classic. Lunch 12:30–2:15 P.M. Mon.–Fri.; 7:30–11 P.M. Mon.–Sat. **Set lunch £15. Set dinner £29.** Credit Cards: MC, V.

Inigo Jones   COVENT GARDEN; P. 2, 3D
14 Garrick St. (tel. 836-6456). Leicester Square Underground. Long heralded as a brilliant chef, Paul Gaylor is a master of nouvelle cuisine and his presentations were among the first to be described as "art on a plate." Rich foods, such as duckling, Norfolk pigeon, and pig's trotter, are transformed by his masterful touch into feather-light creations—but vegetarian gourmets are graced with their own separate menu at £32.50. The wines here are chosen from all wine-producing regions of France. Lunch 12:30–2:30 P.M. Mon.–Fri. Dinner 5:30–11:30 P.M. Mon.–Sat. **Average £55 à la carte. Prix fixe lunch/pre-theater £21.95. Minimum £7.50.** Credit Cards: AE, DC, MC, V.

Jamdani   FITZROVIA; P. 2, 2C
34 Charlotte St. (tel. 636-1178). Goodge St. Underground. Chef Amin Ali, creator of a number of outstanding London restaurants serving Bengali food (Last Days of the Raj in Drury Lane, Covent Garden; Last Days of the Empire in Soho), has surpassed himself with this, his latest venture. Relaxed enough not to feel the need to stick to one cuisine and confident enough to call in celebrated restaurant designers Fitch & Co., he has founded a unique restaurant, a work of art decorated with *jamdani* (woven Indian prints) and with a wonderful menu. Its dishes come from all over the subcontinent and include the innovative *Khargosh achari* (hare cooked in vinegar and spices), to pick out one. London is now a center for the development of Indian Asian cooking, so you should try it while you're here and the best place to do so is at Jamdani. Lunch noon–2:30 P.M. daily. Dinner 6–11 P.M. Mon.–Sat.; 6–10:30 P.M. Sun. **Average £20.** Credit Cards: AE, DC, MC, V.

Jason's Court   MARYLEBONE; P. 1, 2B
Jason's Ct., off Wigmore St. (tel. 274-2997). Bond Street Underground. Chef Shaun Thompson, who trained under Anton Mosimann at the Dorchester, should really be in our celebrated chefs category. If you're interested in trying British cooking at its best-to-outstanding level, don't miss Jason's. Grilled calf's liver with fried onions and bacon resting on creamed potatoes and a light veal gravy is traditional; roast Aylesbury duck basted in wild flower honey with a blackberry and ginger sauce is adventurous. British farm cheeses are *de rigueur* to finish. Lunch noon–2:30 P.M. Mon.–Fri. Dinner 7–10:30 P.M. Mon.–Sat. **Average £25. Set lunch £14.95.** Credit Cards: AE, DC, MC, V.

Joe Allen
13 Exeter St. (tel. 836-0651). Aldwych Underground.

Assuage those pangs of homesickness at Joe Allen, still one of London's most fashionable American restaurants after all these years. It's a place you can safely be seen in while indulging in a good hamburger or perhaps a huge American salad and definitely one of Joe Allen's wonderful puddings. If you come from Chicago you'll miss the Cadillac, though. Open noon–1 A.M. Mon.–Sat.; noon–midnight Sun. **Average £15.** No credit cards.

Kensington Place
201 Kensington Church St. (tel. 727-3184). Notting Hill Gate Underground.

This brasserie, opened a year ago by super-successful restaurant management team Nick Smallwood and Simon Slater, is glass-walled and cool gray and white. The menu is full of both cheap and pricey dishes thought up by chef Rowley Leigh, an award-holding former Roux Brothers trainee. Go for lunch. Evenings are often overrun and the kitchen cannot always cope. Open noon–midnight daily. **Average £17.50.** Credit Cards: MC, V.

Launceston Place
1A Launceston Pl., (tel. 937-6912). Gloucester Road Underground.

Hidden away in a pretty little backstreet, Launceston Place is sister restaurant to Kensington Place. It's perhaps slightly less well known and so marginally less likely to be booked up for its very modern and extremely good value version of a traditional British roast Sunday lunch. Lunch 12:30–2:30 P.M. daily; dinner 7–11:30 P.M. Mon.–Sat. **Average £18. Set Sunday lunch £11.50.** Credit Cards: MC, V.

Mekong
46 Churton St. (tel. 834-6896). Victoria Underground/BR.

The best Vietnamese food in London is served here, which may explain the celebrity-studded clientele. There's a restaurant downstairs and a wine bar upstairs where snacks are served. Tastes are understated, flavors extracted, and aromas released to linger everywhere, enticingly. Lunch noon–2:30 P.M., dinner 6–11 P.M. daily. **Average £15.** Credit Cards: MC, V.

Mr. Kong
21 Lisle St. (tel. 437-7341). Piccadilly Circus Underground.

The respected Mr. Kong is one of the few celebrity chefs of London's Chinatown. Prices in this part of London are now quite high, but for all his fame Mr. Kong doesn't overcharge. This isn't the place to come for chicken and sweet corn—though it's on the menu for anyone who wants it. Order from Mr. Kong's special menu and you'll have a wonderful meal. Booking isn't always necessary, and the restaurant serves very late. Open noon–1:45 A.M. daily. **Average £15.** Credit Cards: AE, DC, MC, V.

Mitchell & O'Brien
2 St. Anne's Ct. (tel. 434-9941). Tottenham Court Road Underground.

A quietly stylish American bar/restaurant with its own deli by the door, Mitchell & O'Brien is currently the darling of every Londoner who's ever claimed to like American food. Pastrami on rye may be the thing to have, but there's good borscht, as well as burgers, plus corned beef hash and other dishes we've enjoyed in New York. The atmosphere is informal but subdued; the very long bar is a place to be seen drinking; the brunch is the best. Restaurant open noon–3 P.M., 6 P.M.–1 A.M., Mon.–Sat.; noon–4 P.M. Sun. (brunch). Bar open noon–11 P.M. Mon.–Fri., 6–11 P.M. Sat. **Average £11.** Credit Cards: AE, DC, MC, V.

New Diamond   CHINATOWN
23 Lisle St. (tel. 437-2517). Piccadilly Circus Underground.
Risen like a phoenix out of the ashes of the old Diamond, the new version has a pretty decor and is more spacious. The food is as good, if not better, and just as varied. This is the Chinatown restaurant that serves duck webs with fish lips. Open noon–3 A.M. daily. **Average £15.** Credit Cards: DC, MC, V.

Orso   COVENT GARDEN; P. 2, 3D
27 Wellington St. (tel. 240-5269). Covent Garden Underground.
This fashionable Chicago-Italian restaurant was opened by Joe Allen. Like his eponymous restaurant around the corner, Orso is in a basement, though it's brightly painted in clinical white. The food is outstanding for London, where Italian food has, until recently at least, been generally mediocre. Ingredients such as buffalo mozzarella are flown in from Italy. The chic dish to order is a small pizza, ludicrously overpriced at £3.50. Open noon–midnight daily. **Average £15.** No credit cards.

Park Room   BELGRAVIA; P. 4, 4B
Hyde Park Hotel, 66 Knightsbridge (tel. 235-2000). Knightsbridge Underground.
A beautiful hotel restaurant with a beautiful view across the park to lift the spirits in the mornings. You can have a light breakfast of fruits, cereals, and yogurt, or an English breakfast that will see you through the day. There's no breakfast dish they don't have, from porridge to kedgeree and kippers, corned beef hash and grilled lambs' kidneys. Dress in style. Breakfast served 7–10:30 A.M. Mon.–Sat.; 8–11 A.M. Sun. Tea served 4–6 P.M. daily. **Set breakfasts £11.75. (English), £9 (Continental). Cream teas £9.** Credit Cards: AE, DC, MC, V.

Pizzeria Condotti   MAYFAIR; P. 2, 3C
4 Mill St. (tel. 499-1308). Oxford Circus Underground.
This Italian pizzeria wins our prize for best pizza house in London. It's now the only restaurant owned by Enzo Apicella, the grand old man of Italian restaurants in London, and it carries all his hallmarks: beautiful design, excellent food, good wines, and polite, efficient service. Open 11:30 A.M.–midnight Mon.–Sat. **Average £10.** Credit Cards: AE, DC, MC, V.

Poons   BLOOMSBURY; P. 2, 2D
15 Woburn Place (tel. 580-1188). Russell Square Underground. (Two Chinatown locations, also: 4 Leicester St., tel. 437-1528; and 27 Lisle St., tel. 437-4549.)

Opened in the heart of Bloomsbury—the university quarter and the site of a good number of tourist hotels—is this, the latest in the Poons chain. The decor is slick, designed around a series of moon gates, and the menu is extraordinary, with the likes of dried tiger lilies and wood ears flavoring the casseroles. Poons's food is always good. Lunch noon–3 P.M., dinner 6–11:30 P.M. daily. **Average £15.** Credit Cards: AE, DC, MC, V.

River Café   HAMMERSMITH
Thames Wharf, Rainville Rd., (tel. 385-3344). Hammersmith Underground.
The opening up of abandoned wharves has attracted several notable restaurateurs over the last year or so—but their restaurants can be hard to find unless you know the area, so get a taxi to this quayside restaurant. Though its menu is based on rustic dishes, the food served here is on a different plane from that of the majority of Italian restaurants in London. Deliciously fresh and authentic ingredients, and an individual way of putting them together into regional Italian dishes tasted only rarely in London, account for its success. The prices are very reasonable for the quality of food. This restaurant is understandably wildly popular and you should book two weeks in advance or at off-peak times. Open 9 A.M.–7 P.M. Mon.–Fri. Lunch served 12:30–3:30 P.M. **Average £20.** Credit Cards: AE, DC, MC, V.

Rules   COVENT GARDEN; P. 5, 3D
35 Maiden Ln. (tel. 836-5314/2559). Covent Garden Underground.
Possibly London's oldest restaurant, Rules opened as an oyster bar in the 18th century. Today it's large and comfortable, predictably traditional in style, with burgundy walls covered with pictures, mirrors, and cartoons. The clientele can be ultra-aristocratic; the service is always ultra-courteous. The menu is sumptuous; the meat section is stamped with the certificate of quality Aberdeen Angus beef and several headings are necessary to deal with all the sub-categories of game. Choosing between the simple (grilled smoked haddock with a poached egg, perhaps) and the rich (red deer with blackberries, strawberries, and raspberries) takes time: this is a menu to dither over because it never disappoints. Open midday to midnight Mon.–Sat. Alcoholic beverages served midday to midnight. **Average £30.** Credit Cards: AE, DC, MC, V.

Saigon   SOHO; P. 2, 3D
45 Frith St. (tel. 437-7109). Tottenham Court Rd. Underground.
A prettily decorated, light, and stylish Vietnamese restaurant with an intimate atmosphere upstairs. Vietnamese cooking is now fashionable in London, and the food here is a tribute to the cuisine: light, imaginative, and subtly and distinctly flavored. Outstanding dishes are the refreshing green papaya salad with nuoc mam sauce and grilled fish with chili, coriander, and spring onions. Open noon–11:30 P.M. Mon.–Sat. **Average £18.** Credit Cards: AE, DC, MC, V.

St. James's Restaurant
ST. JAMES'S; P. 4, 4C
4th Fl., Fortnum & Mason, 181 Piccadilly (tel. 734-8040, ext. 241). Green Park Underground.

The restaurant on the 4th floor is the most elegant of the three restaurants in the Fortnum & Mason department store, with the additional advantage of good views from the windows. The splendid menu features Fortnum's famous lobster bisque, English pies, caviar, and excellent-value roasts served from the trolley for under £10. Fortnum's restaurants are also very good for breakfasts, teas, and high teas. Open 9 A.M.–5 P.M. Mon.–Sat. Lunch served noon–3 P.M. **Average £15** (lunch). Credit Cards: AE, DC, MC, V.

Si Chuen
SOHO; P. 2, 3D
56 Old Compton St. (tel. 437-2069). Piccadilly Circus Underground.

Chef Tsoe-Bing, who opened up here after moving from the Dragon Gate in Gerrard Street, Chinatown, a year or so ago, claims to have introduced Sichuan cooking to London and so, consequently, to the U.K. Sichuan food in London is not outstanding, but Tsoe-Bing's pun pun chicken and tea-smoked duck stand up to scrutiny. Open noon–11:45 P.M. daily. **Average £15.** Credit Cards: AE, DC, MC, V.

Simpson's-In-The-Strand
Grand Divan Tavern
STRAND; P. 5, 3D
Strand (tel. 836-9112). Aldwych Underground or Charing Cross Underground.

Food has been served here since 1848, so Simpson's is entitled to call its menu a "bill of fare." Considering it's such a bastion of rare old English dishes, such as boiled beef with carrots, dumplings and pease pudding, which often appears on the specials list, it's surprising that Simpson's isn't more popular with defenders of English cooking. It's the stuffy formality that puts people off. The tourist trade keeps the daily turnover (25 sirloins of beef, 25 saddles of lamb and 36 roast ducks) ticking over, and what attracts the tourists is the preservation of the old custom of wheeling hot joints of meat on a trolley and carving them at the table. Jacket and tie are essential. Lunch noon–3 P.M., dinner 6–10 P.M., Mon.–Sat. **Average £25. Set lunch and pretheater menu** (6–7 P.M.) £13. Credit Cards: AE, DC, MC, V.

Sutherlands
SOHO; P. 2, C3
45 Lexington St. (tel. 434-3401). Oxford Circuit or Piccadilly Circus Underground.

A stark, minimalist restaurant is the setting the brilliant young British chef Gary Hollihead chooses in which to practice his art. Sample his full repertoire and admire his creative skill in his six-course Menu Surprise (about £40). Lunch noon–2:15 P.M. Mon.–Fri. Dinner 6:15–11:15 P.M. Mon.–Sat. **Average £30.** Credit Cards: AE, MC, V.

Taste of Africa
BRIXTON
50 Brixton Rd. (tel. 587-0343). Brixton Underground.

One of the best African restaurants in Brixton, the center of London's black community. The food is eclectic and authentic—"as hot as it should be," said my African guest—and the list of drinks is diverse. Open noon–midnight Mon.–Sat.; 5 P.M.–midnight Sun. **Average £8.** No credit cards.

Tate Gallery Restaurant
PIMLICO; P. 5, 5D

Millbank (tel. 834-6754). Pimlico Underground/12 bus.
The famous Whistler murals have always made one good reason to visit this historic restaurant; the extraordinary wine list is another. But since its recent reopening after refurbishment the food, which seems immeasurably improved, has become another. From stalwarts like steak, kidney, and mushroom pie to steamed vegetable roly poly served with tomato sauce, rabbit terrine with walnut bread, a few more bright ideas and some reproductions of old recipes, the menu is fundamentally English. Order your wine ahead of the meal if you can—the Tate likes to prepare it properly. And finish with Earl Grey or Darjeeling. Lunch noon–3 P.M. Mon.–Sat. **Set lunch £16.50 (3 courses), £15 (2 courses).** No Credit Cards.

La Tante Claire
CHELSEA; P. 4, 6A

68 Royal Hospital Rd., SW3 (tel. 352-6045). Sloane Square Underground.
A pretty restaurant run by Pierre Koffmann, a respected and dedicated chef who specializes in modern French cooking, for which he has won two Michelin stars. Prices are high, but like most of London's highly creative chefs, Koffmann offers a set price lunch for under £20 and a house wine for under £10. Don't miss them. Lunch 12:30–2 P.M., dinner 7–11 P.M., Mon.–Fri. **Average £40.** Credit Cards: AE, DC, MC, V.

Veronica's
NOTTING HILL GATE

3 Hereford Rd. (tel. 229-5079). Notting Hill Gate Underground, then 31 bus.
The charming Veronica Shaw makes her customers feel like guests in her pretty restaurant. She draws on regional and historical inspiration for her thematic menu, which changes every six weeks. Themes may be a Scottish season at Hogmanay (featuring, for example, venison and native Scottish cheeses); a Spring menu (with Richard II's low-calorie salad of herbs and cresses); or a menu of slightly modernized Tudor recipes. The cooking is excellent. The wine list features many British wines and spirits. Lunch noon–3 P.M. Mon.–Fri. Dinner 7 P.M.–midnight Mon.–Sat. Alcoholic beverages served noon–midnight. **Average £20.** Credit Cards: AE, DC, MC, V.

Waterside Inn
BUCKINGHAMSHIRE

Ferry Rd., Bray, Berkshire (tel. 0628-20691).
Michel Roux, master patissier and holder of three Michelin stars, is chef-patron of the Waterside Inn, overlooking the Thames at Bray in Berkshire. Everything about a meal here—from the *amuses geules* to the petits fours and truffles served with coffee—is delicious. The price of the food is predictably high, except for the set lunch, which is such a gastronomic bargain it should not be missed. Lunch noon–2 P.M. Wed.–Sun.; dinner Easter–Oct. 7–10 P.M. Tues.–Sun. **Average £50. Minimum £30. Set lunch £21.50.** Credit Cards: AE, DC, MC, V.

The White Tower

1 Percy St. (tel. 636-8141). Goodge St./Tottenham Court Rd. Underground.

The oldest Greek restaurant in London opened in 1938, when eating Greek was not fashionable and only the rich and/or famous ate out. Consequently the restaurant's name hardly gives away its ethnic identity: the menu is half French, half Greek with some good English game in season, and the prices are high. The standards of cooking are, however, excellent and the restaurant is always busy. Lunch 12:30–2:30 P.M., dinner 6:30–10:30 P.M. Mon.–Fri. **Average £20.** Credit Cards: AE, DC, MC, V.

10

ENTERTAINMENT

As far as we're concerned, and as far as you're concerned, everything you do on your trip should be classified as "Entertainment." Take a walk through a supermarket and compare it to yours at home. Have the TV or the radio on all the time just to see what the nation is watching and listening to. A TV show here can go on at 12:35 or end at 10:20—it's as if they never heard of half hours. Talk to people about all that stuff you've been reading about in *The Times* or *The Observer* lately. Find out what Londoners think about the issues. Walking around ought to be entertaining all the time. Funny things happen. Weird things the likes of which you've never seen before happen right on the street. Just walking around absorbing all the new stuff should wear you out every day. London is not a city for relaxing. There's simply far too much to do all the time. And all of it is "Entertainment."

However, you do need to know about more specific types of entertainment—something we define as any time someone is performing for your pleasure, whether money is exchanged or not. Entertainment can happen any time of the day or night, and an awful lot of it can be inexpensive or free. In fact, some of the best things in life in London are free.

Church Music

Principal among great, free entertainment in London is music in churches. There are two basic types of doses. The first of course is to attend a service. The Anglican Church (Church of England) is known for its emphasis on music. The big-name churches like **St. Paul's** and **Westminster Abbey** have superior in-house choirs. Services are held daily in the bigger churches, usually morning (matins) and at dusk (evensong). And this is also the best time to see the churches, when they're not full of tourists, when you can hear the acoustics working properly.

Many churches offer free concerts and recitals (a retiring collection may be passed around at the end) at lunchtime or in the evening. Churches that normally have a full music roster are **St. Martin-in-the-Fields, St. Marylebone, St. Bartholomew-the-Great, St. John's, Smith Square** (a former church, now exclusively a concert hall). Of course the sacred music scene really heats up around the holidays. Versions of *The Messiah* or *Ceremony of Carols* or the *St. John Passion* are performed all over town at Christmas and Easter.

Sports

From the sacred to, well, the less sacred, there is sport. Sport in Britain can be endlessly entertaining (the races at Ascot) or merely endless (cricket). As a sociological study it's always good to attend a sporting event in a foreign country. We can't in all good conscience recommend that you go see a football (soccer) match while they are still life-threatening events. We can, however, by all means suggest that you head out to Lord's for a match of cricket (you could go every day for five days straight and still not see the thing decided).

You can go to **horse racing** (try Kempton Park, tel. 0932-782292) or **greyhound racing** (try Wimbledon, tel. 946-2662). You can see **cricket at Lord's** (tel. 289-1611/1615) or at the **Oval** in Kennington (tel. 582-6600). Naturally you'd like to score some tickets for **Wimbledon** beginning the last week in June. Here's how, if you're a plan-aheader: Write in August or September of the *preceding* year for tickets (you'll have to write for 1991 tickets this year) to All England Lawn Tennis and Croquet Club, Box 98, Church Road, Wimbledon, SW19 5AE (tel. 946-2244). A limited number of seats are available on the day; however, people have been known to camp out early (i.e., 5 A.M.) to get them. There are also **regattas** (for rowing sculls) on the Thames, the most famous of which are the Oxford-Cambridge match around Easter and the international competition at Henley-on-Thames (about 15 miles northwest of town), which invariably coincides with Wimbledon. You don't need tickets for either of these events; just find yourself a spot on the riverbank and break open a picnic. The daily papers include advice on the best vantage points from which to watch the races.

Not all sports have to be of the spectator variety. With all the parks around, you can do sports as easily as you can watch other people doing them. For runners there are great loops around Hyde Park and Kensington Gardens and Regent's Park. Another popular route is along the north side of the Thames (but beware of stairs and Embankment traffic noise and fumes). Calmer are the tow paths along the side of Regent's and the Grand Union canals. For serious runners, the **London Marathon** is run on a Sunday in April.

You can let somebody else do the running for you in Hyde Park with a mount supplied by Bathurst Riding Stables (tel.

723-2813), Lilo Blum's Riding School and Stables (tel. 235-6846), or Ross Nye's Riding Establishment (tel. 262-3791). Or you can glide on your own two feet at the Queen's Ice-Skating Club (tel. 229-0172).

If you need more info about such matters, call the Sports Council (388-1277), or talk to the concierge at your hotel. Many major-city health clubs elsewhere in the world have reciprocal agreements with private health clubs in London. If you belong to a swank gym at home, check to see if they have an exchange program that will allow you to use the facilities at a London club.

Theater

Undoubtedly you don't need reminding that London is one of the most important centers for theater of all sorts in the world. The West End is the heart of London's commercial theater scene and is well covered by the international press; we needn't add our recommendation to the clamor, except to point out that West End ticket prices are rocketing and don't always represent the best value for your money unless you absolutely must see the latest Lloyd-Weber/Rice extravaganza or a star turn by Anthony Hopkins or Maggie Smith.

As we discuss in the *Priorities* chapter, a can't-miss bet is to head for the National Theatre's theaters at the **South Bank Centre** or the Royal Shakespeare Company's theaters at the **Barbican Centre.** You can also take an out-of-town overnight junket to the RSC's theaters at **Stratford.** To keep in-town prices down, buy tickets at the half-price booth in Leicester Square. But keep in mind, the hottest shows won't be available there, and there will be a line (very long in summer). There is a lot of great experimental or "fringe" theater in London that might offer anything from a version of Brecht staged à la *Star Wars* to a new play about the gay experience in Soviet Russia, or the debut of a new musical so hot it will move to the West End in no time. Some of the productions are truly top drawer, some are merely "interesting," most at least are worthy of your attention and cash money. Check out the offerings at the **Battersea Arts Centre** (tel. 223-2223), **Bloomsbury Theatre** (tel. 389-9629), **Donmar Warehouse** (tel. 240-8230), **Hackney Empire** (tel. 985-2424), **Holland Park Theatre** (tel. 602-7856), **ICA Theatre** (tel. 930-3647), **Lyric Hammersmith** (tel. 741-2311), **Open Air Theatre, Regent's Park** (tel. 486-2431), **Royal Court** (tel. 730-1745), or **Young Vic** (tel. 928-6363).

Another London-specific brand of theater is **theater in pubs.** Several dozen public houses, upstairs and downstairs, inside and out, offer drama with your drams. The Pub Theatre Network publishes a leaflet listing member pubs; check with the London Tourist Board or phone the network at 622-4553.

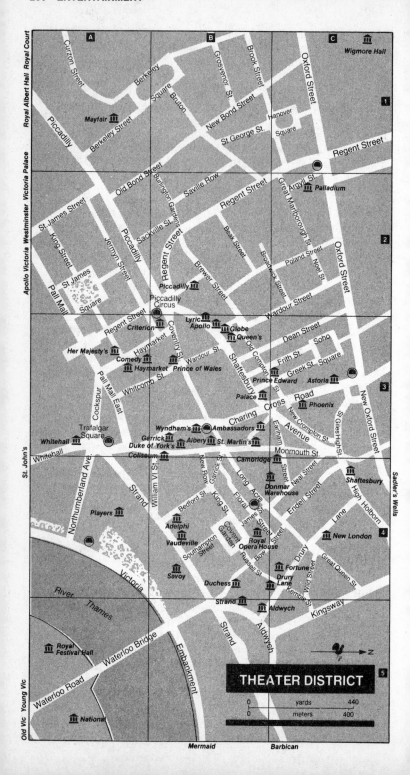

THEATER DISTRICT

Music and Dance

As mentioned above, there's music in the air everywhere in London. For dance, concerts, recitals, opera, you'll run out of evenings long before you run out of choices. In the world of dance, London's premier companies are the **Royal Ballet** and the **Sadler's Wells Ballet.** Both call the Royal Opera House (Covent Garden, tel. 240-1066/1911) home. The Sadler's Wells Theatre (tel. 278-8916) is also noted for its dance programs, as are various theaters at the Barbican and South Bank Centres. London's two most important opera companies are the **Royal,** which performs at Covent Garden (see above), and the **English National,** which performs at the London Coliseum (tel. 831-3161; 240-7200). The **Royal Choral Society** often performs at the Royal Albert Hall (tel. 589-3203), as do many other groups.

In the last ten years London has produced a bumper crop of important dance companies. Among the many, *Michael Clark* and *DV8* are ones to look out for.

There are concert and recital halls all over town. Heavy hitters include the **Royal Philharmonic** at the Barbican (tel. 628-8891) and Royal Festival Hall (tel. 928-3002), the **London Symphony Orchestra** at the Barbican, and the **Academy of St. Martin-in-the-Fields** at Royal Festival Hall and at the church whence comes its name. **Queen Elizabeth Hall** and the **Purcell Room** (tel. for both 928-8800) at the South Bank Centre and **Wigmore Hall** (tel. 935-2141) are places for smaller-scale concerts and recitals.

Nightlife

The pop music scene is a highly visible and highly volatile component of London nightlife. Clubs in London are more than merely places to drink, dance, and check out what everyone else is wearing. While they're doing likewise, the London club scene is a great place to launch a career. The Sex Pistols, The Clash, Boy George, and Sade were prominent fixtures on the club circuit and consequently were spotted by some money-and-connection types who launched them on their various missions to stardom. The London scene lends itself to this type of incestuous self-promotion because it is much more "clubby" than that in most cities this large. That is, in London the clubbers are a small, tight clique with brief "A lists" and no "B lists." The best nights in London clubland are held in warehouses or theaters or wherever the season's entrepreneur/impresario/party organizer can find an empty space whose neighbors (hopefully) won't squeal if the music plays on well into the wee hours. It's kind of guerrilla club-going and is great fun, if you happen to be on the A list, or happen accidentally to happen upon one of these moveable-feast fetes *en passant* as you're walking through deserted streets at 3 A.M.

If you don't have the appropriate credentials (and why should you?), don't be discouraged; there are still plenty of places where the music is hot—or cool, if you prefer—and you can have a damn good time even though half of your fellow partyers aren't on the brink of becoming the Next Big Thing. The best fun is to be had by catching some live music at one of the dozens of music-halls-turned-rock-clubs in town. They feature rhythm-and-blues greats, new wavers, pop stars, reggae, and African bands—London is BIG on ethnic music. Check listings and posters to see what's on tap at the **Academy,** Brixton (tel. 274-1525), the **Astoria** (tel. 434-0403), the **Bass Clef** (tel. 729-2476), **Dingwalls** (tel. 267-4967), **Hammersmith Odeon** (tel. 748-4081), **100 Club** (tel. 636-0933), **Rock Garden** (tel. 240-3961), or **Town & Country Club** (tel. 267-3334).

If jazz is your gig, man, check out the jams at the **Bass Clef** and **100 Club** (see above), **Jazz Cafe** (tel. 359-4936), **Pizza Express** (tel. 439-8722), and **Ronnie Scott's** (tel. 439-0747).

As far as nightclubs go, the top spot changes nearly minute by minute. If you attend well to your *Face* and *Arena* magazine gossip columns, you should have a fair idea of what's the newest hot joint in town. Lots of the clubs feature a different music/entertainment/theme/sexual orientation program each night of the week. Check out the daily listings in *Time Out* and *City Limits* for up-to-the-minute news. In the here-today-gone-tomorrow world of London clubland, any place we might suggest that will still be around by the time this book is published almost automatically can be disqualified as being "the Latest." Keeping this in mind, however, there are some clubs that are fixtures on the scene that consistently serve up good entertainment to satisfy the capricious tastes of London's late-nighters: **Fridge** (tel. 326-5100); **Heaven** (gay) (tel. 839-3852); **Limelight** (tel. 434-0527); **Stringfellows** (tel. 240-5534); **Wag Club** (tel. 437-5534).

Add to this (far-from-complete) list of "Entertainment" film, music in pubs, free festivals, cabaret, comedy, poetry. . . . There is no excuse for you ever to spend a night retiring early in this city. And if you return home from a visit to London relaxed and refreshed, it's your own fault.

11

SHORT TRIPS
FROM LONDON

As mentioned in our list of *Priorities*, it is of the utmost importance to get out of London to see the countryside so dear to an Englishman's heart. We have selected a dozen excursions, which fall into two categories. The first group, including Greenwich, Hampstead, Hampton Court, and Kew Gardens, are excursions all within or just outside the city limits and easily reached by Underground, riverboat (call River Boat Information Service, 730-4812), or other public transport. All four of these can be explored within the confines of a day and do not call for an overnight stay.

The second group, including Bath, Brighton, Cambridge, Oxford, Salisbury, Stonehenge and Avebury, Stratford-upon-Avon, Windsor and Eton, are farther away, have more to see, and therefore warrant an overnight stay. While all can be reached by public transportation, some have attractions spread over a wider area, and/or their best hotels are out of town, and therefore are best enjoyed by car. What we suggest is to take BritRail to your destination, then rent a car there, not in London. You can book the car ahead at home. Budget is a good choice, with offices in Bath (tel. 0225-60518), Brighton (tel. 0273-27351/2), Cambridge (tel. 0223-323838), and Reading for Oxford (tel. 0734-597929), or at one of the airports for other destinations. If you pick up a car outside of the city, you will avoid London's traffic and maze-like road system and the inflated rates of renting a car in town.

Greenwich

BritRail from Cannon St., Waterloo, Charing Cross, and London Bridge to Greenwich. Underground: Docklands Light Railway, then cross at the pedestrian tunnel. Best way in spring and summer is to take the ferry from Westminster or Tower Piers.

Greenwich (pronounced "Grennich") is a little town by the riverside a few miles east of London. There are great buildings to see here. The **Naval College** was designed by Wren, Hawksmoor, and Vanbrugh; some of its rooms, including the Painted Hall and the Chapel, are open to the public. The **National Maritime Museum,** whose most important asset is the **Queen's House,** is the work of Inigo Jones. On the same watery theme, there are two ships to explore. The most impressive is the ***Cutty Sark,*** built in Glasgow in 1869. She is a sleek, still fully rigged clipper ship. Nearby is the ***Gypsy Moth IV,*** which was raced single-handed around the world in 1969 which is by Sir Francis Chichester.

Nearby is the **Royal Observatory,** also Wren-designed, which is full of astronomical instruments, marks the prime meridian (0 degrees longitude), and has been the keeper of Greenwich Mean Time.

Also on view is a beautiful park and the Thames Flood Barrier, a short walk downriver, which is a group of enormous gates used to regulate the flow of water.

The place to eat is **Goddard's Eel and Pie House,** which has been offering up these local delicacies since 1890, or for

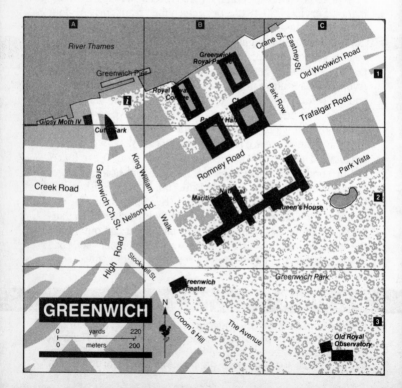

even more atmosphere, stroll among Greenwich's famed fishmongers.

Hampton Court Palace

BritRail from Waterloo Station to Hampton Court, then walk across the bridge; or by riverboat from Westminster Pier in spring and summer.

The easy journey by rail or river takes you out to Henry VIII's palace set in a spectacular park of formal gardens. This, the finest Tudor mansion in England, was built by Cardinal Wolsey and later given to the king. After the Tudors, the court preferred Whitehall until the time of William and Mary, who, notorious for their lack of fondness for that palace, commissioned Christopher Wren in 1699 to do renovations. The State Apartments were severely damaged in 1986, when a fire broke out in the flat of one of the grace-and-favor wards who lived here. Thankfully, much of the furniture and artworks were saved. There are paintings by De la Tour, Tintoretto, Lely, and Verrio among stunning architectural details spanning the centuries. The gardens are laid out with strictly trimmed hedges and tended beds. Visit the Great Vine, a two-hundred-year-old creeper, bring a picnic, or try one of the riverside pubs.

Hampstead

Underground: Hampstead for the town, Archway or Golder's Green, then take bus 210 from either station for Kenwood.

Hampstead Heath is situated in northeast London and is a huge, surprisingly rural plot overlooking the city. In fact, it provides one of the city's best-loved vistas at the top of Parliament Hill, London's highest point, with a sweeping panorama of the Thames valley. At the north edge of the Heath is **Kenwood,** a wonderful art museum housed in a former private mansion largely designed by Robert Adam. The house ended up in the hands of Edward Cecil Guinness, First Earl of Iveagh, who deposited his great art collection here, eventually bequeathing it, along with the house and grounds, to the city. The paintings include works by Gainsborough, Rembrandt, Vermeer, Turner, and Reynolds in a truly lovely setting. Evening music recitals and poetry readings are given in the Orangery. Call (01) 348-1286 for info on Kenwood House; (01) 734-1877 for concert info. There is a pleasant restaurant connected to the house.

Another wonderful residence, operated by the National Trust, is **Fenton House.** A William and Mary structure, its

collection features—aside from paintings and period furnishings—the musical instrument collection of George Henry
Benton Fletcher. The instruments are used to give concerts
at the house periodically throughout the year. There is also
a neat, quiet walled garden in which Shakespeare's plays are
produced several times a summer. For news of these events,
phone the National Trust Office at (01) 222-9251; call (01)
435-3471 for Fenton House info.

Also in the town of Hampstead is **Keats House,** home of
the poet John Keats, off Downshire Hill on Keats Grove.
(Open Monday through Friday 2 to 6 P.M., Saturday 10 A.M.
to 5 P.M., Sunday 2 to 5 P.M.; Monday through Friday only,
1 to 5 P.M. in winter; admission is free.) The house is decorated in an early 19th century style and littered with Keats memorabilia. At the corner of New End Square and Well Walk is
the **Burgh House** (open Wednesday through Sunday 12 to
5 P.M.; admission free), a Queen Anne edifice with original
paneling throughout, as well as exhibitions describing local
history. There is a full roster of lectures and concerts. Call
431-0144 for schedules.

☕ The town of Hampstead is a terrific shopping village of smart
boutiques and galleries which line the High Street. While en
route to any of these points of interest, stop in for a bite or a
beer at **The House on Rosslyn Hill,** 34 Rosslyn Hill. This
busy bar/bistro is open till midnight seven days. Alternately, picnic provisions for the Heath or otherwise can be found at **Rosslyn Deli,** 56 Rosslyn Hill.

Kew Gardens

Underground: Kew Gardens, or by riverboat from Westminster
Pier in summer.

Technically called the Royal Botanic Gardens, these are just
that. Outdoors, laid out in precise, precious beds, or indoors,
displayed in huge hothouses, they are spread out over three
hundred acres on a peninsula formed by a lazy oxbow in the
Thames south and west of the city proper. The garden was
begun in 1731 by the Prince of Wales and was continued by
his widow. Their house, Kew Palace, is also open for inspection and retains its original Georgian furniture. The greatest
work on the garden was done during the reign of George III
by the brilliant landscape architect Capability Brown. The gardens are an important center for botanic and scientific research. Their public attractions include the 18th-century
Orangery; Queen Charlotte's Cottage, a rustic tea house à la
Marie Antoinette's *petite ferme* at Versailles; the Japanese Pa-
goda, copying one in Kyoto; and of course the fantastic 19th-

century greenhouses, some large enough to contain fully grown palm trees.

OVERNIGHTERS

Windsor and Eton

For a map of Windsor and Eton, see atlas page 10.

By rail from Paddington. By car, the M4 to Exit 6, about 30 minutes. Where to stay: **Great Fosters,** Egham (tel.) 0784-433822.

Windsor is the country home of the Queen *et famille* when they want to take a breather from the rigors of Buckingham Palace. Windsor Castle is the principal attraction of the town, and in it you can visit **Queen Mary's Dollhouse,** the **Queen's Gallery,** exhibiting masterpieces from the royal collections (one of the world's great private art collections), and the **State Apartments.** The town is a pretty place, with shops and pubs—and the inevitable pizza joints—along the High Street.

   Eton, home of the famous boy's preparatory school upon whose playing fields the future of the Empire was molded, is across the Thames and is quieter and less trafficked.

   The nicest parts of Windsor, however, are out of the town proper, in **Windsor Great Park.** Here you'll find **Savill Garden,** 36 acres, half formal, half woodland, especially spectacular for rhododendrons and azaleas in spring, roses in summer. Windsor Great Park is also home of the **Guards Polo Grounds,** where, on many weekends, the Prince of Wales can be spotted enjoying a rousing chukker.

 Best places to eat in the area include the **Eton Wine Bar,** the **House on the Bridge,** and, best of all, the **Waterside Inn** in Bray (about 20 minutes away).

The Information office is off High St. in a cul-de-sac behind Madame Tussaud's Exhibition.

Stratford-upon-Avon

For a map of Stratford, see atlas page 11.

By rail from Paddington. By car, the M40 to the A40 to the A 34. About an hour and a half. Where to stay: **Ettington Park Hotel,** Alderminster (tel. 0789-740740).

This of course is the home of the bard, and the entire town is somewhat slavishly given over to Shakespeare mania. The first thing you want to do is get tickets for an evening's performance at the Royal Shakespeare Company whose three theaters occupy a pretty riverside setting; tel. (0789) 295623 (ask about reduced theater-ticket/rail-fare combos). The town itself, once a prosperous and picturesque Cotswold village, is now completely dominated by tourism. The Shakespeare Trust has preserved five properties important to the playwright and his family, and the best way to tour the town is to buy an all-inclusive ticket to see them at your own pace (there are also tour buses available for those without cars). They are **Shakespeare's Birthplace, Nash's House, New Place and garden, Anne Hathaway's Cottage,** and **Mary Arden's House.**

For food try the **Dirty Duck,** a pub across from the RSC theaters overlooking the Avon.

The information center is located at the corner of Bridge and High streets across from the post office.

Oxford

For a map of Oxford, see atlas page 12.

By BritRail from Paddington Station. By car, the M40 to the A40. About an hour in each case. Where to stay: **Le Manoir aux Quat' Saisons,** Great Milton (tel. 0844-27881), or the **Feathers Hotel,** Woodstock (tel. 0993-812291).

Oxford is a great medieval university city situated by the Thames (called the Isis here) and Cherwell rivers. It is easily one of the loveliest and most pleasant towns in all of Europe. Of course the main focus is on the **university buildings** themselves, many built in the 12th to 17th centuries, lining tiny winding streets. There are walking tours and bus tours of the town, or stop in at **Blackwell's bookshop** on Broad Street for a copy of *Vade Mecum,* an insider's guide to the town produced by university students. In addition to the university, there is Britain's oldest **botanic garden** beside the Cherwell, and punts to be hired to travel lazily along same. There are two excellent museums, the **Ashmolean,** with an international collection of artwork, and the **Museum of Modern Art,** with galleries, lectures, and films.

Good food abounds at **Elizabeth Restaurant** and **15 North Parade.** Evenings are full of activity, with theater, film, lectures, and concerts year-round.

Check the Tourist Board Office on St. Aldates by the post office, or call TOURISTLINE OXFORD 244888 for complete information.

Cambridge

For a map of Cambridge, see atlas page 14.

By rail from Liverpool St. Station. By car, the M11 to Exit 11, the A1309 to Cambridge. Where to stay? Try the **Arundel House Hotel** (tel. 0223-67701) in town or, better yet, the **Angel Hotel** in nearby Bury St. Edmunds (tel. 0284-753926)—they also serve some of the best food in the area.

As with its somewhat adversarial twin, Oxford, Cambridge is a medieval university town. The arguments run back and forth, as they have for centuries, over which is the more beautiful. It really is a matter of taste; Cambridge is more compact and prettier than Oxford; the former has wide lawns and gardens sweeping back from the colleges to the sluggish Cam River. There are 32 colleges that make up Cambridge University; among the ones you'll want to see are **King's College**—with its marvelous chapel and choir, **Trinity College, St. John's College,** and **Queen's College.** The **Fitzwilliam (art) Museum,** the **Museum of Classical Archaeology,** the **Scott Polar Research Institute,** and the **Whipple Museum of Science** are each most unique and interesting. Cambridge is full of lovely churches such as **Little St. Mary's, Great St. Mary's,** and the **Round Church.**

The best place for lunch in town is **The Free Press Pub** on Prospect Row. You might like to try punting on the Cam or biking around town. Both types of vehicles can be rented locally.

The Tourist Information Office is on Wheeler St.

Bath

For a map of Bath, see atlas page 16.

By rail from Paddington Station. By car, the M4 to Exit 18, the A46 to Bath. For accommodations, call **The Priory Hotel** (tel. 0225-331922) just a few kms from the city center.

Bath is named, quite simply, for that—or rather for them—the bathhouses and spa built to satisfy this social nicety of which the Romans were so fond. Bath has always been a spa town, reaching its height of fashionability during the Georgian and Regency periods, when its beautiful pale honey-colored buildings were erected. The tourist office is in Abbey Church Yard and arranges walking tours, or you can set off on your own—Bath must be seen on foot for the best effect. Your tour should include the **Roman Baths and Museum** and the **Pump Room** (now a charming restaurant for lunches and teas), both remnants of Bath's past as a chic spa. The 15th-century **Bath Abbey** is a beaut and is just nearby the serene **Parade Gardens.** Bath also has several interesting and unusual museums: **Holburn of Menstrie Museum** (art, furnishings, crafts); the **National Center of Photography;** the **Costume Museum** (devoted to the history of fashion); and **No. 1 Royal Crescent,** a restored 18th-century town house open to the public. Bath is also a terrific shopping town; try the boutiques along the Grand Parade and New Bond Street.

☕ **Clos du Roy** is French and friendly; for simpler fare try the **Pump Room** or the **Canary Tea Shop.**

The tourist center is located at Abby Church Yard.

Salisbury

By rail from Waterloo Station. By car, the M3 to Exit 8, the A303 to the A30 to Salisbury. (Stonehenge, see below, is directly on this route by the exit to the A360 just beyond Amesbury.) For lodging, try the **Red Lion Hotel** (tel. 0722-23334) or the **White Hart Hotel** (tel. 0722-27476). **King's Arms Hotel** (tel. 0722-27629).

Doubtless you have seen at least one of Mr. Constable's famous renderings of **Salisbury Cathedral,** the finest example of Early English Gothic architecture, begun in 1220. But there's much more to the town than that: the **Salisbury and South Wiltshire Museum** is a repository for archaeological finds (many from around and about Stonehenge); **Mompesson House** is a restored 18th-century home with a collection of 18th-century glassware; and just outside of town is **Wilton House,** with interiors by Inigo Jones.

☕ Foodwise, you'll enjoy **Manuel's** for fancy meals, the **Wig and Quill** for pub grub in a 16th-century inn.

The tourist center located in Fish Row has plenty of other suggestions.

Stonehenge and Avebury Stone Circles

Neither can be reached directly by rail. By car, to Stonehenge follow directions to Salisbury and exit at the A360 junction. To

Avebury, take the A4 direct to just outside of the town. From Stonehenge take the A360 to the A361 to Avebury. Close to Avebury is the **Manor House** hotel in Castle Combe (tel. 0249-782206), about twenty minutes away.

The earliest activity at the site of Stonehenge dates back to about 3000 B.C.; the present Neolithic circle was begun about a thousand years later, and was altered and enlarged by various primitive tribes for the next five hundred years. Many people prefer, however, the stone circle at Avebury which surrounds a tiny village, and which was the largest known circle in the world. These things are explained in the **Avebury Museum.** The **Museum of Wiltshire Rural Life** (also in Avebury), housed in The Great Barn, depicts the daily doings of some (somewhat) more recent inhabitants.

For eating, try the **Stones Restaurant** for a light bite in Avebury, or check out the listings for Salisbury. If you are staying near Stonehenge, likewise consult the Salisbury entry.

The Avebury Tourist Information Office is located in The Great Barn.

Brighton

By rail from Victoria Station. By car, the M23 to the A23. The journey should take about an hour and a half. *The* place to stay in Brighton, if not in the whole of south England, is the **Grand Hotel,** King's Rd. (tel. 0273-21188), which has been nursed back to its original glory after a 1985 IRA bombing tried to take out Mrs. Thatcher and the entire Conservative Party in one fell swoop. Right on the water, it fairly oozes British discretion.

Brighton, immortalized in the last decade by the Who's "Quadrophenia," is just the right blend of luxurious resort and ticky-tacky seaside town. The Prince Regent, George IV, put the town on the map by constructing the **Royal Pavilion,** with its Islamic exterior and Chinese interior, it is nothing if not *de trop,* but a stunner nonetheless. Also of interest in town is the **Brighton Art Gallery and Museum,** which runs the gamut from decorative to the fine arts. For performing arts, the **Theater Royal** is the out-of-town testing ground for many West End productions. And for shopping, **The Lanes,** a web of streets behind the Royal Pier, is the place to find fashion and frippery with an aquatic edge.

Try **English's Oyster Bar** on East St. for seafood, or **Le Grandgousier** on Western St. for French cuisine.

The tourist office is at Marlborough House, 54 Old Steine.

12

CITY LISTINGS

Churches

All-Hallows-by-the-Tower   **THE CITY; P. 3, G3**
Byward St.; tel. 481-2928; Mon.–Fri. 9:30 A.M.–5:30 P.M., Sat.–Sun. 10 A.M.–5:30 P.M.

Brompton Oratory   **SOUTH KENSINGTON; P. 4, 5A**
(see London Oratory, below)

Chelsea Old Church   **CHELSEA**
Cheyne Walk; tel. 352-7978, Mon–Sat. 10 A.M.–1 P.M., 2–5 P.M.

Lincoln's Inn Chapel   **HOLBORN; P. 2, 2E**
Lincoln's Inn, Lincoln's Inn Fields; tel. 405-6360; tour Mon.–Fri. 9 A.M., 11 A.M.

London Oratory   **SOUTH KENSINGTON; P. 4, 5A**
Brompton Rd., Thurloe Pl.; tel. 589-4811

Southwark Cathedral   **SOUTH BANK; P. 6, 4G**
1 Montague Pl.; tel. 407-2939

Spanish and Portuguese Synagogue   **THE CITY; P. 3, 3G**
Heneage Lane, Bevis Marks; tel. 289-2573

St. Bartholomew-the-Great   **THE CITY; P. 3, 2F**
Little Britain St.; tel. 606-1575

St. Bride   **THE CITY; P. 3, 3E**
Fleet St.; tel. 353-1301

St. Dunstan in the East   **THE CITY; P. 3, 3G**
Idol Lane, St. Dunstan's Hill, Lower Thames St.

St. Etheldreda's   **HOLBORN; P. 4, 2E**
14 Ely Pl.; tel. 405-1061

St. Giles Cripplegate Church   **THE CITY; P. 3, 2F**
Wood and Fore sts.; tel. 606-3630

St. Martin-in-the-Fields   **SOHO; P. 5, 3D**
5 St. Martin's Lane; tel. 930-0089

St. Mary Abchurch   **THE CITY; P. 3, 3F**
Abchurch Yard, Cannon St.; tel. 626-0306

St. Mary Aldermanbury   **THE CITY; P. 3, 2F**
Aldermanbury and Love Ln.

St. Marylebone Parish Church MARYLEBONE; P. 1, 2B
Marylebone Rd.; tel. 935-7315

St. Mary-le-Bow THE CITY; P. 3, 3F
Bow Lane and Cheapside; tel. 248-5139

St. Paul's Cathedral THE CITY; P. 3, 3F
Ludgate Hill; tel. 248-2705

St. Paul's Church COVENT GARDEN; P. 2, 3D
Covent Garden; tel. 836-5221

Temple Church THE CITY; P. 3, 3E
Fleet St.; tel. 353-1736; Mon.–Sat. 10 A.M. till 4 P.M.

Westminster Abbey WESTMINSTER; P. 5, 4D
Parliament Square; tel. 222-5125; Mon.–Sat. 7:30 A.M.–6 P.M.

Museums and Galleries

Bankside Gallery SOUTH BANK; P. 6, 3F
48 Hopton St.; tel. 928-7521; Tues.–Sat. 10 A.M.–5 P.M., Tues. till 8 P.M., Sun. 1–5 P.M.

Barbican Centre Art Gallery THE CITY; P. 3, 2F
Silk St.; tel. 638-4141; Mon.–Sat. 10 A.M.–6:45 P.M., Sun. 10 A.M.–5:45 P.M.

**Bear Gardens Museum
of the Shakespearean Stage** SOUTH BANK; P. 6, 3F
1 Bear Gardens; tel. 928-6342; Tues.–Sat. 10 A.M.–5:30 P.M., Sun. 2–6 P.M.

**British Library's
National Sound Archive** SOUTH KENSINGTON; P. 4, 4A
29 Exhibition Rd.; tel. 589-6603; Mon.–Fri. 9:30 A.M.–4:30 P.M., Thurs. till 8:45 P.M.

British Museum BLOOMSBURY; P. 2, 2D
Great Russell St.; tel. 636–1555; Mon.–Sat., 10 A.M.–5 P.M., Sun. 2:30–6 P.M.

Courtauld Institute Galleries COVENT GARDEN; P. 2, 3E
Somerset House, The Strand; tel. 580-1015 or 636-2095; Mon.–Sat. 10 A.M.–5 P.M., Sun. 2–5 P.M.

Crafts Council Gallery ST. JAMES'S; P. 5, 4D
12 Waterloo Pl.; tel. 930-4811; Tues.–Sat. 10 A.M.–5 P.M., Sun. 2–5 P.M.

Cricket Memorial Museum MARYLEBONE; P. 1, 1A
Lord's Cricket Ground, St. John's Wood Rd.; tel. 289-1611; Mon.–Sat. 10:30 A.M.–5 P.M.

The Design Museum SOUTH BANK
Butler's Wharf Shad Thames; tel. 403-6933

Dickens House HOLBORN; P. 2, 2E
48 Doughty St.; tel. 405-2127; Mon.–Sat. 10 A.M.–5 P.M.

Dulwich Picture Gallery DULWICH
College Rd.; tel. 693-5254; Tues.–Sat. 10 A.M.–1 P.M., 2–5 P.M., Sun. 2–5 P.M.

Faraday Laboratory Museum MAYFAIR; P. 5, 3C
21 Albermarle St.; tel. 409-2992; Tues. and Thurs. 1–4 P.M.

Freud Museum HAMPSTEAD
20 Maresfield Gardens, Hampstead; tel. 435-2002; Wed.–Sun. 12–5 P.M.

Geffrye Museum HACKNEY
Kingsland Rd.; tel. 739-8368; Tues.–Sat. 10 A.M.–5 P.M., Sun. 2–5 P.M.

The Geological Museum   **SOUTH KENSINGTON; P. 4, 5A**
Exhibition Rd.; tel. 938-8765; Mon.–Sat. 10 A.M.–6 P.M., Sun. 1–6 P.M.

Guards Museum, Wellington Barracks   **WESTMINSTER; P. 5, 4C**
Birdcage Walk; tel. 938-4466; daily 10 A.M.–3:30 P.M., closed Fri.

Hayward Gallery   **SOUTH BANK; P. 5, 4E**
South Bank Centre; tel. 261-0127; Mon.–Wed. 10 A.M.–8 P.M., Thurs.–Sat.
10 A.M.–6 P.M., Sun. 12–6 P.M.

Heinz Gallery   **MARYLEBONE; P. 1, 3B**
21 Portman Sq.; tel. 580-5533; Mon.–Fri. 10 A.M.–1 P.M.

Institute of Contemporary Arts   **ST. JAMES'S; P. 5, 4D**
12 Carlton House; tel. 930-6393; 12–9:30 P.M.

Jewish Museum   **BLOOMSBURY; P. 2, 1D**
Woburn House, Tavistock Sq.; tel. 388-4525; Sun., Tues.–Fri. 10 A.M.–4
P.M.

Kenwood   **HAMPSTEAD**
Hampstead Lane; tel. 348-1286; daily 10 A.M.–5 P.M.

London Dungeon   **SOUTH BANK; P. 6, 4G**
28–34 Tooley St.; tel. 403-0606; daily 10 A.M.–5:30 P.M.

London Experience   **SOHO; P. 5, 3D**
Trocadero, Piccadilly; tel. 439-4938; daily 10 A.M.–11 P.M.

London Planetarium   **MARYLEBONE; P. 1, 2B**
Marylebone Rd.; tel. 486-1121; daily 9 A.M.–5:30 P.M. in summer, 10
A.M.–5:30 P.M. in winter

London Transport Museum   **COVENT GARDEN; P. 2, 3D**
Covent Garden; tel. 379-6344; daily 10 A.M.–6 P.M.

Madame Tussaud's   **MARYLEBONE; P. 1, 2B**
Marylebone Rd.; tel. 935-6861; daily 10 A.M.–5:30 P.M.

Museum of London   **THE CITY; P. 3, 2F**
150 London Wall; tel. 600-3699; Tues.–Sat. 10 A.M.–5:30 P.M., Sun. 2–5:30
P.M.

Museum of Mankind   **MAYFAIR; P. 5, 3C**
6 Burlington Gardens; tel. 437-2224; Mon.–Sat. 10 A.M.–5 P.M., Sun. 2:30–6
P.M.

Museum of the Moving Image   **SOUTH BANK; P. 5, 4E**
South Bank Centre; tel. 401-2636; Tues.–Sat. 10 A.M.–8 P.M., Sun. till 6
P.M.

**The Museum of the
Order of St. John**   **CLERKENWELL; P. 3, 2F**
St. John's Gate, St. John's Lane; tel. 253-6644; Tues., Fri., and Sat. 10
A.M.–5 P.M., Sat. till 4 P.M.

National Army Museum   **CHELSEA**
Royal Hospital Rd.; tel. 730-0717; Mon.–Sat. 10 A.M.–5:30 P.M., Sun. 2–5:30
P.M.

National Gallery   **SOHO; P. 5, 3D**
Trafalgar Sq.; tel. 839-3321; Mon.–Sat. 10 A.M.–6 P.M., Sun. 2–6 P.M.

National Portrait Gallery   **SOHO; P. 5, 3D**
St. Martin's Pl.; tel. 930-1552; Mon.–Fri. 10 A.M.–5 P.M., Sat. 10 A.M.–6
P.M., Sun. 2–6 P.M.

Natural History Museum   **SOUTH KENSINGTON; P. 4, 5A**
Cromwell Rd.; tel. 589-6323; Mon.–Sat. 10 A.M.–6 P.M., Sun. 1–6 P.M.

Old Royal Observatory   **GREENWICH**
Greenwich Park; tel. 858-1167; Mon.–Sat. 10 A.M.–6 P.M., till 5 P.M. in winter, Sun. 2–6 P.M., till 5 P.M. in winter

Osterley Park House   **OSTERLEY**
Thornbury Rd., Osterley, Middlesex; tel. 560-3918; Tues.–Sun. 11 A.M.–5 P.M.

Percival David Foundation
of Chinese Art   **BLOOMSBURY; P. 2, 2D**
53 Gordon Sq.; tel. 387-3909; Mon.–Fri. 10:30 A.M.–5 P.M.

Pollock's Toy Museum   **BLOOMSBURY; P. 2, 2C**
1 Scala St.; tel. 636-3452; Mon.–Sat. 10 A.M.–5 P.M.

Prince Henry's Room   **THE CITY; P. 2, 3E**
17 Fleet St.; tel. 353-7323; Mon.–Fri. 1:45–5 P.M., Sat. 1:45–4:30 P.M.

Public Record Office Museum   **HOLBORN; P. 3, 3E**
Chancery Lane; tel. 876-3444; Mon.–Fri. 10 A.M.–5 P.M.

The Queen's Gallery   **WESTMINSTER; P. 5, 4C**
Buckingham Palace Rd.; tel. 799-2331 ext. 3351; Tues.–Sat. 10:30 A.M.–5 P.M., Sun. 2–5 P.M.

Queen's House, National Maritime Museum   **GREENWICH**
Romney Rd., Greenwich; tel. 858-4422; Mon.–Sat. 10 A.M.–6 P.M., Sun. 12–6 P.M.

Ranger's House   **GREENWICH**
Chesterfield Walk, Blackheath; tel. 853-0035; Feb.–Oct. 10 A.M.–5 P.M.

Royal Academy   **MAYFAIR; P. 5, 3C**
Burlington House Sq.; tel. 439-7438; daily 10 A.M.–6 P.M.

The Royal Albert Hall   **SOUTH KENSINGTON; P. 4, 4A**
Kensington Gore; tel. 589-8212; 10 A.M.–8 P.M.; March–Sept.

Royal Britain   **CLERKENWELL; P. 3, 2F**
Aldersgate St.; tel. 588-0588; daily 9:30 A.M.–5:30 P.M.

Royal College of Music   **SOUTH KENSINGTON; P. 4, 4A**
Prince Consort Rd.; tel. 589-3643; museum hours Mon. and Wed. 11 A.M.–4:30 P.M. by appt.

Royal Geographic Society   **SOUTH KENSINGTON; P. 4, 4A**
1 Kensington Gore; tel. 589-5466; Mon.–Fri. 10 A.M.–1 P.M. and 2–5 P.M.

Royal Institute of British Architects   **BLOOMSBURY; P. 2, 2C**
66 Portland Pl.; tel. 580-5533

The Royal Mews   **WESTMINSTER; P. 5, 4C**
Buckingham Palace Rd.; tel. 930-4832 Wed.–Thurs. 2–4 P.M.

Science Museum   **SOUTH KENSINGTON; P. 4, 5A**
Exhibition Rd.; tel. 589-3456; Mon.–Sat. 10 A.M.–6 P.M., Sun. 11 A.M.–6 P.M.

Scotch Whiskey House   **MAYFAIR; P. 5, 4C**
17 Half Moon St.; tel. 629-4384; Mon.–Fri. 9:30 A.M.–5:30 P.M.

Serpentine Gallery   **HYDE PARK; P. 4, 4A**
Kensington Gardens, Hyde Park; tel. 402-6075; Mon.–Fri. 10 A.M.–6 P.M., Sat. and Sun. 10 A.M.–7 P.M., till 4 in winter.

Sir John Soane's Museum   **HOLBORN; P. 2, 2E**
13 Lincoln's Inn Fields; tel. 405-2107; Tues.–Sat. 10 A.M.–5 P.M.

South Bank Crafts Centre　　　　　SOUTH BANK; P. 5, 4E
　Royal Festival Hall; tel. 928-0681; Tues.–Sun. 12–7 P.M.

Space Adventure　　　　　　　　　SOUTH BANK; P. 6, 4G
　64–66 Tooley St.; tel. 378-1405; daily 10:30 A.M. till 5:45 P.M.

Syon House and Park　　　　　　　　　　　ISLEWORTH
　Brentford, Middlesex; tel. 560-0881; Easter to Sept. Sun.–Thurs. 12–4:15
　P.M.; Oct. Sun. only 12–4:15 P.M.; Closed Oct.–Easter.

The Tate Gallery　　　　　　　　WESTMINSTER; P. 5, 5D
　Millbank; tel. 821-1313; Mon.–Sat. 10 A.M.–5:50 P.M., Sun. 2–5:50 P.M.

Theatre Museum　　　　　　　　COVENT GARDEN; P. 2, 3D
　Russell and Wellington sts.; tel. 836-7891; Tues.–Sun. 11 A.M.–7 P.M.

**Thomas Coram Foundation
for Children**　　　　　　　　　　BLOOMSBURY; P. 2, 2D
　40 Brunswick Sq.; tel. 278-2424; Mon.–Fri. 10 A.M.–4 P.M.

Tower Bridge　　　　　　　　　　　　　THE CITY
　Tel. 403-3761; daily 10 A.M. till 6:30 P.M., till 4:45 P.M. in winter

Victoria and Albert Museum　　SOUTH KENSINGTON; P. 4, 5A
　South Kensington; tel. 589-6371; Mon.–Sat. 10 A.M.–5:50 P.M., Sun.
　2:30–5:50 P.M.

The Wallace Collection　　　　　MARYLEBONE; P. 1, 2B
　Hertford House, Manchester Sq.; tel. 935-0687; Mon.–Sat. 10 A.M.–5 P.M.,
　Sun. 2–5 P.M.

Whitechapel Art Gallery　　　　　　　　　EAST END
　Whitechapel High St., tel. 377-0107; Tues.–Sun. 11 A.M.–5 P.M., Wed. till
8 P.M.

William Morris Gallery　　　　　　　WALTHAMSTOW
　Lloyd Park, Forest Rd., Walthamstow; tel. 527-5544 ext. 4390; Tues.–Sat.
　10 A.M.–1 P.M. and 2–5 P.M., first Sun. of each month 10 A.M.–12 P.M. and
　2–5 P.M.

Historic Sites
Bank of England　　　　　　　　THE CITY; P. 3, 3G
　Threadneedle St.; tel. 601-4878; Mon.–Fri. 10 A.M.–6 P.M.

The Banqueting House　　　　　WHITEHALL; P. 5, 4D
　Whitehall; tel. 930-4179; Tues.–Sat. 10 A.M.–5 P.M.; Sun. 2–5 P.M.

Big Ben　　　　　　　　　　　WESTMINSTER; P. 5, 4D

Buckingham Palace　　　　　　WESTMINSTER; P. 5, 4C
　The Mall; Changing of the Guard, Mon.–Sat. 11:30 A.M., Sun. 10:30 A.M.

The Cabinet War Rooms　　　　　WHITEHALL; P. 5, 4D
　Clive Steps, King Charles St.; tel. 930-6961; daily 10 A.M.–5:15 P.M.

The Central Criminal Court　　　　THE CITY; P. 3, 3F
　Old Bailey and Newgate sts.; tel. 248-3277; galleries Mon.–Fri. 10:30
　A.M.–1 P.M., 2–4 P.M.

The Charterhouse　　　　　　　CLERKENWELL; P. 3, 2F
　Charterhouse Sq.; tel. 253-9503; tours Apr.–Jul., Wed. 2:45 P.M.

Commonwealth Institute　　　　　　　KENSINGTON
　230 Kensington High St.; tel. 603-4535; Mon.–Sat. 10 A.M.–5:30 P.M., Sun.
　2–5 P.M.

Crosby Hall　　　　　　　　　　　　　CHELSEA
　Cheyne Walk; tel. 352-9663; Mon.–Sat. 10 A.M.–12 P.M., 2:15–5 P.M., Sun.
　2:15–5 P.M.

Gray's Inn HOLBORN; P. 2, 2E
Gray's Inn Pl.; tel. 405-8164; gardens open Mon.–Fri. 12–2:30 P.M.

Guildhall THE CITY; P. 3, 2F
Gresham St.; tel. 606-3030; Mon.–Sat. 10 A.M.–5 P.M., Sun. (May–Sept. only) 10 A.M.–5 P.M.

Hampton Court Palace HAMPTON COURT
East Molesey, Surrey, Hampton Ct.; tel. 977-8441; daily 9:30 A.M.–6 P.M.

Her Majesty's Tower of London
(see the Tower of London, below)

Hogarth's House CHISWICK
Hogarth Lane, Great West Rd.; tel. 994-6757; Mon., Wed.–Sat. 11 A.M.–6 P.M., Sun. 2–6 P.M.

Houses of Parliament WESTMINSTER; P. 5, 4D
Palace of Westminster; tel. 219-4272 or 219-3574

International Stock Exchange of the United Kingdom and the Republic of Ireland Limited THE CITY; P. 3, 3G
Old Broad and Threadneedle sts.; tel. 588-2355; Mon.–Fri. 9:45 A.M.–3:30 P.M.

Kensington Palace KENSINGTON
Kensington Gardens; tel. 937-9561; Mon.–Sat. 9 A.M.–4:15 P.M., Sun. 1–5 P.M.

Leadenhall Market THE CITY; P. 3, 3G
Gracechurch St.; 7 A.M.–6 P.M.

Leighton House KENSINGTON
12 Holland Park Rd.; tel. 602-3316; Mon.–Sat. 11 A.M.–5 P.M.

Lincoln's Inn (See Lincoln's Inn Chapel above)

Linley Sambourne House KENSINGTON
18 Stafford Terrace; tel. 937-0663; open May–Oct., Wed. 10 A.M.–4 P.M., Sun 2–5 P.M.

Lloyd's THE CITY; P. 3, 3G
1 Lime St.; tel. 623-7100; Mon.–Fri. 10 A.M.–2:30 P.M.

Mansion House THE CITY; P. 3, 3G
Mansion House Pl.; tel. 626-2500; by written appt. only

New Palace of Westminster WESTMINSTER; P. 5, 4D
(see Houses of Parliament, above)

Old Bailey THE CITY; P. 3, 3F
(see The Central Criminal Court, above)

Old War Office WHITEHALL; P. 5, 4D
Whitehall; tel. 218-9000

Operating Theatre of Old St. Thomas's Hospital SOUTH BANK; P. 6, 4G
St. Thomas St.; tel. 407-7600 (ext. 2739); Mon., Wed., Fri. 12:30–4 P.M.

Parliament Square WESTMINSTER; P. 5, 4D

Royal Exchange THE CITY; P. 3, 3G
Cornhill and Threadneedle sts.; tel. 283-7101; Mon.–Fri. 11:30 A.M.–1:45 P.M.

Royal Hospital Chelsea CHELSEA
Royal Hospital Rd.; tel. 730-0161; Mon.–Sat. 10 A.M.–12 P.M., 2–4 P.M.

Royal Opera House   COVENT GARDEN; P. 2, 3D
  Covent Garden; tel. 240-1066

Smithfield Market   THE CITY; P. 3, 2F
  Mon.–Thurs. 5–10 A.M.

St. Bartholomew's Hospital   THE CITY; P. 3, 2F
  West Smithfield; tel. 601-8888; Open daily 10 A.M.–8 P.M.

Staple Inn   HOLBORN; P. 2, 2E
  High Holborn; tel. 242-0106

The Temple   THE CITY; P. 3, 3E
  Crown Office Row; tel. 353-4355

Thames Barrier Visitor Centre   WOOLWICH
  Unity Way, Woolwich; tel. 854-1373; Mon.–Fri. 10:30 A.M.–5 P.M., Sat. and
Sun. till 5:30 P.M.

The Tower of London   THE CITY; P. 3, 3G
  Tower Hill; tel. 709-0765; Mon.–Sat. 9:30 A.M.–5 P.M., Sun. 2–5 P.M., winter
Mon.–Sat. till 4 P.M., closed Sun.

University of London   BLOOMSBURY; P. 2, 2C
  Montague Pl.; 387-7050

Westminster Abbey   WESTMINSTER; P. 5, 4D
  Parliament Sq.; tel. 222–7110; Mon.–Fri. 8 A.M.–6 P.M., Sat. 9 A.M.–2:45
P.M., Sun. for services

Parks and Gardens

Chelsea Physic Garden   CHELSEA
  Royal Hospital Rd.; tel. 352-5646; Apr.–Oct. Wed. and Sun. 2–5 P.M.

Dorset Fields   MARYLEBONE; P. 1, 2B
  Dorset Square

Green Park   P. 5, 4C

Holland Park   KENSINGTON
  Kensington High St.

Hyde Park   P. 4, 3–4A-B

Kensington Gardens   P. 4, 3–4A

London Zoo   MARYLEBONE; P. 1, 1B
  Regent's Park; tel. 722-3333; daily 9 A.M.–dusk, winter from 10 A.M.

Lord's Cricket Ground   MARYLEBONE; P. 1, 1A
  St. John's Wood Rd.; tel. 289–1611; Apr.–Sept.

Ranelagh Gardens   CHELSEA
  Royal Hospital Rd.

Regent's Park   MARYLEBONE; P. 1, 1A, B, C

St. James's Park   WESTMINSTER; P. 5, 4C-D

Victoria Park   HACKNEY

13

TRAVEL ARRANGEMENTS

The best way to insure smooth sailing throughout your trip is to do as much advance planning as possible; it also tends to get you that much more involved in and excited about your impending voyage.

Do talk to friends who have been there. Do do some reading (novels, histories, magazines, newspapers) on the subject of London specifically, or Britain generally. Do plan to arrive in Britain with at least £100 per person (in cash or traveler's checks), so you needn't be bothered changing money at the airport. Do buy your airline tickets as far in advance as possible to get the best rate. Do make hotel reservations (and theater reservations and even dinner reservations if you only have a week in town and want to eat at the best places) ahead of time.

This section is a roundup of important matters to attend to in the weeks or months prior to your departure.

For Information . . .

You may (just possibly) need information additional to that within the covers of this volume. The best place to go to is the **British Tourist Authority (BTA)** office in your area. The BTA is truly a crackerjack organization; they know everything about travel in Britain and are most kind and eager to help you. By all means write or phone them to pick their collective brain.

BRITISH TOURIST AUTHORITY OVERSEAS OFFICES

Australia
Midland House
171 Clarence St.
Sydney NSW 2000
Tel. (02) 29-8627
Telex: 20762 BTA SYD AA

Canada
94 Cumberland St.
Suite 600
Toronto, Ontario, M5R 3N3
Tel. (416) 925-6326
Fax: (02) 262 1414

Fax: (416) 961 2175

Ireland
123 Lower Baggot St.
Dublin 2
Tel. 614188

New Zealand
Dilworth Building
3rd floor
Customs and Queen sts.
Auckland 1
Tel. (09) 31 446
Fax: (09) 776 965

United States
625 N. Michigan Ave.
Suite 1510
Chicago, IL 60611-1977
Tel. (312) 787-0490
Fax. (312) 787-7746

Cedar Maple Plaza
Suite 210
2305 Cedar Springs Rd.
Dallas, TX 75201–1814
Tel. (214) 720-4040
Telex: 4952106
Fax: (214) 871 2665

World Trade Center
Suite 450
350 South Figueroa St.
Los Angeles, CA 90071
Tel. (213) 628-3525
Telex: 466655 BTA L5A C1
Fax: (213) 687 6621

40 West 57th St.
New York, NY 10019
Tel. (212) 581-4700
Telex: 237798
Fax: (212) 265 0649

Disabled visitors will find London and Great Britain most accessible and accommodating. The Royal Association for Disability and Rehabilitation (RADAR) is a good source of information and can be reached at 25 Mortimer St., London, W1N 8AB; tel. 637-5400. Holiday Care Service, 2 Old Bank Chambers, Station Rd., Horley, Surrey RH6 9HW; tel. (0293) 774535 also has free facility and accommodations information. Another good resource is ARTSLINE. This is an organization with listings of galleries, museums, and theaters that have facilities for those with special needs. In some cases, transportation to and from cultural events can be arranged. The ARTSLINE number is (01) 625-5666/7. The Automobile Association (AA) publishes a book assisting with holiday planning called the *AA Traveller's Guide for the Disabled.* It can be obtained by writing to the Automobile Association, Fanum House, Basingstoke, Hampshire, RG21 2EA.

Transportation

Thankfully, London is one of the easiest places to get to from just about anywhere on the planet; if you can get to an airport or a pier, you can get there.

Sailing to London
Until completion of the Chunnel (the English Channel tunnel to link England with France), the only way for foreigners to get to the island is by some form of oversea transport. If you have time, patience, and money the North Atlantic Crossing is still a very genteel five-day voyage made regularly by the *Queen Elizabeth 2* (phone Cunard in the United States 800-5-CUNARD), and occasionally by other superliners. Some people choose to sail one way and fly the other; in fact, British Airways and Cunard offer a package including flying the Concorde one way and sailing the *QE2* the other way, thus allowing the traveler the experience of

crossing the Atlantic as quickly and as slowly as possible in the same trip.

Flying to London

Certainly, most people will be flying to London. There are several daily flights from every major North American and South Pacific city offered by a variety of airlines. For those of you trying to rack up frequent-flyer miles, check to see whether your favorite airline travels to London in order to add several thousands to your tally, or perhaps to cash in on those bimonthly puddle-jumper flights that have added up over the past year. If your airline does not fly to London, it may have a reciprocal arrangement with one that does, so it's worth a phone call to check.

Most well-traveled individuals agree that unless you have a special reason for preferring another airline (like your Uncle Joe can get you cheap tickets), it is always best to fly with the national airline of your destination. The native carriers tend to have the best landing arrangements and on-the-ground facilities at their home town airports. This is an especially fortunate choice in the case of travel to London. Whether you are flying coach or Concorde, British Airways is an exceptionally good company and offers an exceptionally wide range of imaginative, competitively priced package tours to London.

Because London is such a popular destination, it is possible to find charter flights from most major cities for up to half off the fare of a regularly scheduled flight. Most charter companies operate by agreeing to buy up a certain number of seats—or in some cases an entire plane of seats—at a discounted rate and then pass the savings on to you. Most companies are quite legitimate and offer a good product at a good price. Check the travel section of a reputable newspaper for advertisements. Rates can vary considerably as, obviously, can service.

If you are booking a charter, there are several things you need to find out: **1)** Will you be flying on a scheduled flight? **2)** What airline and type of airplane will you be flying on? **3)** How far in advance can you/must you pick up your ticket? **4)** What form of payment is acceptable? Credit card? Check? Cash only? **5)** Is a deposit necessary? How much? How soon? **6)** What guarantee do you have that the flight will leave on the date and at the time (barring unavoidable delays) agreed upon? **7)** What arrangements can be made for refund of money in case of a canceled flight?

If you're at all uneasy about the answers you receive to these questions, call the Better Business Bureau to check if they have a file on the charter company in question.

Perhaps in your business you have sent important documents by overseas courier. This means someone picks up your package, flies with it to London, and hand-delivers it to the addressee by the next morning. Many overseas freight companies will "hire" you to be a courier by paying part or all of the cost of your flight in return for your picking up and delivering a package. Sometimes there are time restrictions—you can only fly on a certain day and stay for a week or two—or luggage restrictions—you can only bring a carry-on bag. But this is by far the cheapest way to fly. (Couriers with extra-special packages have been sent on Concorde.) Don't worry, if you deal with a well-known service, you won't be caught transporting drugs or weapons or classified computer chips; it is a perfectly acceptable and legitimate business. The easiest way to find out which companies will fly you this way is to look in the phone book for listings of international courier companies in your city and start calling. If the first company doesn't service London (most of the important ones do), ask them to suggest someone who does.

A final tip. The traditional flight from North America to Europe leaves between 6 and 9 P.M., and you arrive in London, beat and bleary eyed, between 6 and 9 A.M. the next morning. You get into town by 10, but can't check into your hotel till noon and are left to roam the streets till then, an easy mark for jet lag. There is a more civilized way to do it. The most civilized way, of course, is the Concorde, which takes 3½ painless hours and will have you in London just in time for cocktails. For those with important business to attend to at the other end, give the Concorde serious consideration. Arriving fresh and alert and ready to work could make all the difference to your deal. For those of you searching for a special-occasion splurge, this is a supremely special way to travel. The one danger is that once you've flown the Concorde, it's easy to be spoiled by the speed and service. If you're susceptible to these types of things, do try to keep a clear head.

Faster Than a Speeding Bullet (Well, Almost)

It's morning at the Concorde Club, JFK. Texans are making their one-last-calls to the home office giving last-minute instructions in twangy tones. Others sidle up to the breakfast buffet for a melon or Danish or perhaps a pre-boarding Bloody, and grab a copy of the *Times* (New York, London, or Financial).

On board the pilot gives us the lowdown on flying high and fast as Caroline serves a fresh glass of Cuvee Rene Lalou Millesime. The screens are ticking off the meters and miles: Mach 0.78. There go the Hamptons. —22 degrees C. Looks like a nice morning on Cape Cod.

3,380 miles to go. There goes Nantucket. Just hit Mach 1. Here comes the food. There goes the New World. Mach 2. 55,000 feet. —58 degrees C. Screaming across the Atlantic. 2,910 miles to go. "Up here we have the sky to ourselves," purrs the pilot. We burn fuel. We get lighter. We fly higher. More champagne? 59,000 feet. Don't mind if we do.

If you don't have that kind of money to spend, take an early-morning flight over instead of an evening flight. It should arrive early in the evening the same day. If you're going to be late, be sure to call your hotel to let them know this, so they will save your reservation. This way you can have a shower, a meal, a good night's rest, and be ready to hit the ground running in the morning.

ARRIVING IN LONDON

At Heathrow

Now that you've decided how you're going, you need to know where you're going. Although there are transportation information desks at each airport, it's best to arrive prepared. When you make your reservations, ask your hotel to suggest the best way to get to it from whichever airport.

Heathrow is London's busiest airport, about 15 miles west of the city. The fastest, cheapest way to get into town is by **Underground** (which travels a pleasant aboveground route for much of the journey): follow the signs in the terminal that are indicated by the Underground symbol, a red circle with a horizontal slash cutting across it. For about £2 the Piccadilly line will take you to central London in 45 minutes to an hour's time.

If you prefer to go by **bus,** London Transport runs an Airbus service from all terminals. Look for the signs indicating "Airbus" outside the terminal. Airbus Route A1 goes to southwest London, Airbus A2 goes to northeast London. If you're not sure which to take, ask the driver when you get on. The trip takes an hour and costs about £3. If you're arriving at night, go to the Heathrow Central Bus Station—a building in the center of the ring of terminals 1, 2, and 3—and take night buses N56 and N97.

If you must take a **taxi,** the fare to central London will hover around £20, not including tip. There may be extra charges for luggage and nighttime or weekend service. London cabbies are usually quite honest, but it's always best to get an estimate of the total fare before you get into a taxi, so there will be no surprises at the other end.

If you are planning to rent a **car** (and we strongly advise against it, except for out-of-London trips), book it in advance (i.e., at home before you leave) with an international company. You can book a car in the United States or Canada and pre-pay in dollars at a guaranteed rate, so you won't have to worry about fluctuating exchange rates. If you wait till you arrive, check with Budget (01-759-2216) or catch the shuttle bus to Swan National Car Rentals. The extra ten-minute ride to their offices could save you considerably (01-897-3232).

At Gatwick

Gatwick is London's second airport and popular with many budget carriers. The best way by far to get into town from Gatwick is the **Gatwick Express,** a train service to Victoria Station in southwest London where you can make connections for the Underground or get a taxi. The trip takes about a half hour and will cost about £7.50.

Green Line Flightline buses operate between Gatwick and Victoria Bus Station. The journey takes a little over an hour, depending on traffic, and costs £3.50. Again, Budget is a good choice of rental car at Gatwick (0293-540141), as is Swan (0293-513031).

Formalities

You will need a valid **passport,** which will be inspected and stamped at customs upon arrival.

Arriving as a visitor, it is unlikely that you will have anything to **declare**—unless you're bringing a case of Jack Daniel's as a hostess gift. You are allowed to bring 1 liter of liquor and four hundred cigarettes. You may not bring meat or poultry (unless fully cooked) or any type of plant material into the country. Pets must have a rabies license and are subject to a long period of quarantine immediately prior to arrival, so no matter how attached you are to one another, it's best to leave your furry pals at home.

If you are visiting Britain for a short period of time and are planning to drive, a valid **driver's license** from your home country will suffice. It is also important that you bring it because you will need to produce it when you rent a car. If you are planning to be in Britain longer than a year, you will need an International Driver's License.

The Seasons in London

London, the capital of fog, Macs (Macintosh raincoats), and brollies (Brit for umbrellas), has an undeserved reputation for bad weather. In the southeast of the island as it is, clouds tend to dump their burden on the Irish Sea, in Wales, and in Cornwall, so often London will be fair when the weather map for the rest of the country looks bleak. The one thing certain about London's weather, however, is its unpredictability. Autumn of 1988 was cold and damp; summer of 1989 was one of the warmest, sunniest on record. Go try and figure.

If you look at Britain on a world map, you may be surprised to see that latitudinally it is quite far north. The Gulf Stream keeps it warm. Winter will occasionally bring snow but rarely enough to last more than a day or two. Spring tends to be chilly, with rain through Mar. and into April. The weather breaks late in April and can be fine from then through the summer. Autumn (the Brits do not say "fall") can bring some of the year's best weather, from Sep. nearly through Oct.: crisp, sunny days and cool nights.

Bring sweaters and overcoats from Oct. through Mar. From April through Sep. bring a variety of clothing; summer days can be hot and muggy, and many places are not air-conditioned, so bring lightweight clothes. But pack several sweaters and a pair of warmish trousers for cooler evenings or a cold-weather front. Umbrellas are better than raincoats because rain tends to be sporadic, so you can just pop up your brolly, then put it down again, as the clouds roll in and out but won't be caught in a hot, heavy raincoat when the sun returns to warm things up again.

When you're packing be sure to include a few more dressy outfits if you plan to frequent theaters and upscale restaurants. If you have business in London, a professionally correct look is essential for both men and women. The habit of wearing sneakers to work, then changing into wing tips or pumps, has not caught on here yet, and the City's businessfolk stand very much on ceremony. Unless you're here signing recording contracts for your heavy-metal band, it's best to err on the side of conservatism in business dress.

Weather Information

Climate	Jan.	Feb.	Mar.	Apr.	May	Jun.	Jul.	Aug.	Sep.	Oct.	Nov.	Dec.
Average daily temperature												
°C	4	4	6	9	12	15	16	16	14	11	7	5
°F	39	39	43	48	54	59	60	60	57	52	45	41
Average rainfall												
milimeters	86	65	59	58	67	61	73	90	83	83	97	90
inches	3.3	2.5	2.3	2.2	2.6	2.4	2.8	3.5	3.2	3.2	3.8	3.5
Average daily sunshine hours												
	2	2	4	5	6	7	6	5	4	3	2	1

Money Matters

The basic unit of currency in Britain is the pound sterling whose value fluctuated in 1989 but was at about US $1.55–$1.60 at print time.

Rule Number 1: The most important thing to remember about changing money: Do it only once. In other words, never buy pounds with dollars and then dollars back again with the same pounds. Every time you make a transaction, you lose five to ten percent, so if you change the same money twice, you could easily lose up to twenty percent.

Rule Number 2: Never change money at a hotel or a bureau de change. If you run short on a weekend, use a credit card or change only the absolute minimum until you can get to a bank. Virtually every bank in London will change money. Banks are open Mon.–Fri., 9:30 A.M.–3:30 P.M. Some are open Sat. A.M. as well. There are 24-hour banks at Heathrow and Gatwick.

Most places in the city will accept traveler's checks. The best kind to get are those sold by Barclay's Bank because there is no service charge (usually one percent for other brands) levied when you buy them. Credit cards are also widely accepted, although it is always wise to check with a hotel or restaurant when you make your reservations. Most department stores and major shops will take credit cards, as will BritRail and many bus companies. It is essential to have a credit card when renting a car.

Additionally, it is possible to get cash or traveler's checks using a credit card. If you don't have one already, get a PIN (Personal Identification Number) for your credit card. This will enable you to withdraw money from automatic-teller machines at London banks that honor your credit card in exactly the same way you withdraw money with your bank cards from a cash machine at home. To find out which London banks service your card, call your credit card's service information number (check, too, that your PIN number has the right amount of digits). In all cases, there will be a limit on the amount of pounds you can withdraw per week, and there will be a per-transaction service charge.

American Express card holders can cash a personal check at selected AmEx travel centers in London. To do so, you must present, along with your check, your AmEx card and a piece of ID—driver's license or passport.

It is possible to get a cash advance, up to your available credit limit, with a Visa or MasterCard. This can be done at banks displaying the card's logo. The credit card companies view these transactions as loans and will charge you interest starting from *the day you receive the cash advance,* whether you pay your bill on time or not.

Among the cards, Visa and MasterCard (called Access in Britain) are most widely accepted, followed closely by AmEx and less closely by Diners Club and finally Carte Blanche.

V.A.T.

Value Added Tax is a 15 percent surcharge imposed on all goods and most services (i.e., hotel and restaurant bills). It is possible, although truly a pain in the neck, for non-British citizens to be refunded for VAT costs on goods but not on services. How to go about this is explained in the Shopping section. All prices quoted in this book are inclusive of VAT unless otherwise specified.

TIPPING

A ten to 15 percent tip is customary in restaurants, hotels, and taxis. Often your hotel or restaurant bill will include a service charge and should be labeled accordingly. If the service was good, of course you are welcome to add more; if it was bad, you can request to have a certain percentage subtracted—but be prepared for a verbal scuffle. Tipping the barman in a pub is not necessary.

1990 Events

January

London International Boat Show, Jan. 4–14, 1990, Earls Court Exhibition Centre, Warwick Rd., London SW5
contact: National Boat Shows Ltd., Boating Industry House, Vale Rd., Oaklands Park, Weybridge, Surrey KT13 9NS; tel. Weybridge (0932) 854511

West London Antiques Fair, Jan. 18–21, 1990, Kensington Town Hall, Hornton St., London W8
contact: Caroline Penman, Penman Antiques Fairs, Box 114, Haywards Heath, West Sussex RH16 2YU; tel. Lindfield (044 47) 2514

Rugby Union: England v. Ireland, Jan. 20, 1990, Rugby Football Union Ground, Twickenham, London
contact: Rugby Football Union, Twickenham, Middlesex TW1 1DZ; tel. 892–8161

World of Drawings and Watercolours Fair, Jan. 24–28, 1990, Park Lane Hotel, Piccadilly, London W1

February

Art 90, Feb. 1–4, 1990, Business Design Centre, Upper St., Islington, London N1
contact: Sue Bond Public Relations, 46 Greswell St., London SW6 6PP; tel. 381–1324

Crufts Dog Show, Feb. 8–17, 1990, Earls Court Exhibition Centre, Warwick Rd., London SW5
contact: Crufts Dog Show Office, The Kennel Club, 1 Clarges St., London W1 8AB; tel. 493-6651

Rugby Union: England v. Wales, Feb. 17, 1990, Rugby Football Union Ground, Twickenham, London
contact: Rugby Football Union, Twickenham, Middlesex TW1 1DZ; tel. 892–8161

March

Chelsea Antiques Fair, Mar. 13–24, 1990, Chelsea Old Town Hall, King's Rd., Chelsea, London SW3
contact: Caroline Penman, Penman Antiques Fairs, Box 114, Haywards Heath, West Sussex RH16 2YU; tel. Lindfield (044 47) 2514

International Contemporary Art Fair, Mar. 29–Apr. 1, 1990, Olympia, Hammersmith Rd., London W14
contact: Charlie Robinson, Interbuild Exhibitions Ltd., 11 Manchester Sq., London W1M 5AB; tel. 486-1951

April

Start of the London to Beijing Motor Challenge, Apr. 7, 1990, Starts Marble Arch, London W1, finishes Beijing, China
contact: David Pattison, Secretary, London to Beijing Motor Challenge, Jules Verne Travel Promotions Ltd, 21 Dorset Square, London NW1; tel. 723–6556

Devizes to Westminster International Canoe Race, Apr. 13–16, 1990, starts at Wharf Car Park, Wharf St., Devizes, Wiltshire to County Hall Steps, Westminster Bridge Rd., London SE1

Westminster Antiques Fair, Apr. 19–22, 1990, Royal Horticultural Halls, Greycoat St. and Vincent Sq., London SW1
contact: Caroline Penman, Penman Antiques Fairs, Box 114, Haywards Heath, West Sussex RH16 2YU; tel. Lindfield (044 47) 2514

London Marathon, Apr. 22, 1990, London
contact: Andy Ritchie, Entry Coordinator, London Marathon, Box 262, Richmond, Surrey TW10 5JB; tel. 948-7935

May

Royal Windsor Horse Show, May 10–13, 1990, Home Park, Windsor, Berkshire
contact: Francis Crawley, Shows Box Office, 4 Grove Parade, Buxton, Derbyshire SK17 6AJ; tel. Buxton (0298) 72272

Bath International Festival, May 25–Jun. 10, 1990, Bath, Avon
contact: Philip Walker, Bath Festival Office, Linley House, 1 Pierrepont Place, Bath, Avon BA1 1JY; tel. Bath (0225) 462231

June

Bath International Festival, May 25–Jun. 10, 1990, Bath (see above).

Greenwich Festival, Jun. 1–17, 1990, Greenwich, London SE10
contact: Tim Baker, Box Office, 25 Woolrich New Road, London SE18 6EU; tel. 854–8888 ext. 2316

Beating Retreat by the Massed Bands of the Scottish Division, Jun. 12–14, 1990, Horse Guards Parade, Whitehall, London SW1
contact: Retreat Booking Office, Headquarters The Scottish Division, The Castle, Edinburgh EH1 2YT; tel. 031–336 1761 ext. 4279

Grosvenor House Antiques Fair, Jun. 13–23, 1990, Grosvenor House, Park Lane, London W1
contact: Evan Steadman and Partners Ltd, The Hub, Emson Close, Saffron Walden, Essex CB10 1HL; tel. Saffron Walden (0799) 26699

Grosvenor House Antiques Fair, Jun. 14–24, 1989, Grosvenor House, Park Lane, London W1
contact: Evan Steadman and Partners Ltd., The Hub, Emson Close, Saffron Walden, Essex CB10 1HL; tel. Saffron Walden (0799) 26699

Trooping the Colour—The Queen's Official Birthday Parade, Jun. 16, 1990, Horse Guard's Parade, Whitehall, London SW1. Advance booking is required and tickets are allocated by ballot; apply in writing between January and end of February.

contact: The Brigade Major, HQ Household Division, Horse Guards, Whitehall, London SW1A 2AX.

Horse Racing: Royal Ascot, Jun. 19–22, 1990, Ascot Racecourse, Ascot, Berkshire
contact: The Secretary, Grand Stand Office, Ascot Racecourse, Ascot, Berkshire SL5 7JN; tel. Ascot (0990) 22211

Lawn Tennis Championships, Jun. 25–Jul. 8, 1990, All England Lawn Tennis and Croquet Club, Wimbledon, London SW19
contact: All England Lawn Tennis and Croquet Club, Church Rd., Wimbledon, London SW19 5AE; tel. 946-2244

July

Henley Royal Regatta, July 4–8, 1990, Henley-on-Thames, Oxfordshire
contact: The Secretary, Henley Royal Regatta Headquarters, Regatta House, Henley-on-Thames, Oxfordshire RG9 2LY; tel. Henley-on-Thames (0491) 572153

City of London Festival, Jul. 8–25, 1990
contact: City Arts Trust, Bishopsgate Hall, 230 Bishopsgate, London, EC2M 4QM; tel. 377-0540

Royal Tournament, Jul. 11–28, 1990, Earls Court Exhibition Centre, Warwick Rd., London SW5
contact: Royal Tournament Office, Horse Guards, Whitehall, London SW1A 2AX; tel. 930-6009

August

West London Antiques Fair, Aug. 16–19, 1990, Kensington Town Hall, Hornton St., London W8
contact: Caroline Penman, Penman Antiques Fairs, Box 114, Haywards Heath, West Sussex RH16 2YU; tel. Lindfield (044 47) 2514

September

Chelsea Antiques Fair, Sept. 11–22, 1990, Chelsea Old Town Hall, King's Road, Chelsea, London SW3
contact: Caroline Penman, Penman Antiques Fairs, Box 114, Haywards Heath, West Sussex RH16 2YU; tel. Lindfield (04447) 2514

October

Horse of the Year Show, Oct. 1–6, 1990, Wembley Arena, Wembley, London
contact: Francis Crawley, Shows Box Office, 4 Grove Parade, Buxton, Derbyshire SK17 6AJ; tel. Buxton (0298) 72272

National Brass Band Championships of Great Britain, Oct. 6–7, 1990, various venues including Royal Albert Hall, Kensington Gore, London SW7
contact: Anne-Marie Sizer, Boosey and Hawkes Band Festivals Ltd, Deansbrook Road, Edgware, Middlesex HA8 9BB; tel. 951-0747

November

Lord Mayor's Procession and Show, Nov. 10, 1990, The City, London
The route runs from the guild-hall to the Royal Courts of Justice.

City of London Antiques Fair, Nov. 20–25, 1990, Barbican Exhibition Centre, Silk St., London EC2
contact: Caroline Penman, Penman Antiques Fairs, Box 114, Haywards Heath, West Sussex RH16 2YU; tel. Lindfield (044 47) 2514

December

Olympia International Showjumping Championships, Dec. 13–17, 1990, Olympia, Hammersmith Rd., London W14
contact: Francis, Shows Box Office, 4 Grove Parade, Buxton, Derbyshire SK17 6AJ; tel. (0298) 72272

The following major art exhibitions are on in 1990: **Frans Hals,** Jan. 13–Apr. 8, 1990, at the Royal Academy of Arts, Piccadilly, London W1, tel. 439–7438. **The Image of the Hurricane** runs Apr. 10–Oct. 31, 1990, at the Royal Air Force Museums, Hendon, London NW9, tel. 205–2266.

The **Shakespeare Theatre Season** runs from Mar. to the end of the year at the Royal Shakespeare Theatre, Swan Theatre, and the Other Place, Stratford-upon-Avon (tel. for Stratford-upon-Avon 0789–295623.)

The **Henry Wood Promenade Concerts 1990** (The Proms) will go from Jul. 20 to Sep. 15, 1990, at the Royal Albert Hall, Kensington Gore, London SW7. (Contact: Nicola Goold, Orchestral Promotions and Publicity Officer, BBC Symphony Orchestra, Room 426, 16 Langham St., London W1A 1AA; tel. 927–4296.) The **Open Air Theatre** Season in Regent's Park is Jun.–Sep.

Bank Holidays in 1990 are Jan. 1, Apr. 13 (Good Friday), Apr. 16 (Easter Monday), May 7 (May Day), May 28 (Spring Bank Holiday), Aug. 27 (Summer Bank Holiday), Dec. 25 (Christmas Day), Dec. 26 (Boxing Day).

BUSINESS BRIEF

Business in Britain is much like British weather—predictably unpredictable. A typical British weather forecast will advise you to expect "sunshine with intermittent showers" or "rain with occasional sunshine." Only rarely will it predict a real storm.

You'll find that it's much the same when you're doing business with the inhabitants of this tight and tidy little isle. The British—be they English, Scot, or Welsh—are a polite people. Like their weather, their moods may vary between pleasant and dour, but it takes a great deal of adversity to provoke them into a noisy or disagreeable storm.

British reserve is confusing to many Americans, who are far more prone to express a current mood, whether it is delight, displeasure, or disappointment. The British, one soon begins to believe, must surely be great poker players.

This brief piece is meant to serve as an umbrella—a "brolly," if you will—for those Americans (and others) who are fortunate enough to find themselves "doing business" in the United Kingdom. In a modest way it is meant to shield you during those occasional showers and to give you a sense of security when all is sunny and bright. It may even help you avoid one of those infrequent storms.

Let's' get down to business:

- Recognize first of all that the British actually *like* most Americans (whether they show it overtly or not). They respect most of us (but not all of us), they dislike some of us (but not most of us), and they are occasionally confused by the whole bloody lot of us. Try as they will, they find it difficult to fit us into a proper (that is, "British") mold. This ambiguity about "you Americans" stems from the fact that we're truly alike in many basic ways, yet we are also so very, very different.
- Keep in mind that a firm "no" will be rendered every bit as politely in Britain as an enthusiastic "yes". In other words, don't assume that your deal has been concluded until hands have been shaken or a letter of intent has been signed—either of which is worth its weight in pounds sterling or gold.
- Don't be surprised that most of them (English, Scot, or Welsh) are more class-conscious than many Americans, al-

though this is more evident in their dealings with each other than with visiting Americans. Again, as above, they find it difficult to catagorize the "typical" American—but they will *always* place a high value on good manners.

- Also keep in mind that many if not most of your British counterparts place an even higher value on solid experience than on university degrees. Experience, they feel, speaks for itself, while flaunting one's education is terribly bad form. Many successful British men and women hold *no* university degrees, but it would be a grave mistake to assume that yours gives you any sort of superiority.

- Don't be thrown if you encounter a bit more sexism in Britain than you might find in the States. In all likelihood you will find fewer women in mangerial positions, and in many meetings and conferences you'll find none at all (excepting the "tea lady," of course).

- Don't be loud, either in dress or speech. Although some of the British dress rather badly, they often express surprise when an American is conservatively dressed and neatly groomed. They also believe—or *pretend* to believe—that we're much too brash, although they secretly know that's often not true. They'll deny it, of course, but many of them secretly admire us for some of the qualities they tend to deride.

- Avoid, if possible, discussing British politics—but be forewarned that the British will discuss yours. Many of them are convinced they understand American politics better than you do, and they're equally convinced that you know nothing of theirs. That may well be true—but politics, like religion, has no place in a business discussion.

- Avoid also any criticism of the royal family (even if they don't) and try to sidestep any comparison between British and American "football" or cricket and baseball—at least until your business has been concluded.

- Don't underestimate the British—*any* of them—for under that scruffy tweed jacket or Savile Row suit beats a heart that is both clever and canny. Person for person, and acre for acre, they've managed their affairs better than most—and they've been at it for hundreds of years.

- Don't mistake civility for servility, pomposity for lack of ability, or good manners for weakness. There are exceptions, of course, and broad generalities are dangerous—but British business acumen is a fact.

- Above all, consider yourself lucky if you're planning a business trip to Great Britain. The country is a constant delight, the natives are civilized, the language is almost the same as yours, and the weather is *usually* mild.

CULTURAL TIME LINE

A.D. 43	Roman trading station at "Londinium" on the north banks of the Thames.
286–87	Roman admiral Carausias in a revolt against Diocletian proclaims himself emperor and makes Londinium his capital.
449	Britain conquered by Germanic tribes (Angles, Saxons, and Jutes).
675	All Hallows by the Tower Church founded.
796	Britain united under Egbert.
1016	London becomes the capital for the Anglo-Saxon kings.
1066	Battle of Hastings. Norman conquest of England. William the Conqueror crowned in Westminster Abbey.
1078	Tower of London built.
Early 12th century	London a city republic under Henry I.
1157	Hanseatic trading post on the banks of the Thames.
1170	Murder of Thomas Becket, Archbishop of Canterbury.
1192	Office of Lord Mayor established.
1215	King John signs the Magna Carta.
1245–69	Westminster Abbey rebuilt in Gothic style.
1272–1307	Under Edward I, Inns of Court established.
1332	Two houses of Parliament established.
1337–1453	Hundred Years War.
1440	Eton College founded by Henry VI.
1455–85	Wars of the Roses: dynastic struggle between houses of York and Lancaster for the throne.
1476	William Caxton: first book printed in England.
1483	Richard III allegedly has his nephews murdered in the Tower of London.
1512	Houses of Parliament destroyed by fire.
1518	College of Physicians founded.
1529	Cardinal Wolsey presents his Hampton Court Palace to Henry VIII.
1534–1535	Church of England established under Henry VIII. Execution of Sir Thomas More.
1558–1603	Reign of Queen Elizabeth I. London's rise as commercial and cultural center.
1588	Defeat of the Spanish Armada; Gower's *Armada* portrait of Elizabeth I.

1599	Globe Theatre built in Southwark, south bank of the Thames.
c. 1600	Inigo Jones (1573–1651), first English architect, travels to Italy, studies Palladian style, designs Banqueting House (1622).
1605	Gunpowder Plot: Guy Fawkes tries to blow up Parliament.
1611	Publication of King James Bible.
1635	Rubens: *Apotheosis of Charles I* (Ceiling, Banqueting House).
1649	End of civil wars between supporters of Parliament and Royalists. Charles I beheaded. Cromwell becomes Lord Protector. Commonwealth established.
1652	First London coffee shop.
1660–85	Stuart Restoration.
1665–66	Great Plague and Great Fire of London. Four-fifths of the city destroyed.
1669	Christopher Wren appointed Surveyor General; redesigns many churches destroyed by fire.
1675	Greenwich ("Old Royal") Observatory founded.
1680–81	King Square (Soho) built.
1689	Henry Purcell's opera *Dido and Aeneas.*
1694	Bank of England incorporated by royal charter to finance war against France.
1702	London's first daily newspaper, *The Daily Courant,* printed on Fleet Street.
1709	Richard Steele founds *The Tatler.*
1710	St. Paul's Cathedral (redesigned by Christopher Wren).
Mid-18th century	English industrial revolution begins.
c. 1740	Chippendale's furniture shop opens on St. Martin's Lane.
1753	British Museum founded.
1759	Kew Gardens established.
1768	Royal Academy of Arts founded; Joshua Reynolds (1723–1792), first president.
1722	James Gibbs begins St. Martins-in-the-Fields church.
1775–1783	American Revolutionary War of Independence.
1780	Newgate Prison burned during the Gordon riots.
Early 19th century	First train service in London; development of Port of London.
1805	Lord Nelson's victory at Trafalgar.
1814	Sir John Soane's Dulwich Picture Gallery, London's first public art gallery.
1817	Statues and friezes from the Parthenon first exhibited at the British Museum (Elgin Marbles). Keats resides at Wentworth Place in Hampstead (Keats Museum).

1824	National Gallery founded.
1837	Queen Victoria makes Buckingham Palace the official royal residence; Dickens and his family move to Doughty Street in Bloomsbury (Dickens Museum); Carlyle writes *The French Revolution* at 24 Cheyne Row, Chelsea.
1843	John Ruskin: *Modern Painters,* Vol. 1.
1849	Karl Marx moves to London.
1851	Great Exposition; Crystal Palace.
1852	New Houses of Parliament open, designed by Charles Berry.
1861	William Morris establishes a firm to revive pre-industrial crafts and design.
1863	First London metro line completed.
1869	*Cutty Sark,* fastest tea clipper of its day, built.
1871	Albert Hall completed.
1878	Obelisk from Heliopolis ("Cleopatra's needle") unveiled at Victoria Embankment.
1897	Queen Victoria's Diamond Jubilee.
1899–1902	Boer War.
1900	*Daily Express* founded.
1914–18	World War I.
1914	Vaughan Williams: *London Symphony.*
1915	Zeppelin air raid on London.
1918	Women's suffrage in England.
1927	Virginia Woolf: *To the Lighthouse;* Bloomsbury Group.
1938	Chamberlain signs Munich pact with Hitler.
1939–1945	World War II.
1940	57 nights of continuous aerial bombing (the blitz). Churchill becomes prime minister.
1949	Orwell: *1984.*
1953	Queen Elizabeth crowned in Westminster Abbey.
1974	IRA bombs damage Parliament.
1979	Margaret Thatcher becomes Prime Minister
1981	Marriage of Prince of Wales and Lady Diana Spencer.
1982	Falkland Island campaign.
1986	Marriage of Prince Andrew and Miss Sarah Ferguson (now the Duke and Duchess of York).

Chronology of Reigns
Norman (1066–1189)

William the Conqueror	1066–1087
William II (Rufus)	1087–1100
Henry I (Beauclerc)	1100–1135
Stephen	1135–1154

Plantagenet

Henry II	1154–1189
Richard I	1189–1199
John (Lackland)	1199–1216
Henry III	1216–1272
Edward I	1272–1307
Edward II	1307–1327
Edward III	1327–1377
Richard II	1377–1399

House of Lancaster

Henry IV	1399–1413
Henry V	1413–1422
Henry VI	1422–1461
	1470–1471
	(restored)

House of York

Edward IV	1461–1469
	1471–1483
Edward V	1483
Richard III	1483–1485

Tudor

Henry VII	1485–1509
Henry VIII	1509–1547
Edward VI	1547–1553
Mary I	1553–1558
Elizabeth I	1558–1603

United Kingdom House of Stuart

James I	1603–1625
Charles I	1625–1649

Commonwealth & Protectorate

Oliver Cromwell	1653–1658
Richard Cromwell	1658–1659

House of Stuart
(Restoration)

Charles II	1660–1685
James II	1685–1688
(Glorious Revolution)	1688
Mary II & William III	1689–1702
Anne	1702–1714

House of Hanover

George I	1714–1727
George II	1727–1760
George III	1760–1820
George IV	1820–1830
William IV	1830–1837
Victoria	1837–1901

House of Saxe-Coburg

Edward VII	1901–1910

House of Windsor

George V	1910–1936
Edward VIII	1936
George VI	1936–1952
Elizabeth II	1952–present

VITAL INFORMATION

EMERGENCIES
In case of disaster call 999. Rape Crisis Center, 837-1600.

Hospitals
With 24-hour emergency rooms;
Charing Cross Hospital (tel. 846-1234)
St. Thomas Hospital (tel. 928-9292)
Westminster Hospital (tel. 828-9811)
St. Bartholomew's Hospital (tel. 601-8888)
Royal Free Hospital (tel. 794-0500)
The National Health Service (Britain's socialized medical plan) does not cover foreigners. If you receive minor medical services, often the doctors or nurses will not charge you because the trouble of filling out the forms is not worth the small amount of revenue to be generated therefrom. For major medical services, you will be expected to pay the rate charged to private patients. Check to see if any of your existing policies cover overseas medical care, and if so, what kind and how much. If you feel you need more insurance just in case, contact any major insurance broker listed in your phone book, or contact your credit card's service department. Most credit cards have emergency medical-service programs—sometimes free to card members. It is possible to take out medical insurance once you are here, but it is time-consuming and costly; we advise you to attend to this matter back home.

If You Lose Your Passport
Report it immediately to the police and to your embassy:

Australia High Commission, Australia House, the Strand (tel. 438-8738)
Canadian High Commission, Canada House, 1 Grosvenor Square (tel. 629-9492)
New Zealand High Commission, New Zealand House, Haymarket (tel. 930-8422)
United States Embassy, 24 Grosvenor Square (tel. 491-3506)

If You Lose Your Travelers' Checks
Report it to the office of the dispensing organization (i.e., Barclay's Bank or American Express). Bring along the list of numbers of your checks (which you remembered to keep in a safe place SEPARATE FROM YOUR CHECKS) and some form of identification (passport).

If You Lose Your Credit Card
Call:
American Express (tel. 0273-696933)
Diner's Club (tel. 0252-516261)
MasterCard (Access) (tel. 0702-351303)
Visa (tel. 0604-230230)

Lost Property
Report it to the nearest police station (ask a policeman in the street or check the phone book for its location). Or direct written inquiries to Metropolitan Police Lost Property Office, 15 Penton Street, N1.

If you lost the item on the bus or Underground, report in person to Lost Property Office, 200 Baker Street, NW1 5RZ, to fill out a form.

Airline Offices

Air Canada, 140 Regent Street (tel. 759-2636); British Airways, 75 Regent Street (tel. 897-4000); Pan Am, 193 Piccadilly (tel. 409-0688); TWA, 200 Piccadilly (tel. 636-4090)

London Tourist Board Information Centres

Victoria Station Forecourt

Harrods Department Store, Brompton Road, Knightsbridge

Selfridges Department Store, Oxford Street

Tower of London, West Gate

Heathrow Terminals 1,2,3, Underground Concourse, and Terminal 2, Arrivals Concourse

For London Tourist Board Telephone Information Service, phone 730-3488.

For Travel Elsewhere in Britain

British Travel Centre, 12 Regent Street (tel. 730-3400)

Northern Ireland Tourist Board, 11 Berkeley Street (tel. 493-0601)

Scottish Tourist Board, 19 Cockspur Street (tel. 930-8661)

Wales Tourist Board, 34 Piccadilly (tel. 409-0969)

For BritRail general information (tel. 922-6632), or call the station whence your train is departing, listed in the phone book.

For Green Line (bus) coaches from Victoria Station, call 668-7261.

Post Offices

Main post offices are open Monday to Friday from 9 A.M. to 5:30 P.M., Saturday from 9 A.M. to 12:30 P.M. Additionally, stamps can be bought at post office substations at newsstands or tobacconists that display the red and yellow "Post Office" sign. Lines are usually very long at the main-branch post offices, so it's often better to get your stamps when you buy your paper. Some main post offices also handle Girobank foreign (money) exchange.

Telephones

Try not to make phone calls from your hotel room; you will be charged ridiculous rates. It's better to find a public telephone, of which there are two types in England:

1) Pay phone into which you insert coins from 2 pence to £1.
2) Phonecard Phones. These are a great invention and are operated by a phonecard, which can be purchased in units from 10 to 200 at the price of 10 pence a unit from main post offices, some newsagents who display the phonecard sign, and at some hotels. The phonecard is about the size of a credit card and has much the same function, allowing you to "charge" the cost of your call up to the amount of units listed on its surface. Any unused units will be stored on the phonecard, which can be reused until all the units have been eaten up.

British Telecom (the phone company) is not the greatest in the world. You'll find that for every completed call you make, you will probably have to dial the number once or twice to get a proper connection, and calls have the unfortunate habit of being cut off in mid-conversation. There's nothing you can do, but be patient and keep dialing.

For London directory assistance: 142; elsewhere in Britain: 192

For overseas operator assistance: 155

For international calls: dial 010, then The country code

For Australia, 61

For Canada, 1

For New Zealand, 64

For the United States, 1

Phone rates within the U.K. are most expensive weekdays from 8 A.M. to 1 P.M., less expensive weekdays from 1 P.M. to 6 P.M., cheapest weekdays from 6 P.M. to 8 A.M. and all day and all night Saturday and Sunday.

Rates for international calls are lowest from 8 P.M. to 8 A.M. weekdays and all day and all night Saturday and Sunday. For Australia and New Zealand, the lowest rates are daily from midnight to 7 A.M. and from 2:30 P.M. to 7:30 P.M.

Useful Phone Numbers

Weather: 246-8091

Time: 123

Teletourist (listing of daily events): 246-8041

Road Conditions (within an 80-km radius): 246-8021

Financial and Business News: 246-8026

Samaritans (for medical emergencies): 283-3400

Release (for legal assistance): 603-8654

Police Headquarters, New Scotland Yard: 230-1212

Electricity

Most hotels have hair dryers and irons or pressing services. If you're bringing electrical appliances—keep these to an absolute minimum—you will probably need to buy an adapter to change the voltage (from 110–120 volts, 60 cycles for North America) to 220–240 volts, 50 cycles, the British unit. Many hotels have in-the-wall outlets for electric razors that will take either 110 or 220. If you need to get an adapter, you can buy one at a hardware store at home or in London.

Index

Academy of St. Martin-in-the-Fields, 94, 201
Act of Supremacy, 140
Air travel to London, 221–223
Airline offices, 239
All-Hallows-by-the-Tower, 55
American Memorial Chapel, 64
Ancient civilizations, 130
Antique shops, 170–171
Art Exhibitions, 230
Arts Centre, 54
Avery Stone Circles, 210–211

Ballet, 33, 98, 201
Bank holidays, 230
Bank of England, 11, 47, 66
Bankside, 156
Bankside Power Station, 160
Banqueting House, 41, 74
Barbican Centre, 47, 54, 100, 199
Barristers, 144
Bath, 209–210
Battersea Arts Centre, 199
Bayswater, hotel, 19
Bear Gardens Museum of the Shakespearean Stage, 160
Bearbaiting, 160
Beatles' manuscripts, 31
Belgravia, 12, 33, 102–114
    hotels, 16, 21, 23–24
Bethnal Green Museum of Childhood, 42
Bevis Marks, 55
Bicycle, 37
Big Ben, 76, 84
Birdcage Walk, 87
Bloomsbury, 12–13, 31, 127–137
Bloomsbury Festival, 132
Bloomsbury Group, 128
Bloomsbury Square, 127
Bloomsbury Theatre, 132, 199
Boat rental, 126
Borough Market, 156, 158
Botanical garden, 113
Bow Bells, 58
Brick lane, 32
Brighton, 211
British Library, 129, 130
British Library's National Sound Archive, 106–107
British Museum, 120–121, 129–131
    description, 31
British terms, 7
Broadgate, 67
Brunswick Gardens, 151
Buckingham Palace, 9, 12, 34, 35
Bugle House, 91
Bunhill (Bone Hill) Fields, 138
Bus, 36–37
Business, 65–68, 231–232
    bank holidays, 230
    district, 12

Cabinet War Rooms, 35
Cambridge, 209
Camden, 12
Camden Lock, 32
Camden Town, 39
Canals, 39
Car rental, 37
Carlton Gardens, 118
Carnaby Street, 88, 91
Cathedral Church of St. Savior and St. Mary Overie, 157

Cecil Count, 100
Central Criminal Court, 68
Ceremony of the Bath, 53
Ceremony of the Keys, 52
Chancery Lane, 144
Changing of the Guard, 9, 31, 42, 74, 87
Chapel of Edward the Confessor, 83
Chapel of the Kings, 83
Chapel Royal of Saint John the Evangelist, 53
Charing, 94
Charing Cross, 73, 94
Charterhouse, 13, 139–140
Chartism, 138
Chelsea, 9, 12, 16, 33, 35, 102–114
    Fulham Road, 104
    hotels, 16, 21–22, 25
    shopping, 33–34, 104
Chelsea Bridge, 113
Chelsea Flower Show, 113
Chelsea Old Church, 114
Chelsea Pensioners, 112
Chelsea Physic Garden, 44, 113
Chelsea Royal Hospital, 33, 45, 112–113
Chelsea Wharf, 114
Cheyne Walk, 114
Children, sightseeing, 42
Children's Playground, 42, 126
Chinatown, 88, 100
Chiswick, 8
Chiswick House, 41
Chronology of Reigns, 236–237
Chubb vaults, 53
Church of the Order, 142
Church music, 197–198
Churches, listing of, 212–213
Churchill's Underground, 75–76
Circuses, 90
City, 8–9, 12, 16, 32, 33, 46–69
    boundaries of, 46; business, 65–67; churches, 32, 33, 55, 57–58; lawyers, 68–69; map of, 48; museum, 32; pubs, 65, 69; Smithfield Market, 47, 49; St. Paul's, 60–65; Tower, 49–50, 52–53
City listings, 212–218
    churches, 212–213; historic sites, 216–218; museums and galleries, 213–216; parks and gardens, 218
City of London Information Centre, 65
Class system, 3–4
Clerkenwell, 12, 13, 138–146
Clerkenwell Green, 138
Clerkenwell Heritage Centre, 142
Clerkes Well, 138
Clink Street, 159
Clore Gallery, 34, 85
Clothiers, 98–99
Coastal trading schooner, 159
Collegiate culture, 106
Commonwealth Institute, 152
Constitution Hill, 34
Courtauld Institute Galleries, 95
Covent Garden, 12, 16, 32, 33, 41, 95–98
    hotels, 27
Craftsmen's Potters Shop, 91
Credit cards, 17
    lost, 238
Cricket, 128, 134–135, 198

memorial museum, 135
Cripplegate, 138
Crosby Mall, 114
Crown Jewels, 42, 53
Cruises, 34, 39, 42
Cultural time line, 233–237

Design Museum at Butler's Wharf, 156
Diamond Sutra, 128
Dickens, 142–143, 145
Dickens House, 139, 142–143, 145
Docklands, 39
Dole, 1
Domesday Book, 145
Dorset Fields, 134
Downing Street, 74–75
Dress collection, 150
Duels, 124

Earls Court, 147
East End, 8, 51
tours, 39
Eaton, 207
Edward the Confessor, 9, 70
shrine, 83
Electricity, 240
Elgin marbles, 128, 130
Eliot, George, 114
Embankment Gardens, 95
English Rococo, 92
Entertainment, 179–202
church music, 197–198; dance, 201; music, 201; nightlife, 201–202; sports, 198–199; theater, 199–200
Ethnography Department of the British Museum, 120–121
Events, 1990, 227–230
Exhibition of 1851, 107
Exhibition Road Gallery, 106

Faraday Museum, 44, 123
Fenton House, 205–206
Financial district, 32, 65–67
Fitzroy, 132
Fleet River, 138
Formalities, 224
Foundling Hospital Art Treasures, 128
Freud Museum, 44

Galleries, listing, 213–216
Galleries, mansion, 43
Gallows, 127
Gardens, 218
Geological Museum, 107
Gibbons, Grinling, 112
Globe, 155–156
Good Hope House, 72
Goulders Hill Park, 40
Gray's Inn, 13, 143, 144
Great Bell of Bow, 58
Great Bell of Westminster, 76
Great Exhibition of 1851, 104–105
Great Fire, 9, 54, 56, 138, 147
Great Plague, 9, 56, 147
Green Park, 8, 124, 138
Greenwich, 203–205
Greyhound racing, 198
Guards Museum, 86–87
Guildhall, 47

Hackney Empire, 199
Hampstead, 8, 205–206
Hampton Court Palace, 45, 205
Harrods, 110
Hays Dock, 156

Hays Galleria, 157
Hays Wharf, 155, 157
Hayward Gallery, 155, 161
Hayward, John, 58
Henry VII's chapel, 83–84
Highgate, 8
Highwaymen, 124
Hippies, 98–99
Historic sites, listings of, 216–218
Hogarth, William, tour, 41
Holborn, 12, 13, 138–146
Holburne stream, 138
Holland House, 153
Holland Park, 13, 16, 41, 153–154
description, 32
Holmes, Sherlock, 134
Horse racing, 198
Hospitals, 238
Hotels, 14–30
air-conditioning, 16; Belgravia, 21, 23–24; B&Bs, 15; Chelsea, 16, 21–22, 25; Covent Garden, 27; credit cards, 17; Kensington, 17, 23, 25–26; Knightsbridge, 17, 18, 19, 23, 24–25; listings of, 14; location information, 17; Marylebone, 19–21; Mayfair, 16, 18, 22; out of town, 27–30; price, 14, 15; private bath, 15; reservations, 14, selections, 17–30; Soho, 23–24; South Kensington, 16, 22–23; standards, 16; St. James's, 16, 20, 26
Hougomont Farm, 86
House of Commons, 78–79
House of Lords, 78
House of St. Barnabas, 91
Houseboats, 114
Houses of Parliament, 12, 35, 77–79
Hyde Park, 8, 35, 124–126
character of, 124, 126
Serpentine Gallery, 126
Hyde Park Corner, 34
H.M.S. *Belfast,* 156

Information 238–240
airline offices, 239; bank holidays, 230; business, 231–232; credit cards, lost, 238; cultural time line, 233–237; electricity, 240; emergencies, 238; hospitals, 238; hotel listings, 14; money matters, 225–226; passport, lost, 238; phone numbers, 239–240; post offices, 239; property, lost, 238; seasons, 224–225; special events, 227–230; telephones, 239; tipping, 226; tourist board, 239; travelers checks, lost, 238; V.A.T., 226; weather, 225
Inns of Court, 138, 143–145, 146
Institute of Contemporary Arts (ICA), 117
International Shakespeare Globe Centre, 160
International Stock Exchange, 66–67
Islington, 12

Jewish Museum, 132
Jones, Inigo, tour, 41, 160

Keats, John, 206
Kensington, 13, 32, 147–154
hotel, 17, 23, 25–26; map, 149; museums, 34–35
Kensington Gardens, 8, 35, 102, 117, 126, 147

Kensington Gore, 102
Kensington Palace, 32, 45, 148, 150–151
Kensington Palace Gardens, 151
Kensington Square, 151
Kenwood, 205
Kew Gardens, 206–207
King's Road, 104, 111–112
Kite Flying, 42
Knights, 139–142
Knights Arcade, 110
Knights Hospitalar, 141–142
Knightsbridge, 102
  hotels, 17–19, 23, 24–25; shops, 109–110

Lambeth, 156
Laser concerts, 134
Law, 68–69
Lawrence, T.E., 84
Leadenhall Market, 67
Leicester Square, 41, 99–100
Leighton House, 32, 148, 152–153
Lincoln's Inn, 143, 144
Lincoln's Inn Chapel, 41
Lindisfarne Gospels, 130
Linley Sambourne House, 32, 148, 152
Little Angel Marionette Theatre, 42
Little Venice, 39
Lloyd's Bank Law Courts Branch, 69
Londinium, 9, 46, 62
London Dungeon, 157
London Experience, 101
London International Financial Futures Exchange (LIFFE), 66
London Pavilion, 101
London Planetarium, 42, 44, 134
London Symphony, 54, 201
London Transport Information, 37
London Transport Museum, 33, 97
London University, 13, 16
London Wall, 12
London Zoo, 39, 42, 53, 128, 136
Long Water, 126
Lord's Cricket Ground, 135
Lovely Ritas, 37

Madame Tussaud's, 42, 101, 128, 134
Magna Carta, 78, 130, 145
Mall, 31, 117
Maltese Cross, 142
Mansion Galleries, 43
Mansion House, 66
Maps: Bath, atlas 16; Belgravia, So. Kensington, Chelsea, 103; City, 48; Cambridge, atlas 14–15; Great Britain, atlas 9; Greater London, atlas 8; Greenwich, 204; Hyde Park, 125; Kensington, 149; London, atlas 1–6; London Orientation, 10–11; London Underground, atlas 7; Oxford, atlas 12–13; St. James, Mayfair, the Parks, 116; St. Paul's Cathedral, 61; Soho & Covent Garden, 89; Stratford Upon Avon, atlas 11; Theater District, 200; Tower of London, 50; Westminster & Whitehall, 71; Westminster Abbey, 81; Windsor & Eton, atlas 10
Marathon, 198
Marble Arch, 34, 127
Markets, 32
Marx Memorial Library, 138

Marylebone, 8, 12–13, 31, 127–137
  hotels, 19–21
Marylebone Cricket Club, 134
Master of the Revels, 141
Mayfair, 12, 115–116
  hotels, 16, 18, 22
Michelin House, 110–111
Military Knights Hospitalar, 141
Military museum, 113
Monasteries, dissolution of, 139, 140, 141
Monks, 139–142
Montagu House, 129
Mummies, 129
Museum of London, 47, 54
Museum of Mankind, 120–121, 129
Museum of the Moving Image (MOMI), 155, 162
Museum of the Order of St. John, 141–142
Museums and Galleries, 213–216
Music, 43–44, 91, 201
Music halls, 100

Nash House, 117
National Army Museum, 113
National Film Theatre, 155, 161
National Gallery, 41, 85, 88, 90, 92–93
  description, 32
National Maritime Museum, 204
National Portrait Gallery, 32, 90, 93–94
National Theater Company, 161, 162
National Trust, 86
Natural History Museum, 42, 107–108
Naval History, 156
Nightlife, 201–202
Ninevah Galleries, 130
Norman crypt, 58
Northampton Square, 142
Notting Hill, 32; hotels, 14, 16
Nottingham House, 148, 150

Old Admiralty, 73
Old Bailey, 33, 47, 68
Old Curiosity Shop, 139
Old Royal Observatory, 44
Old Treasury Building, 74
Old Vic, 162
Old War Office, 73
Open Air Theatre, 153, 199, 230
Opera House, 97–98
Operating Theatre of Old St. Thomas's Hospital, 158
Oratory, 109
Order of St. John, 13
Orienting yourself, 8–13
  map, 10–11
Oxford, 208
Oxford Circus, 90–92
Oxford Street, 90–91

Paddington, 14
Palace Gardens Terrace, 151
Pall Mall, 117, 118·
Park Lane, 34
Parks, 8, 12, 115–126, 218
Parliament, 76–79
Parliament Hill, 40
Parliament Square, 31, 34, 76, 86
  description, 35
Passes, 37
Passports, lost, 238
Pavillion's Lawn Room, 135
Pepys, Samuel, 69
Percival David Foundation of Chinese Art, 128, 131–132

Peter Leonard Assoc., 91
Petrie Museum of Egyptian
    Archaeology, 131
Petticoat lane, 32
Piccadilly, 16, 119–120
Piccadilly Circus, 32, 100–101
Pimlico, 8
Planetarium, 42, 44, 134
Poet's Corner, 84
Pollock's Toy Museum, 42, 137
Pop concerts, 105
Portobello Antiques Market, 154
Post Offices, 239
Premier Box Office, 99
Prince Henry's Room, 69
Priorities, 31–35
Public Record Office Museum, 138,
    144
Pubs, 47, 65, 67–68, 69, 84, 86, 92,
    111, 114, 123, 145, 146, 154,
    159, 160, 163, 208, 209, 210
Purcell Room, 161, 201

Queen Elizabeth Hall, 161, 201
Queen's Collections, 87
Queen's Gallery, 31, 34, 87
Queen's House, 41
Queen's Life Guard, 73–74

Ranelagh Gardens, 33, 104, 113
Records, 91, 106–107
Reflexology, 98
Regattas, 198
Regent Street, 16, 90, 121–122
Regents Park, 8, 128–129, 135–136
    Open Air Theatre, 196
Reigns, chronology of, 236–237
Restaurants, 175–196
    breakfast, 183, 185; British,
    182–183; chefs, 179–180; cuisines
    in the news, 180–181; districts to
    eat in, 176–178; customs and
    etiquette, 184; ethnic, 181; lunch,
    183, 185; restaurants to be seen
    in, 178–179; selections, 185–196;
    tea, 183, 185
Ricci, Sebastiano, 112
Riverboats, 39
Romans, 9
Roof Garden, 151
Rosetta Stone, 128, 130
Rossetti, D.G., 114
Rotherhithe, 156
Royal Academy, 117, 120
Royal Albert Hall, 35, 102, 105–106
Royal Ballet, 33, 98, 201
Royal College of Art, 106
Royal College of Music, 106
Royal Exchange, 66
Royal Festival Hall, 155, 161
Royal Geographic Society, 106
Royal Hospital, 33, 45, 112–113
Royal Institute of British Architects,
    41
Royal Mews, 31, 34, 87
Royal Academy of Music, 134
Royal National Theater, 44
Royal Observatory, 204
Royal Opera House, 33
Royal Parks, 8, 31, 115–117,
    124–126
Royal Shakespeare Company (RSC),
    34–35, 54
    backstage tours, 44
Royal Tennis Courts, 135
Russel Square, 128

Sadler's Wells Ballet, 33, 98, 201

Sadler's Wells Theatre, 142
Salisbury, 210
Savile Row, 121
Science and Technology, 44
Science Museum, 44, 107
Scotch Wiskey House, 123
Seasons, 224–225
Serpintine Gallery, 126
Shakespeare Globe Museum, 44,
    156
Shakespeare's will, 145
Ship travel to London, 220–221
Shopping, 164–174
    antiques, 170–171; auctioneers,
    171; clothing, 165–169; cosmetics
    and toiletries, 169–170; furnishings,
    171–172; index to shops, 172–174
Shorts Gardens, 98
Sir John Soane's Museum, 41, 139,
    145
Sightseeing, 31–35
Sloan Street, 110
Smith Square, 198
Smithfield Market, 32, 47, 49
Society of Apothecaries of London,
    113
Soho, 12, 32, 33, 88–101
Soho Square, 91
South Bank, 8, 13, 155–163
    Hays Wharf, 155
South Bank Centre, 13, 34, 94, 155,
    156, 161, 199
South Bank Crafts Centre, 162
South Kensington, 12, 33, 102–114,
    147
    hotels, 16, 22–23
    shopping, 33–34
South Sea artifacts, 129
Southwark, 9, 155, 156, 159
Southwark Cathedral, 44, 157–158
Southwark Heritage Information
    Centre, 159
Space Adventure, 157
Spanish and Portuguese Synagogue,
    55, 57
Speakers Corner, 126
Special events, 227–230
Spitalfields, 32
Sports, 198–199
Stepney, 9
Stock Exchange, 12
Stone of Destiny, 83
Stone of Scone, 83
Stonehenge, 210–211
Strand, 9
Stratford, 199
Stratford-upon-Avon, 207–208
St. Barnabas-in-Soho, 92
St. Bartholomew-the-Great, 47, 198
St. Bartholomew's Hospital, 41
St. Bride's, 57
St. Dunstan in the East, 57
St. Dunstan's Hill, 57
St. Edward's Tower, 40
St. Etheldredas, 139, 146
St. Giles Cripplegate Church, 55
St. Giles's Fields, 88
St. James's, 12, 115–116
    hotels, 16, 20, 26
St. James's Hospital, 124
St. James's Palace, 118
St. James's Park, 8, 124
St. John's, 84, 198
St. John's Gate and Museum, 139,
    141
St. Katharine's Dock, 54
St. Martin's Lane, 100

St. Martin-in-the-Fields, 94, 198
St. Mary Abbot's Church, 106
St. Mary Abchurch, 45, 57–58
St. Mary Aldermanbury, 58
St. Marylebone, 133 *see also*
   Bloomsbury
St. Marylebone Parish Church, 134
St. Mary-le-Bow, 58
St. Paul's, 12, 40, 60–65
   ambulatory, 64; description, 33;
   dome, 63–64; Golden Gallery, 65;
   Stone Gallery, 65; music, 197;
   watch, 60; Whispering Gallery, 65
St. Paul's Church, 44
Swinburne, A.C., 114
Swiss Centre, 100

Tate Gallery, 35, 85–86
   description, 34
Taxis, 37
   night tour, 34
Telephones, 239
Temple, 46, 47, 68–69
Temple Church, 69
Thames, 8, 9, 16
   cruises, 34, 39, 42
   view of, 53
Thatcherism, 1, 4
Theater, 34–35, 199–200
   open air, 153, 199
   sporting events, 101
   theatre museum, 41, 44, 97
   tours, 44
Thomas Coram Foundation, 41,
   136–137
Thorney Island, 70
Tickets, 99
   half price, 100, 117
Tipping, 226
Tomb of the Unknown Warrior, 83
Touring, 38–45
   by night, 34; Charterhouse, 139;
   Clerkenwell, 139, 142; for the view,
   40; history of Hogarth's London,
   41; Jones, Inigo, 41; kids' London,
   42; mansion galleries, 43;
   organized tours, 38–40; rockers'
   London, 43–44; science and
   technology, 44; theatrical, 44;
   thematic tours, 40–45; Tower, 49,
   52; Victorian, 45; walking, 39–40,
   46–47, 139; Wall Walk, 54; Wren,
   Christopher, 45
Tourist Board, 239
Tourist information, 219–220
Tower, 32, 34, 49–50, 52–53
   Bell Tower, 52; Bloody Tower, 53;
   Garden Tower, 53; description, 35;
   53; Tower Green, 53; Tower Hill,
   53; White Tower, 53
Tower Records, 101
Toy museum, 137
Trafalgar Square, 9, 12, 34, 72–73

Transportation, 36–37
   flying, 221–223; sailing to London,
   220–221
Travel, 239
Travel arrangements 219–230, 239
   arriving, 223; events, 227–230;
   formalities, 224; information,
   219–220; money matters, 225–226;
   seasons, 224–225; transportation,
   220–223; *see also* Information
Travelcard, 37
Travelers checks, lost, 238
Trips, 203–207
   Greenwich, 203–205; Hampstead
   205–206; Hampton Court Palace,
   205; Kew Gardens, 206–207;
Trips, overnight, 207–211
   Avebury Stone Circles, 210–211;
   Bath, 209–210; Brighton, 211;
   Cambridge, 209; Eton, 207; Oxford,
   208–209; Salisbury, 210;
   Stonehenge, 210–211; Stratford-
   upon-Avon, 207–208; Windsor, 207
Tube, 36
Turner, J.M.W., 114
Tyburn, 127–128

University of London, 128, 131–132
Underground, 36

V.A.T., 164–165, 226
Vauxhall Bridge, 8
Vegetable market, 32
Verrio, Antonio, 112
Victoria and Albert Museum, 102,
   108–109
Victoria Embankment, 35
Victoria London, 45
Victoriana, 152–153

Wakefield Tower, 53
Wallace Collection, 128, 133
Waterloo Bridge, 8, 156
Waxworks, *see* Madame Tussaud's
West End, 9
Westminster, 8, 9, 12, 31, 35, 70–87
Westminster Abbey, 44, 80–84
   church music, 197; description, 35
Westminister Abbey School, 84
Westminister Bridge, 35
Westminster Cathedral, 40
Whitehall, 12, 31, 70–87
Wigmore Hall, 137, 201
Wimbledon, 8, 198
Windsor, 207
World's End, 114
Wren, Christopher, 45, 57, 58, 59,
   160, 204

Young Vic, 162, 199

Zoo, 39, 42, 53, 128, 136

LANGUAGE / 30

For the International Traveler

32 languages! A basic language course on 2 audiocassettes and a phrase book Only $14.95 each + shipping

Nothing flatters people more than to hear visitors try to speak their language and LANGUAGE / 30, used by thousands of satisfied travelers, has you speaking the basics quickly and easily. Each LANGUAGE / 30 course offers:

- approximately 1½ hours of guided practice in greetings, asking questions and general conversation
- proven effective method

Order yours today.

Arabic	Greek	Korean	Spanish
Chinese (Mandarin)	Hebrew	Latin	Swahili
Czech	Hindi	Norwegian	Swedish
Danish	Hungarian	Persian (Farsi)	Tagalog (Pilipino)
Dutch	Indonesian	Polish	Thai
Finnish	Irish	Portuguese	Turkish
French	Italian	Russian	Vietnamese
German	Japanese	Serbo-Croatian	Yiddish

THE ONLY GUIDES YOU'LL EVER NEED — WHEREVER YOU'RE GOING!

Savvy, refreshing, modern and insightful, BANTAM TRAVEL GUIDES are an exciting new way to travel. Literate and lively, and focusing on the things that make a destination special, BANTAM TRAVEL GUIDES are available in two easy-to-use formats: trade size to plan a trip and gain in-depth understanding of what your destination has to offer, and pocket size — perfect to carry along!

Here's what BANTAM TRAVEL GUIDES offer:

* Full-color atlases — plus black and white maps
* Respected travel writers — and food critics
* In-depth hotel and restaurant reviews
* Indexed listings, invaluable advice, weather charts, mileage tables, and much, much more!

Don't miss these BANTAM TRAVEL GUIDES:

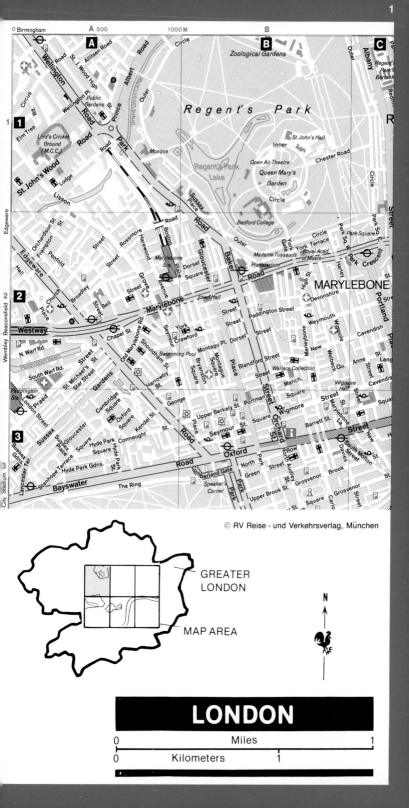

© RV Reise - und Verkehrsverlag, München

GREATER LONDON

MAP AREA

N

LONDON

Miles

Kilometers

FAST FACTS

Greater London's size (area) .... 610 square mile

Greater London's population 6,800,00

London's Underground is the oldest subway system
in the world. The first section opened .... Jan. 10, 186

Number of licensed taxis in London .... about 15,00

Queen Victoria was the longest reigning
British monarch 1837–190

King George III was the longest reigning king 1760–182

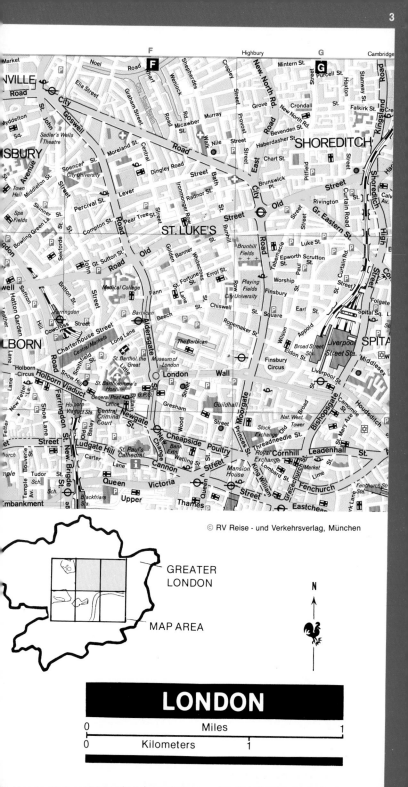

© RV Reise - und Verkehrsverlag, München

GREATER
LONDON

MAP AREA

N

LONDON

| 0 | Miles | 1 |
| 0 | Kilometers | 1 |

4

White City Stad

3

Bayswater

The Ring

H y d e

Kensington

Gardens

Serpentine
Bridge

The Long Water

Serpentine

The Serpentine

The Lido

P a r k

Road

4

Rotten

Row

South Carriage Drive

South Carriage Drive

Road

Kensington

Knightsbridge

Royal
Albert
Hall

Exhibition

Trevor Place

Ennismore Gdns.

Prince's
Ennismore
Gardens

P.Consort
Rd.

Imp. Coll.

Ennismore
Gdns.

Brompton
Square

Cheval Place

Basil Street

Hans Crescent

Road

Sloane

Lowndes

Wilton Pl.

Kinnerton St.

Cr.

Lowndes St.

Cadogan

Belgrave

Halkin St.

Grosvenor Cr.

Square

Upper Belgrave

Place

Belgrave Place

St.

Chapel St.

Constitution

Buckingham Pala
Gardens

Grosvenor

Place

Duke of
Wellington Place

Imp. College Rd.

Science Museum

Geol. a. Natural
History Museum

Victoria and Albert
Museum

Beauchamp Pl.

Egerton
Terrace

Hans
Place

Pont

Street

Cadogan

Chesham

Street

Place

Lyall Eaton

Street Eaton

Eaton

Chester

Square

BROMPTON

BELGRAVIA

Turloe Place

Thurloe

South
Ter.

Square

Walton

Mossop
St.

Milner

Square

Draycott

King's

South Eaton
Place

Elizabeth

Street

Eaton Terrace

5

Harrington Rd.

Pelham St.

Pelham C.

Sloane

Pl.

Cadogan

Pl.

Sloane

Chester St.

Burne

Square

Sydney

Road

Inkworth

Elysan

Draycott

Av.

Sloane

Road

Lr. Sloane

St.

Pimlico Rd.

Buckingham

Summer
Square

Onslow

Onslow
Gdns

Square

Street

Elystan Pl.

Duke of York's
HQ

6

Fulham

Cale

Chelsea

Square

Britten

St. Luke's Church

St.

King's

Chelsea Bridge Rd

Chelsea
Barracks

Ebury Bridge Rd.

Sutherlan

Warwi

CHELSEA

Burton's Court

Roy. Hosp. Rd.

Fulham

A

Fulham

B

Brighton

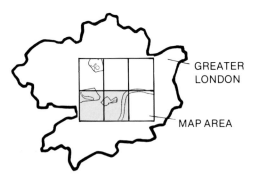

GREATER
LONDON

MAP AREA

C

Brewer

Glasshouse Street
Royal Academy
Burlington House
Piccadilly Coventry
Circus
D
Somerset House
Victoria
Embank
E
Lisle
Cranbo
Panton
Orange
St.
Bedford St.
Strand
Lancaster
Regent
Haymarket
Pall Mall East
Cockspur
St. Martin's La.
William IV St.
St. Martin
in the
Fields
J. Adam
Savoy
Cleopatra's
Needle
National
Gallery
Nelson's
Column
Trafalgar
Square
Charing Cross
Stn.
Waterloo Bridge
National
TV Centre

ST. JAMES'S
King Street
St. James's
Square
Carlton Ho. Terrace
Pall Mall
Whitehall
Northumberland
Av.
Hungerford Bridge
Royal
Festival
Hall
Queen
Elizabeth Hall
Upper
Cornwall
Stamford

Marlborough Ho.
Horse Guard's
Av.
Jubilee Gdns.
Roupell
Brad
Wooton

Lancaster Ho.
St. James's
Palace
St. James's
Park
The Treasury
Downing St.
Home a. Foreign
Offs.
Ministry of
Defence
SOUTH BANK
Waterloo
Sta.
Waterloo
The
Webb

The Mall
Queen
Victoria
Memorial
St. James's Park Lake
Government Offices
The
County Hall
Belvedere
York Road
Marsh
Frazier Street

Birdcage
Wellington Barracks
Buckingham
Petty
France
Walk
George St.
St. Parliament
Bridge St.
Westminster
Bridge
Westminster
Abbey
Houses of
Parliament
St. Thomas's
Hospital
Royal St.
Westminster
Pearman
Morley St.

New Scotland
Yard
Old Pye St.
Smith St.
Storey's
Gate
Square
Palace
Lambeth
Palace
Archbishop
Park
LAMBETH
Kennington
G.M.
Harmwor

Westminster
Cathedral
Greycoat Pl.
Horseferry
Peter
Street
Marsham
Dept. of
Enviroment
Road
Street
Lambeth
Lambeth High
St.
Lambeth
Walk
Walnut Tree Walk
Fitzalan St.
Brook

WESTMINSTER
Francis
Greencoat
Vincent
Square
Rochester
Row
Tothill St.
Millbank
Lambeth
Bridge
Fire Brigade HQ
Lollard St.
Walcot

PICO
Way
Denbigh
Bridge
Road
Westm. School
Playground
Vincent Street
Regency Street
Erasmus St.
John
Islip
Street
Tate Gallery
Embankment
Blacky
Prince
Street
Vauxhall
Street
Sancroft
Street
Kennington
Road
Reedwo
St.
Monk

St.
Charlwood
Drive
Charlwood
Street
Moreton
Street
Vauxhall Bridge
River Thames
Albert
Vauxhall
Tyers
VAUXHALL
Courtenay
Street
Kennington Road
Kenni

D Brighton **E** Camberwe

N

LONDON

0	Miles	1
0	Kilometers	1

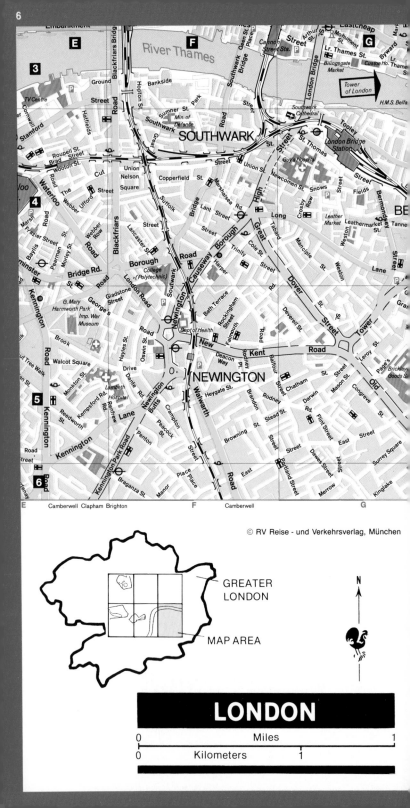

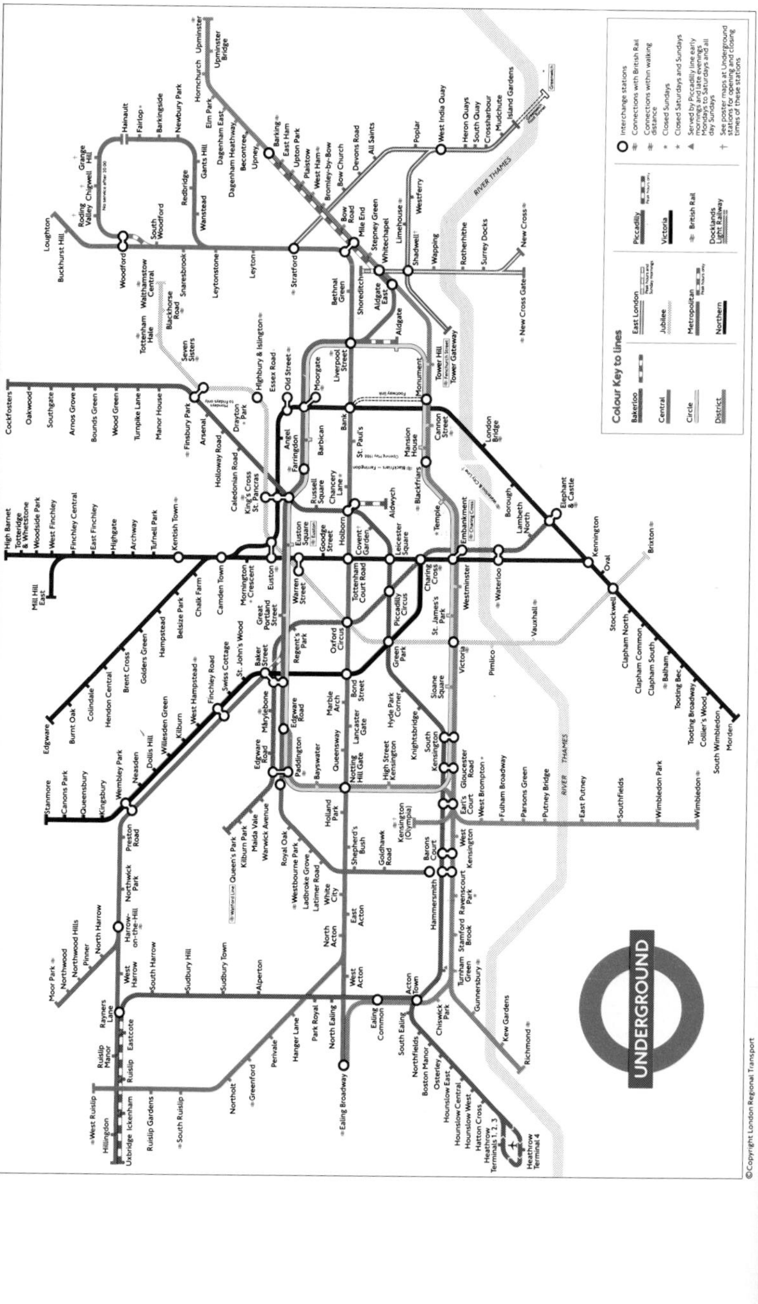
UNDERGROUND
Colour Key to lines
Bakerloo
Central
Circle
District
East London
Jubilee
Metropolitan
Northern
Piccadilly
Victoria
British Rail
Docklands Light Railway
Interchange stations
Connections with British Rail
Connections within walking distance
Closed Sundays
Closed Saturdays and Sundays
Served by Piccadilly line early mornings and late evenings Mondays to Saturdays and all day Sundays
See poster maps at Underground stations for opening and closing times of these stations
RIVER THAMES
Cockfosters
Oakwood
Southgate
Arnos Grove
Bounds Green
Wood Green
Turnpike Lane
Manor House
Finsbury Park
Arsenal
Holloway Road
Caledonian Road
King's Cross St. Pancras
High Barnet
Totteridge & Whetstone
Woodside Park
West Finchley
Finchley Central
East Finchley
Highgate
Archway
Tufnell Park
Kentish Town
Mill Hill East
Camden Town
Chalk Farm
Belsize Park
Hampstead
Golders Green
Brent Cross
Hendon Central
Colindale
Burnt Oak
Edgware
Stanmore
Canons Park
Queensbury
Kingsbury
Wembley Park
Neasden
Dollis Hill
Willesden Green
Kilburn
West Hampstead
Finchley Road
Swiss Cottage
St. John's Wood
Baker Street
Marylebone
Edgware Road
Paddington
Bayswater
Queensway
Notting Hill Gate
Holland Park
Shepherd's Bush
White City
East Acton
North Acton
West Acton
Ealing Broadway
Ealing Common
Acton Town
Chiswick Park
Turnham Green
Stamford Brook
Ravenscourt Park
Hammersmith
Barons Court
West Kensington
Earl's Court
Gloucester Road
South Kensington
Sloane Square
Victoria
Pimlico
Vauxhall
Stockwell
Clapham North
Clapham Common
Clapham South
Balham
Tooting Bec
Tooting Broadway
Colliers Wood
South Wimbledon
Morden
Brixton
Oval
Kennington
Elephant & Castle
Lambeth North
Borough
London Bridge
Waterloo
Embankment
Charing Cross
Westminster
St. James's Park
Green Park
Piccadilly Circus
Leicester Square
Covent Garden
Holborn
Aldwych
Temple
Blackfriars
Mansion House
Cannon Street
Monument
Bank
St. Paul's
Chancery Lane
Russell Square
Euston Square
Euston
Warren Street
Goodge Street
Tottenham Court Road
Oxford Circus
Regent's Park
Great Portland Street
Mornington Crescent
Bond Street
Marble Arch
Lancaster Gate
Hyde Park Corner
Knightsbridge
High Street Kensington
Kensington (Olympia)
Goldhawk Road
Angel
Old Street
Moorgate
Barbican
Farringdon
Liverpool Street
Aldgate
Aldgate East
Tower Hill
Tower Gateway
Highbury & Islington
Essex Road
Drayton Park
Seven Sisters
Tottenham Hale
Blackhorse Road
Walthamstow Central
Bethnal Green
Mile End
Stratford
Leyton
Leytonstone
Snaresbrook
South Woodford
Woodford
Buckhurst Hill
Loughton
Roding Valley
Chigwell
Grange Hill
Hainault
Fairlop
Barkingside
Newbury Park
Gants Hill
Redbridge
Wanstead
Shoreditch
Whitechapel
Stepney Green
Bow Road
Bow Church
Bromley-by-Bow
West Ham
Plaistow
Upton Park
East Ham
Barking
Upney
Becontree
Dagenham Heathway
Dagenham East
Elm Park
Hornchurch
Upminster Bridge
Upminster
Devons Road
All Saints
Poplar
West India Quay
Heron Quays
South Quay
Crossharbour
Mudchute
Island Gardens
Limehouse
Westferry
Shadwell
Wapping
Rotherhithe
Surrey Docks
New Cross
New Cross Gate
Fulham Broadway
Parsons Green
Putney Bridge
East Putney
Southfields
Wimbledon Park
Wimbledon
West Brompton
Gunnersbury
Kew Gardens
Richmond
South Ealing
Northfields
Boston Manor
Osterley
Hounslow East
Hounslow Central
Hounslow West
Hatton Cross
Heathrow Terminals 1, 2, 3
Heathrow Terminal 4
Uxbridge
Hillingdon
Ickenham
Ruislip
Ruislip Manor
Eastcote
Rayners Lane
West Ruislip
Ruislip Gardens
South Ruislip
Northolt
Greenford
Perivale
Hanger Lane
Park Royal
North Ealing
Alperton
Sudbury Town
Sudbury Hill
South Harrow
West Harrow
Harrow-on-the-Hill
North Harrow
Pinner
Northwood Hills
Northwood
Moor Park
Northwick Park
Preston Road
Queen's Park
Kilburn Park
Maida Vale
Warwick Avenue
Royal Oak
Westbourne Park
Ladbroke Grove
Latimer Road
Watford Line
Greenwich

8

HERTFORDSHIRE

ESSEX

ENFIELD

BARNET

HARROW

HARINGEY

WALTHAM FOREST

REDBRIDGE

HAVERING

HILLINGDON

BRENT

CAMDEN

HACKNEY

ISLINGTON

NEWHAM

BARKING AND DAGENHAM

EALING

KENSINGTON AND CHELSEA

CITY OF WESTMINSTER

TOWER HAMLETS

HAMMERSMITH AND FULHAM

CITY OF LONDON

GREENWICH

BEXLEY

HOUNSLOW

SOUTHWARK

LAMBETH

RICHMOND UPON THAMES

WANDSWORTH

LEWISHAM

River Thames

MERTON

KINGSTON UPON THAMES

SUTTON

CROYDON

BROMLEY-

KENT

SURREY

Inner London

N

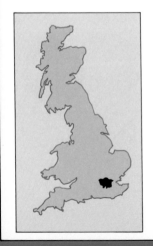

GREATER LONDON

0   miles   5

0   kilometers

GREAT BRITAIN

| miles | 50 |
| kilometers | 120 |

N

Scotland:
Scrabster
Ullapool
Kyle of Lochalsh
Inverness
Mallaig
Aberdeen
Montrose
Oban
Dundee
Dunoon
Glasgow
Edinburgh
Ardrossan
Prestwick

North Sea

Dumfries
Stranraer
Blyth
Newcastle
Sunderland
Carlisle
Workington
Whitehaven
Hartlepool
Middlesborough

Irish Sea

Barrow
Scarborough
Heysham
Lancaster
Fleetwood
Bradford
York
Preston
Leeds
Hull
Liverpool
Manchester
Goole
Holyhead
Immingham
Grimsby
Ringway
Sheffield
Chester
Stoke-on-Trent
Nottingham
Boston
Derby
Shrewsbury
Kings Lynn
Great Yarmouth
Wolverhampton
Leicester
Norwich
Aberystwyth
Birmingham
Birmingham International
Lowestoft
Coventry
Worcester
Stratford upon Avon
Northampton
Cambridge
Ipswich
Fishguard
Felixstowe
Milford Haven
Swansea
Sharpness
Luton
Colchester
Harwich
Pembroke Dock
Newport
Stansted
Port Talbot
Cardiff
Bristol
Reading
Heathrow
London
Barry
Bath
Ramsgate
Barnstaple
Dover
Gatwick
Folkestone
Southampton
Shoreham
Brighton
Exeter
Poole
Newhaven
Plymouth
Weymouth
Cowes
Portsmouth
Penzance
Fowey

English Channel

| **A** | **B** | **C** |

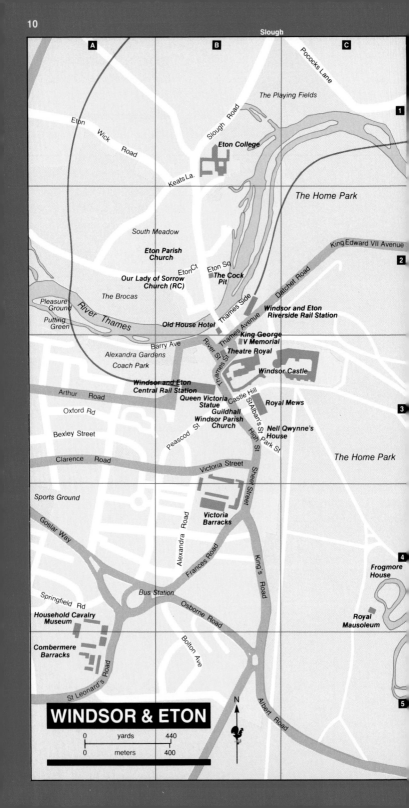

Slough

Pococks Lane

A B C

The Playing Fields

1

Eton Wick Road

Slough Road

Eton College

Keats La.

The Home Park

King Edward VII Avenue

2

South Meadow

Eton Parish Church

Eton Ct. Eton Sq

Our Lady of Sorrow Church (RC)

The Cock Pit

The Brocas

Pleasure Ground

River Thames

Putting Green

Thames Side

Detchet Road

Windsor and Eton Riverside Rail Station

Old House Hotel

Barry Ave

Thames Avenue

King George V Memorial

Alexandra Gardens

River St

Thames St

Theatre Royal

Coach Park

Windsor Castle

Windsor and Eton Central Rail Station

Arthur Road

Queen Victoria Statue

Castle Hill

Royal Mews

3

Oxford Rd

Guildhall

Windsor Parish Church

St Albans St

Park St

High St

Nell Qwynne's House

Bexley Street

The Home Park

Clarence Road

Victoria Street

Sports Ground

Alexandra Road

Sheet Street

Gosiar Way

Victoria Barracks

4

Springfield Rd

Frances Road

Bus Station

King's Road

Osborne Road

Frogmore House

Household Cavalry Museum

Combermere Barracks

Bolton Ave

Royal Mausoleum

St Leonard's Road

Albert Road

N

5

WINDSOR & ETON

| 0 | yards | 440 |
| 0 | meters | 400 |

Alcester

A St. Andrew's Cres. St. Martin's Close **B** **C**

Rail Station

1

Orchard Way

Shottery Road

Albany Road

Wellesbourne Grove

Alcester Road

Evesham Road

Broad Walk

Evesham Place

Grove Road

Arden Street

Greenhill Street

2

Broad Street

Chestnut Walk

Rother Street

Mansell Street

West Street

Bull Street

Windsor Street

Old Town

Church Street

Scholar's Lane

Shakespeare Institute

Meer Street

Street

Shakespeare Centre

Ely Street

Bell Ct.

Wood Street

Shakespeare's Birthplace

Great William St.

3

The Other Place Theatre

Chapel Street

Chapel Lane

High Street

Henley Street

Union St.

Guild Street

Tyler Street

John St.

Payton Street

Southern Lane

Sheep Street

i

Museum

Bridge Street

World of Shakespeare Theatre and Cinema

Stratford Upon Avon Canal

Swan Theatre

Waterside

Royal Shakespeare Theatre

Bancroft Gardens

Warwick Road

4

Bowling Green

River Avon

Bancroft Place

Cricket Ground

Recreation Ground

Bridge Foot

Bancroft Place

Old Tramway Walk

Swan's Nest Lane

River

Clopton Bridge

Bridgeway

Shipston Road

Avon

Tiddington Road

Banbury Road

→N

5

STRATFORD -UPON-AVON

0 yards 110
0 meters 100

Birmingham

Warwick

Banbury

Woodstock Banbury

St. Margarets Road

Ba

Banbury

Woodstock

Road

St. Bernards Road

River Thames

Little Clarendon St.

St. C
C

St. John St.

Ashmolea
Museun

Beaumo

Rail Station

Hythe Bridge St.

Worctr. St.

George

Park End Street

New Road

Swindon

Botley Road

Hollybush

Paradise St. Castle S

Oxpens Road

T

OXFORD

N

| 0 | yards | 440 |
| 0 | meters | 400 |

A **B** **C**

1

2

3

4

5

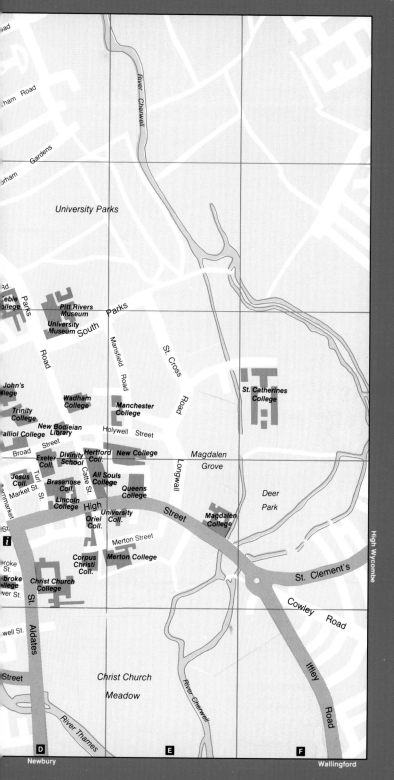

River Cherwell

ham Road

Gardens

orham

University Parks

Rd.

eble
ollege

Parks

Pitt Rivers
Museum

University
Museum

South

Parks

St. Cross

Road

Mansfield

Road

John's
llege

Road

St. Catherines
College

Wadham
College

Trinity
College

Manchester
College

New Bodleian
Library

alliol College

Holywell   Street

Broad

Street

Divinity
School

Hertford
Coll.

New College

Magdalen

Exeter
Coll.

Grove

Jesus
Coll.

Turl

St.

Brasenose
Coll.

All Souls
College

ormarket

Market St.

Lincoln
College

Queens
College

Longwall

Deer

Park

St.

High

University
Coll.

Oriel
Coll.

Magdalen
College

Street

i

Merton Street

roke
St.

roke
llege

Corpus
Christi
Coll.

Merton College

ver St.

St.

Christ Church
College

St. Clement's

Aldates

Cowley   Road

well St.

Street

Christ Church

Meadow

River Cherwell

Iffley

Road

High Wycombe

River Thames

CAMBRIDGE

Lady Margaret Rd.

Castle Street

Chesterton Lane

Magdalene

Bedford

Madingley Rd.

Northampton Street

Magdalene St.

New Park Street

Bridge Street

Queens Road

St. John's

Park

Je

Bridge of Sighs
St. Johns Bridge

River Cam

St. John's St.

Trinity

Trinity Street

Sidney St

The Backs

Trinity Bridge

Green Street

Garret Hostel Br.

Market

**Trinity
Hall**

**Gonville
and
Caius**

Kings Parade

**University
Church**

Petty
Cur

Clare Bridge

Clare

**King's College
Chapel**

i

King's

Exchan

King's Bridge

Benet St.

West Road

Queen's

Kings Parade

**Corpus
Christi**

River Cam

The Backs

Pembroke St

Queen's
Bridge

Silver Street

Mill Lane

Trumpington Street

Pemb

Little St. Mary's La.

N

Museum

Queens Road

Peterhouse

**Fitzwilliam
Museum**

| 0 | yards | 220 |
| 0 | meters | 200 |

A   B   C

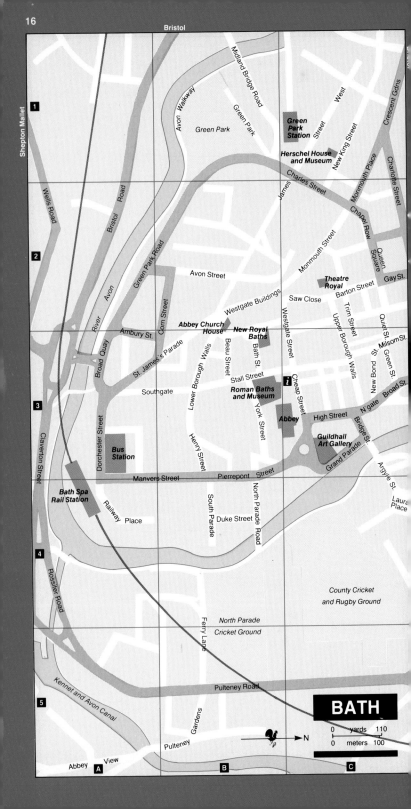

Bristol

Shepton Mallet

Midland Bridge Road

Avon Walkway

Green Park

Green Park

West

Crescent Gdns

Green Park Station

Herschel House and Museum

Street

New King Street

Charles Street

Monmouth Place

Charlotte Street

Chapel Row

Wells Road

James St

Monmouth Street

Queen Square

Gay St.

Bristol Road

Avon Street

Theatre Royal

Barton Street

Trim Street

Upper Borough Walls

Quiet St.

Milsom St.

Green St.

Green Park Road

Westgate Buildings

Saw Close

Westgate Street

New Bond St

Corn Street

Abbey Church House

New Royal Baths

River Avon

Ambury St.

Broad Quay

St. James's Parade

Beau Street

Lower Borough Walls

Bath St.

Stall Street

Roman Baths and Museum

Cheap Street

High Street

N'gate

Broad St.

Bridge St.

Abbey

Guildhall Art Gallery

Grand Parade

Argyle St.

Southgate

York Street

Dorchester Street

Bus Station

Henry Street

Manvers Street

Pierrepont Street

Laura Place

Bath Spa Rail Station

Railway Place

South Parade

Duke Street

North Parade Road

Claverton Street

County Cricket and Rugby Ground

Ferry Lane

North Parade Cricket Ground

Rossiter Road

Kennet and Avon Canal

Pulteney Road

Pulteney

Gardens

Abbey

View

BATH

0 yards 110
0 meters 100

N

A   B   C